POLISH ANALYTICAL PHILOSOPHY

International Library of Philosophy and Scientific Method

A Catalogue of books already published in the
International Library of Philosophy and Scientific Method
will be found at the end of this volume.

POLISH
ANALYTICAL
PHILOSOPHY

*A Survey and a Comparison with
British Analytical Philosophy*

by

HENRYK SKOLIMOWSKI

*Associate Professor of Philosophy
University of Southern California*

LONDON
ROUTLEDGE & KEGAN PAUL
NEW YORK : THE HUMANITIES PRESS

First published 1967
by Routledge & Kegan Paul Ltd
Broadway House, 68–74 Carter Lane
London, E.C.4

Printed in Great Britain
by Richard Clay (The Chaucer Press), Ltd
Bungay, Suffolk

FM

CONTENTS

Contents

Contents

ACKNOWLEDGEMENTS

THIS book has its origin in the generosity of St. Antony's College, Oxford. My warm thanks go to the Warden of the College, Mr. F. W. Deakin, and to the Fellows, for their encouragement and substantial financial aid when I was at Oxford. To the British Council in London I owe gratitude for a grant-in-aid which enabled me to finish the book.

The number of people who contributed in one way or another to the final shape of the book is really too great to allow mention of all of them. At Oxford I was greatly benefited by Professor Ayer's incisive criticisms of the early drafts of the manuscript. Mr. Anthony Quinton has been most patient in his thorough reading of every chapter. His many suggestions very considerably improved the content and the form of the book.

In Poland I owe gratitude especially to Professor Tadeusz Kotarbiński and the late Professor Kazimierz Ajdukiewicz, who were very generous with their time in discussing various chapters.

In particular warm thanks are due to Mrs. Evelyn Gluck who helped in more than one way in shaping the final version. My greatest indebtedness, however, I owe to my wife, Jacqueline, who was throughout the entire period of writing an inspiration, a critic, and a benevolent censor. Without her this book would have taken much longer and would have been much poorer.

I also wish to thank Professor Bernard Williams and Mr. Ted Honderich, the editors of the series, for valuable suggestions and improvements.

To the *Journal of the History of Ideas* I wish to express my gratitude for permission to reprint 'Analytical-Linguistic Marxism in Poland' (Vol. XXVI, No. 2, April–June 1965); and to the *Personalist* for permission to reprint 'Praxiology—the Science of Accomplished Acting' (Vol. 46, No. 3, Summer 1965).

INTRODUCTION

EVEN small nations have their great periods. Poland's great period of intellectual and cultural exuberance occurred during the Renaissance, in the fifteenth and sixteenth centuries; then she was not quite so small and not quite so insignificant. In the twentieth century, although a small and insignificant country, Poland again experienced a period of intellectual and cultural awakening. Philosophy in particular was the field where talent was abundant and the calibre of contributions surprisingly high. Analytical philosophy was the embodiment of what was best and most accomplished in the Polish philosophy of that time. Although it was practised with ratiocinative rigour, it did not become so narrowly restricted that philosophical problems become strangled rather than solved, as was the case with the Vienna Circle; and although it was preoccupied with minute and often piecemeal analyses, it arrived, in the way of traditional philosophy, at more general and more systematic conclusions. These, moreover, could not be easily discarded as 'bad' metaphysics.

This philosophy originated with Kazimierz Twardowski, a pupil of Brentano. Polish analytical philosophers learnt much, however, from Bertrand Russell. Inspired by *Principia Mathematica*, which was regarded as opening up new vistas for philosophy based on inquiry into logic and language, Polish philosophers and logicians carried on independent investigations along the same lines. Research into the relationship between logic and language, and sometimes between logic, language, and reality became the kernel of Polish analytical philosophy.

Apart from the logicians, whose accomplishments have already been incorporated into the body of logic, Polish philosophers through the persistent application of logic and continuous analysis of language arrived at results which in cogency of argument, coherence of structure, and rationality of approach are in the best Western European intellectual tradition, and can stand comparison with the finest achievements of twentieth-century rational philosophy. However, a provincial language has prevented the dissemination of their ideas and also an appreciation of the value of their contributions.

This work has three aims:

1. To trace the origins and describe the nature of analytical philosophy.
2. To examine in detail the sources, development, and contributions of the Polish analytical movement.
3. To relate Polish to British analytical philosophy.

With Polish philosophy, as indeed with all 'provincial' philosophies, a major problem is to integrate its features into one comprehensive framework and to relate it to 'central' philosophies, because only then can the achievements of provincial philosophies be understood and appreciated. In the present case British analytical philosophy has been chosen as the point of reference.

It should be emphasized that the main purpose is to describe the development of Polish philosophy, analytically oriented, and not the development of Polish logic. It may well be, as some scholars would claim, that the contributions of Polish logicians can be considered unique in the history of modern logic, and that they form the most valuable part of Poland's share in contemporary philosophy; this aspect of Polish philosophy, however, is neither examined nor assessed here. Consequently, this book may come as a disappointment to those who expect it to be an account of modern logic in Poland. The pages which follow were written not for logicians only, but for philosophers in general. One underlying motive of my undertaking has been to show that, in addition to logic, Polish philosophers have tackled some fundamental problems of philosophy.

True, the growth of the Polish analytical movement is so intertwined with the development of logic that the movement might be considered as a logical movement; on the other hand, it can be conceived as a trend characterized by its hyper-conscious attitude towards language. The latter is precisely the standpoint of this investigation. By emphasizing the rôle of language in the development of Polish analytical philosophy, it has been possible to link it with the entire contemporary analytical movement. Logic is thus treated as a supplementary element and only in a descriptive way.

The study covers the period from 1895, when Twardowski moved to Lwów, until the early 1960s, when the analytical movement became emasculated.

Since the period is a long one, abounding in achievements, many events and many names have had to be left unmentioned in order to preserve clarity of exposition. To have made a simple mention of them for the sake of compiling a complete and impressive list was felt to be unnecessary and unrewarding. Consequently, only the major figures have been selected and only the major features of their work have been examined.

It has not been possible here to follow up all the implications of analytical philosophy in Poland, to trace its influence on the whole intellectual life, its social significance and its liberalizing effect in times when the ideological cliché reigned. Yet in some chapters I felt it necessary to demonstrate that this philosophy, in spite of its technical character, did not remain the sole property of a small circle of 'initiated rabbis', and that in spite of its preoccupation with highly sophisticated cognitive problems it did leave an important imprint on society.

Warsaw—Oxford—Los Angeles

TO

JACQUELINE

I

ON THE ORIGINS AND CHARACTER OF

ANALYTICAL PHILOSOPHY

I BASIC CHARACTERISTICS OF ANALYTICAL PHILOSOPHY

As the incomparable David Hume said so well, 'It is certain that the easy and obvious philosophy will always, with the generality of mankind, have the preference above the accurate and abstruse.' Unfortunately, this seems to be true not only with 'the generality of mankind', but with the generality of philosophers also. For this reason, among others, analytical philosophy is in disfavour with the generality of mankind and the generality of philosophers. Is it because one doesn't like to like what one doesn't quite understand? On the other hand, a hostile critic may be partly justified in his distaste for analytical philosophy because his question 'What is analytical philosophy?' is hardly ever adequately answered. Concise aphorisms employed for this purpose lend an air of definiteness but are far from accurate or adequate. Since it seems to me that analytical philosophy cannot be summed up in one phrase, and since it seems to be considerably and significantly different from other contemporary philosophies, I shall attempt to enumerate its characteristics. It is my contention that there are not many analytical philosophies, but only one, embodying, indeed, many divergent trends. These trends, however, have enough in common to sharply distinguish analytic philosophy from other contemporary philosophies. I shall thus seek to establish the central features of divergent analytical trends which I call in their entirety analytical philosophy. Before specifying these central characteristics, a word should perhaps be said about some popular definitions of analytical philosophy.

I

One such was solemnly enunciated by Wittgenstein and obstinately repeated by many others, namely that analytical philosophy is solely concerned with an *activity* aiming at the clarification of the meaning of philosophical propositions. This definition has some virtues. It is concise and elegant, and the aesthetic appeal of brief and elegant definitions is a factor of some importance. Mathematicians are often motivated in their research not by a desire to discover truth, but by a desire to formulate their proofs in a neat, elegant, and aesthetically satisfying form. Mathematicians, I contend, can afford to be satisfied with the aesthetic merit of their formulae, but philosophers and historians of philosophy cannot.

For this reason I do not think that the description of analytical philosophy as 'the philosophy of analysis' will do either. The phrase does not convey much, particularly because the term 'analysis' has been used so differently and abused on so many occasions that it has become almost meaningless. Furthermore, an investigation into the nature of analytical philosophy conducted in this way would have to start with an analysis of the concept of 'analysis'; and this being so, it would be necessary to determine what kind of analysis is to be applied in analysing the concept of 'analysis'. *Regressus ad infinitum* quite clearly emerges if such a procedure is followed.

Nor do I think either that analytical philosophy can be exclusively characterized as 'words, words, words': that is, that it can be identified with Oxford linguistic philosophy. The latter, like the Vienna Circle or the teaching of Wittgenstein, is only a part of the whole analytical movement.

That movement is a complex phenomenon and does not, as I have said, allow for a concise definition. I propose to reserve the name 'analytical philosophy' for that species of twentieth-century philosophy which is distinguished by the following characteristics:

1. Its recognition of the active rôle of language in philosophy —what, in other words, could be called its hyper-conscious attitude towards language.
2. Its piecemeal attitude towards philosophical problems.
3. Its cognitive character.
4. Its intersubjective treatment of the process of analysis.

The above characteristics (which will be developed and elucidated in the course of this chapter) seem sufficient to differentiate analytical philosophy from other apparently similar types of philosophies on the one hand, and necessary on the other to warrant giving any philosophy the title 'analytical'.

It should be observed that these characteristics are not unique in the sense that we cannot find them in other philosophies; on the contrary, each of them individually can be found in some other philosophy. What is unique is their configuration, that is to say their simultaneous appearance within the body of analytical philosophy.

Regarding the first characteristic, it is important to note that language in analytical philosophy is understood not only as a means, but also as an aim of philosophical inquiry; is conceived not only as a container, but also as a shaper of ideas. The hyperconscious attitude towards language may be considered to be the novel element of analytical philosophy and its main characteristic. Complementary to it, and in a way derivative from it, is the fact that analytical philosophers can be divided into different groups according to their relation to language. In Chapter VI the four types will be distinguished.

What, it may be asked, is so special about paying attention to language during the course of one's philosophical inquiry? After all, from Plato and the sophists on, philosophers for centuries showed a great deal of sensitivity to language as a container and transmitter of ideas. British empiricists in particular went so far as to state explicitly the importance of language in practising philosophy. Bacon said that the idols of the market place, 'which have crept into the understanding through the alliances of words and names', are the most troublesome. These idols exist because men believe that their reason governs words, whereas in fact, as Bacon pointed out, words often govern reason. Hobbs was even more to the point when he asserted that reasoning in philosophy is 'nothing but reckoning of the consequences of general names agreed upon for the marking and signifying of our thoughts'.

These, however, were only verbal declarations and did not lead either to an improvement of philosophy or to a change in the style of philosophizing. That was to come about only in the twentieth century. Philosophers of the past, though some of them made allowances for the special rôle of language in philosophy, continued to philosophize in the same style as those who did not exhibit any special interest in language.

The contrast between seventeenth-century philosophers who

3

talked about the importance of language in philosophy and philosophers of the twentieth century who possessed a genuine knowledge of the function of language and used it for the improvement of their philosophy is similar to one which can be observed in the history of medicine. From the time of Hippocrates, or even earlier, physicians have talked solemnly and profoundly about the biological–mechanical processes of the human body. But only since the anatomy of the human body became known through dissection, the circulation of the blood was discovered, and various other physiological and psychological processes were identified by empirical analyses, has there been any adequate consciousness of these biological–mechanical processes or, in modern language, the psychosomatic functioning of the human body. Earlier medical 'theories' can be regarded as phantasmagoria or simply as metaphysical speculations. There is beyond doubt a qualitative difference between modern medicine and the medicine of the past; and undoubtedly analytical philosophy is similarly based on a qualitatively new understanding of the way language functions.

How this knowledge was acquired or this new attitude towards language arrived at is a question of the origins of analytical philosophy. In my opinion the maturation of a new attitude towards language began to crystallize in science. In the next section, dealing with the origin of analytical philosophy, this problem will be further discussed.

The second characteristic of analytical philosophy is its piecemeal attitude towards philosophical problems; there is a predilection for tackling rather small issues, which are elaborated with thoroughness and precision. This is in contrast to the holistic attitude, which may be identified with constructing huge philosophical syntheses, usually by means of picturesque analogies and at the expense of logic. This concentration on small issues does not, of course, preclude arriving at solutions to large problems as a residue of particular analyses. What is characteristic is a shift of emphasis; the answer to large problems is to be derived from thorough analyses of particular and detailed sub-problems. In this respect analytical philosophy is a philosophy without presuppositions. It is quite plain that the more we assume at the beginning of a philosophical inquiry, the more we can 'prove' afterwards; and conversely, the less we assume, the less we are capable of proving later. The philosophical systems of the past

4

illustrate this point only too well; they were able to prove much because much was uncritically assumed in their presuppositions. Since analytical philosophy assumes very little to start with, it is not able to 'prove' much afterwards. This is why it does not offer ready solutions to many a traditional problem. These solutions are not to be derived from its assumptions, but rather are to be reached through thorough analyses of the matter in question.

There is another reason for the fact that analytical philosophy does not offer dogmatic solutions to complex philosophical problems. The standards of exactitude, the demands for clarity, the requirements of stringency in proofs have been drastically raised in analytical philosophy. And above all, the insistence on full meaningfulness for philosophical assertions has acquired something like the force of law. Because we are engaged in the pursuit of truth, and because we desire our activity to be worthy of its name, we must be certain about the meanings of our assertions. In a word, the stringent demands of 'respectability' postulated for philosophical activity imply restraint in making sweeping assertions. This restraint in turn implies seeking for the answers to whole problems through the analysis of partial ones. Thus, the piecemeal character of analytical philosophy is, in a sense, a function of its respectability.

Our third claim is that analytical philosophy is a cognitive type of philosophy. This means that it is directed towards the exploration of the external world, which is being investigated for the sake of the acquisition of knowledge, and not for any other reason. There is no desire to prove the preordained order of nature or the greatness of God. In addition to being cognitive, analytical philosophy often aspires to be scientific. However, 'scientific philosophy' should not be used as another name for analytical philosophy, for at least three reasons.

1. There have been philosophers who undoubtedly should be described as 'analytical' but who have not attempted to make philosophy a science: for example, G. E. Moore, the late Wittgenstein, the Oxford philosophers of ordinary language, or the major philosophers of the Polish analytical movement.

2. Philosophy, in fact, had aspired to be scientific before the twentieth century, although unquestionably there is a difference in content between earlier philosophies which attempted to be

scientific (for example, Comte's positivism) and the twentieth-century scientific philosophies.

3. Among contemporary philosophies, there are schools of thought which have very little to do with analytical philosophy but which nevertheless claim to be schools of scientific philosophy. Marxist philosophy is the most obvious case in point. Its advocates insist that it is the 'only true' scientific philosophy.

From these instances it follows that its scientific character is a secondary attribute of analytical philosophy, and not a defining characteristic. However, when scientific philosophy is defined in terms of scientific method, and when its structure is designed after that of the physical or even formal sciences (this is the primary understanding of contemporary scientific philosophy), then we can easily observe a convergence between scientific and analytical philosophy. The most successful practitioners of this kind of scientific philosophy, such as Russell, Carnap, and Reichenbach, can be considered analytical philosophers as well. Scientific philosophy, in the sense specified, is a department of analytical philosophy.

The cognitive character of any philosophy implies something more than an aspiration to be scientific. The division of all philosophy into cognitive and non-cognitive can be seen as one of the fundamental divisions throughout the history of philosophy. From Socrates on, we can see a distinctive split among philosophical schools. Before Socrates, the exploration of the world external to man was considered philosophy's main task. With him there began a search into the nature of man, his place in the universe, his goals, his destiny; and the purpose of philosophy then became, more often than not, to establish the uniqueness of man, to distinguish and defend his values, or to justify man's tragic existence and find for him some measure of comfort and consolation.

Thus it could be said roughly that cognitive philosophy is concerned with the search for truth, it attempts to carry its investigations in an intersubjective manner, and it adheres to the tenets of rationalism; whereas non-cognitive philosophy is developed to help man to live, and is often supported by a variety of irrationalistic arguments appealing to intuition, the emotions, and sometimes to extra-sensory perceptions.

From the cognitive character of analytical philosophy seems to follow its epistemological realism and a certain tendency towards empiricism. It is difficult to maintain grand idealistic designs and to endow the Absolute with various attributes, if at the same time we have to specify clearly the meaning of the Absolute itself and the nature of its attributes. A tendency towards empiricism sometimes takes a crude form, as in the Vienna Circle; usually, however, it exhibits a more refined form which consists in testing the consequences of a philosophical theory against the tenets of epistemological realism. If the consequences of a philosophical theory too obviously clash with reality, or with logic, or with common sense, then the theory is rejected as too fantastic.

The fourth characteristic of analytical philosophy is its intersubjective treatment of the process of analysis. It employs the kind of analysis which is intersubjectively meaningful in virtue of the language in which it is carried out. The employment of this type of analysis distinguishes it from other philosophies which base their investigation on analyses of different kinds. Phenomenology, for example, conceives of analysis as the penetration of 'essences'; existentialism conceives of analysis as revealing the 'existential dimension'. In neither of the two is analysis understood as being dependent upon and objectively related to language, but rather as based on individual and personal experience. It appears that private languages—the media of subjective analyses—in which meanings of words are determined solely by the individual user, would be futile for any consistently cognitive philosophy. Furthermore, how can these private languages be characterized and distinguished? Presumably by emphasizing their intentional departure from ordinary language. Would this not imply the use of the common intersubjective language as a point of departure? Then the characteristics and peculiarities of private languages would have to be accounted for on a metalanguage level in no other way but by assuming an intersubjective common language. In short, the concept of analysis which is not related to an intersubjective language is at best bound to be entangled in inconsistencies and at worst may be useless for the actual process of analysis. Perhaps a different term is needed for that activity which is performed subjectively and which is not related to common language; the term 'analysis', on the other hand, should be limited to analyses via intersubjective language as in analytical philosophy.

7

2 ON THE ORIGINS OF ANALYTICAL PHILOSOPHY

A. *The action-reaction scheme as an explanation*

No philosophy can be fully comprehended unless we understand its origins and the environment from which it emerged. An examination of the above with respect to analytical philosophy, makes it clear that the characteristics mentioned above are essential for its unequivocal and adequate description.

The actual beginning of analytical philosophy can be taken as the publication of Bertrand Russell's 'On Denoting' in 1905. In successive years, further impetus and reinforcement was given to the analytical movement in England; it was clearly in the course of the struggle with idealism that the movement acquired its shape. However, I shall suggest that the roots of analytical philosophy reach much deeper, and that its development in an embryonic way occurred during the two preceding centuries. More specifically, I shall defend these views.

I. *The origin of analytical philosophy is not entirely due to Britain and British philosophers* and cannot be explained adequately only in terms of the pursuing of one tradition or the breaking down of another.

II. *Analytical philosophy was stimulated and came into being through science*, particularly through the development of eighteenth-century botany, chemistry, physics, nineteenth-century non-Euclidean geometries, and above all mathematical logic.

It is true that analytical philosophy or, more precisely, a philosophical movement subsequently recognized as 'analytical philosophy', was born in Britain. The British idealism of the second half of the nineteenth century was a reaction against empiricism, naturalism, and materialism, all of which were the philosophical consequences of nineteenth-century achievements in the natural sciences. Analytical philosophy, it is said, notably in the hands of Russell and Moore, was itself a reaction against idealism.

The wave of idealism started in England with the publication in 1865 of J. H. Stirling's book, *The Secret of Hegel*. Stirling himself was perfectly frank about his apologetic intentions. He wished to reveal to the public the secret of Hegel, who 'has no object but to restore Faith—Faith in God, Faith in the immortality of the Soul, and the freedom of the will—nay, Faith in Christianity as the revealed religion'. In a word, English idealism was a response to the expansion of the natural sciences, an attempt to restore faith, to support the human values apparently threatened by new scientific discoveries. This can also be seen in the philosophies of McTaggart and Bradley.

Bradley's main books, *The Principles of Logic* and *Appearance and Reality*, abound with powerful and precise arguments which seemingly refer to the external world. When we examine the source of his philosophizing, however, we can argue that it was an ethical impulse which gave vitality to Bradley's metaphysical system. This is explicitly and somewhat ironically expressed in his essay, 'My Station and its Duties', where he defined metaphysics as 'the finding of bad reasons for what we believe upon instinct'.

McTaggart provides an even more striking case. When we consider the content of his principal book, *The Nature of Existence*, with its clearly stated and very precisely deduced ontological arguments, we might again suppose that he was trying to give an account of the world. However, when we turn to the source of his philosophical endeavours, we find that ethical and religious questions also gave rise to his metaphysical speculations—that, in short, consolatory purposes were his main ones. 'The utility of Metaphysic,' he wrote, 'is to be found rather in the comfort it can give us . . . in the chance that it may answer this supreme question (whether good or evil predominates in the universe) in a cheerful manner, that it may provide some solution which shall be a consolation and an encouragement.'[1]

Without forcing the issue, we may indeed say that English idealism originated entirely as a reaction against the materialistic consequences of the growth of the natural sciences. But to explain the emergence of analytical philosophy in terms of a reaction against the prevailing idealism is to tell only a part of the story. The analytical movement should also be viewed in the wider context of European philosophy. We should consider various processes and phenomena which occurred in Europe at the time when the campaign against the theory of internal relations was launched in Britain. The emergence of analytical philosophy will then appear as a natural and almost inevitable phenomenon, as a part of the whole European cultural and scientific tradition; also, the element of novelty in analytical philosophy will appear as indisputable and obvious.

[1] J. McTaggart, *Philosophical Studies* (London, 1934), pp. 184 ff.

9

On the Origins and Character of Analytical Philosophy

At the turn of the century, one of the most striking changes in Europe was the process of secularization of intellectual and cultural life. Interest in religion and in religious issues shrank drastically. Gilbert Ryle, in his introduction to *Revolution in Philosophy*, describes the process as it occurred in Britain.

> Between the time when Bradley was an undergraduate and the time when I was an undergraduate the population of intellectuals and particularly of academic intellectuals in the British Isles had changed from being a predominantly clerical to an almost entirely lay population. In Bradley's youth most Fellows of colleges were in orders, and a big proportion of the undergraduates came from, and were destined to go to, the vicarage and the manse. The burning theoretical issues were between theologians and theologians, or else between theologians and antitheologians. Beneath and behind even the more purely philosophical divisions of opinion lay the division between faith and doubt. By the 1920's all of this had gone. Almost all university teachers were laymen; almost all undergraduates came from lay homes and looked forward to secular careers.[2]

The same process of the secularization of intellectual life ran parallel in most European countries, so that the ground for non-religious, non-idealistic down-to-earth philosophy had been prepared.

At the same time many values, often the basic prerequisites of grandiose philosophical systems, were undermined by social, artistic, and scientific changes. The emergence of a new social class, the proletariat, changed social patterns and existing social values; drastic changes in the arts led to the disintegration of the classical forms and the classical patterns of aesthetic evaluation; the feeling of a crisis in science, particularly in classical physics, led to the assertion that scientific theories are only convenient devices to help us to sort out experience, 'neither true nor false, but useful', and led also to doubt the unshakability and certainty of science.

Another factor which prepared the ground for the rise of analytical philosophy was the unprecedented increase in the number of periodicals in the second half of the nineteenth century. As the sciences developed and new branches and even new sciences came into being, and as scientific activities became more and more institutionalized in specialized societies, new periodicals were

[2] G. Ryle (ed.), *Revolution in Philosophy* (London, 1957), p. 2.

established for the promotion of specific branches of knowledge. Philosophers no longer had to write for popular periodicals which covered the multitude of related or sometimes unrelated fields of learning and were designed for the educated layman as well as for the specialist. With the growth of the number of periodicals, and owing to the fact that new theories often required a new technical language, various specialists, philosophers among others, could and had to use the language of their own disciplines—more professional, more precise, but for that very reason less comprehensible to the 'general reader'. This led to the professionalization of philosophy; thus philosophy or, at any rate, analytical philosophy became a philosophy for philosophers.

It is clear, therefore, that the emergence of a minimalistic philosophy, non-committal, critical and cautious, was in many ways prepared for and determined by various processes, great and not so great, which took place in Europe at the turn of the century.[3]

There is still another question to be answered. How did this philosophy acquire its distinctive form? Why did it become the philosophy of analysis and particularly the philosophy of linguistic analysis? This question leads us to consider the development of science during the last two centuries.

B. *The development of science as a necessary prerequisite*

The changes in the structure of economic, social, intellectual, and religious life in Europe already discussed do not explain the philosophically novel element in analytical philosophy, namely its hyper-conscious attitude towards language. Never before were philosophers so acutely aware of the importance of language in philosophy, of the snares and traps of language and of its uses and abuses. Once these were perceived, the hyper-conscious attitude

---

[3] Since, in my opinion, analytical philosophy does not have to be inseparably linked with scientific philosophy and in particular does not have to be considered as an extension of logical positivism, I have not felt it necessary to discuss the origins of the Vienna Circle. It is perfectly true that the teachings of Ernst Mach in Vienna at the turn of the century—his empiricism, his attempt at the scientific treatment of philosophical problems, his insistence on sobriety and meaningfulness in philosophical inquiry—were to become fundamental traits of the doctrines of the Vienna Circle, and no doubt had some indirect influence on analytical philosophy at large. But, since the origins of analytical philosophy are not the same thing as the origins of logical empiricism, although some people tend to think they are, the importance of Mach ought not to be overrated.

became the main factor in changing the philosophical landscape. Other factors, although also new, for example mathematical logic, seem to be correlated and, in a sense, subordinated to the main one.

The acquisition of this attitude towards language was not due to the achievement of one philosopher nor of a group of philosophers, but rather should be attributed to the development of science over the last two centuries.

As mentioned above, philosophers since Plato have paid a good deal of attention to linguistic considerations. And, as has also been mentioned, British philosophers sometimes formulated the rôle of language in philosophy in a startlingly contemporary way. In actual fact, some passages of Locke's *Essay Concerning Human Understanding* (Book III) seem to indicate that he was quite close to a complete understanding of the rôle of language in philosophical discourse. His ideas, however, were not developed by his successors, and consequently did not come to fruition; it appears that they were too premature for his time. With many new ideas in various departments of human thought, the process of their maturation is a long and often complicated one. Such was the process of crystallizing the linguistic approach to philosophy. The maturation of this process was to happen outside philosophy. It took about two centuries of scientific experience before the vague philosophical programmes of the seventeenth century could be fulfilled.

When scientists observed that language is not transparent, is not only a means of expression, but sometimes a force which shapes the content of our ideas, this immediately facilitated advances in science. This is quite apparent from the time of Linnaeus' reform of botany about 1750. There are even earlier indications, however, of a correlation between the progress of scientific theories and deliberate terminological 'break-throughs'.

By terminological 'break-through' I mean first a recognition that language is a kind of prison which hampers our theoretical activity, and secondly, an adoption of some linguistic reforms which ultimately lead to an advancement of the science. Old terminology and old concepts are, as a rule, inadequate for the description of the new content of scientific discoveries. The more clearly the language of a science is recognized as a conceptual prison, the more successfully can the scientist break down some of its constraining walls. *The history of science in the last two centuries is, in a sense, the history of breaking down the walls of the prison of language.*

This process of terminological break-through may already be observed at the beginning of the seventeenth century. William Gilbert, called the father of magnetism since he introduced and to a large degree shaped its terminology, is a case in point. He wrote in the introduction to his treatise *De Magnete*:

> We sometimes employ words new and unheard of, not . . . in order to veil things with a pedantic terminology and to make them dark and obscure, but in order that hidden things which have no name and that have never come into notice, may be plainly and fully published.[4]

Gilbert's lack of respect for established language and established categories allowed him to describe certain phenomena which otherwise could not have been described.

Galileo's achievements were no doubt largely due to his experimental genius, but also in part to his courage in dismantling the ladder of the Aristotelian categories of physics. What is first of all desirable, he wrote, is 'to find and explain a definition best fitting natural Phenomena'. He keenly perceived the problem of finding a proper language adequate for the new content of scientific inquiry. In a somewhat poetic manner he wrote:

> Philosophy is written in this vast book which stands forever open before our eyes, I mean the universe; but it cannot be read until we learn the language and become familiar with the character in which it is written.[5]

It was, of course, the language of mathematics which he recommended and afterwards applied with such success that it was to dominate physics during the following centuries. It might reasonably be claimed that, without introducing the quantitative language to physics (by means of which various relationships could be precisely expressed and thus precisely established, because they could have hardly been established if they could not have been adequately expressed), Kepler and Newton could not have formulated their laws.

From about 1750 the advances of knowledge achieved through

[4] William Gilbert, *De Magnete* (London, 1600); English trans. (New York, 1958), p. L.

[5] Galileo Galilei, 'Il Saggiatore', question 6, in *Discoveries and Opinions of Galileo*, trans. S. Drake (New York, 1957).

13

or, at any rate, in connection with the creation of new languages of the various sciences were striking and continuous. About 1740 Linnaeus accomplished his reform of nomenclature in botany. In this undertaking he seemed to be quite aware of the importance of introducing adequate names and definitions for the development of his science. He wrote:

> Botanists seem to me never to have touched upon nomenclature as a subject of study, and therefore this path of their science remains still unexplored. . . . There have been no laws laid down by which names could be made or defended.[6]

Linnaeus' reform of the language of botany had far-reaching consequences for the further development of that science. The number of botanical names, which had been growing since the time of Theophrastus, had, by the eighteenth century, multiplied to such an extent that it overwhelmed botanists. Linnaeus' system, resulting from his reform of the nomenclature, described every plant by two names: those of species and genus. In this way long, cumbersome, and ambiguous descriptions were replaced by short, logically unequivocal, and botanically adequate names.

Next came the reform of the language of chemistry initiated by T. Bergman about 1775, but brought to significant fruition by Lavoisier. When Lavoisier chose chemistry as the main pursuit of his life, he sought incessantly for logical clarity and cohesion of thought as well as for unambiguous and precise language. This was to a large extent achieved in his *Traité élémentaire de chimie* of 1784,[7] the first modern textbook of chemistry. In this treatise Lavoisier attacked 'the prejudice for which we originally have to thank the Greek philosophers, that all bodies in nature should be composed of only three or four elements'.[8] In the same treatise, he proposed to use the word *element* 'for all substances which we cannot decompose further, because only in this way can we in fact recognize them'. This is a memorable definition, since the whole development of chemistry was based on it. Lavoisier's revolutionary changes in chemistry were accompanied by his full recognition of the importance of language for expressing the content of chemical theories. This was stated by him *expressis verbis*

---

[6] *Correspondence of Linnaeus and Other Naturalists*, ed. Sir J. E. Smith (London, 1821), Vol. II, pp. 256–8.

[7] A. L. Lavoisier, *Traité élémentaire de chimie*, 2nd edn., Vol. I (Paris, 1793).

[8] Ibid., p. xv.

in his address delivered in 1787 and entitled 'Memoir on the Necessity of Reforming and Perfecting the Nomenclature of Chemistry'. Lavoisier said in this Memoir:

> That method which is so important to introduce into the study and teaching of chemistry is closely linked to the reform of its nomenclature. A well made language, a language which seizes on the natural order in the succession of ideas will entail a necessary and even a prompt revolution in the manner of teaching ... thus it is that the logic of a science is related essentially to its language.

It is quite clear therefore that the idea of the significance of language in 'making' science started to emerge at least 150 years before the appearance of analytical philosophy. The crystallization of this idea is particularly striking in the nineteenth century—in non-Euclidean geometries, physics, and mathematical logic.

Before examining the contribution of these sciences to the emergence of analytical philosophy, let us notice an interesting fact connected with Lavoisier's revolution in chemistry. His ideas about language turned out to be fruitful beyond expectation and stimulated remarkably the development of this science. We should not forget, however, that he was considerably influenced by Condillac's *Logique* of 1780, and quoted extensively from this work in *La Méthode de nomenclature chimique* of 1787 and in other papers.

Because Condillac exerted a rather strong influence on Lavoisier, it is perhaps worth while saying a few words on his ideas about language. First of all, it should be observed that Condillac's interest in language was not only technical. A true son of the French Enlightenment, he aimed at a total reform of learning through a reform of education. Language was to play the most important part in this reform. More specifically, the reform of language was to bring about a radical improvement in education. This linguistic reform was based on three principles:

1. In a manner similar to that of Descartes, the basic elements of a complex subject are to be discerned.
2. In a manner similar to that of Linnaeus and other naturalists, all the elements are to be classified according to logical, that is to say natural connections 'which subsist beneath all the welter of phenomena, all the chaos of irrelevant experience'.
3. A language should be constructed for a science, a language

based on the above classification and designed 'to fix the thing in the name' and thus 'cementing' memory to nature.

It is a well-known fact that Condillac, in his philosophy and particularly in his ideas about language, was himself influenced by John Locke. Therefore, although it would be somewhat hazardous to say that Locke's ideas directly influenced analytical philosophy, we may say that through their influence on Condillac, then in turn on Lavoisier, the development of chemistry, and the new approach towards language, they indirectly had some influence on the growth of analytical philosophy. We see here an interesting case of the mutual influence of science and philosophy. Locke's ideas, through Condillac, stimulated Lavoisier and brought about an advancement in chemistry. Then, having been dissolved into the bloodstream of science, these ideas later influenced philosophy.

The development of geometry in the nineteenth century was another step towards the full recognition of the significance of language in 'making' science. For a long time mathematicians had sought a proof of Euclid's fifth axiom (i.e. that through one point, only one line can be drawn parallel to a given straight line). At the beginning of the nineteenth century, two mathematicians, Lobachevsky and Bólyai, showed undeniably that this axiom is unprovable and in the process created new systems of non-Euclidean geometry. Lobachevsky assumed that through one point an infinite number of lines can be drawn parallel to a given straight line. At the same time he retained all the other axioms of Euclid. From this hypothesis, he afterwards deduced a set of theorems which were shown to be non-contradictory and which led to the construction of a new kind of geometry. After this break-through, it was relatively easy to create further systems of geometry. Thus Riemann's geometry also was based on a rejection of Euclid's fifth axiom and on the assumption that through a given point, the number of straight lines parallel to a given line is none.

At first most mathematicians treated Lobachevsky's geometry as a kind of logical curiosity. But when its, so to say, deductive fertility was fully realized and new geometries appeared one after another, and when the applications of such non-Euclidean geometries had been demonstrated, the general opinion changed. It was admitted that geometrical axioms are not synthetic *a priori* intuitions, as Kant claimed, and are not imposed upon us with such force that we cannot conceive of their opposites, or build a theoretical edifice upon them. It was admitted furthermore that geometrical postulates can be chosen conventionally and that one geometry cannot be more true than another, but may be, as some claimed, more convenient. It appears that the development of geometry at that time outran our intuition concerning the nature of the subject. And it appears also that language played a considerable part in this undertaking—what could not be conceived of was unexpectedly formulated in language and established as a pillar for a new foundation. A linguistic violation—because this is what it was at first—resulted in a profound conceptual change in our outlook. There is no doubt that the assertion that an infinite number of straight lines parallel to a given line can be drawn through a given point, was at first a linguistic freak if not an outright linguistic violation. From the point of view of ordinary language at that time, it was inconceivable and therefore unsayable. Once it was said and proved conceivable, it could not but lead to deep reflection upon the nature of language.

Thus investigations into the nature of geometry led not only to a different idea about the significance and nature of axioms, but also to more general reflections on the nature of science and of language. Through these investigations mathematicians began to perceive that the proper treatment of geometry is tied up with a new understanding of the language of geometry. This, of course, was extended to other sciences, physics in particular. The emergence of conventionalism may be regarded as an official and universal recognition of the influence of language on scientific theories and, indirectly, on human thought.

Pondering on the nature of physics, scientist–philosophers (Le Roy and Poincaré particularly) arrived at the conclusion that every system of physics has a hypothetical-deductive structure, which means that the system is dependent on a set of hypotheses on which it is constructed. Because hypotheses *ex definitione* are introduced in a partly arbitrary manner, a system of physics is not necessarily a reflection of reality, but rather a development and transformation of those concepts which were used for the formulation of the hypotheses. By investigating the nature of hypotheses and the rôle of conventions in physics, Poincaré and others pinpointed some of the peculiar features of the language of physics; exhibiting these features meant emphasizing their importance;

and emphasizing their importance meant at the same time sharpening our sensitivity towards language.

On the other hand, physicists themselves began to grasp what may be called the 'logical structure' of physical theories. They began to perceive the same logical structure in phenomena which were supposed to be different in kind. This was clearly expressed by Hertz when he wrote on Maxwell's theory.

> Maxwell's theory is Maxwell's system of equations. Every theory which leads to the same system of equations, and therefore comprises the same possible phenomena, I would consider as being a form or special case of Maxwell's theory; every theory which leads to different equations, and therefore to different possible phenomena, is a different theory.[9]

Grasping the logical structure was a way of showing that facts which seemed radically different were similar when reformulated in the *appropriate* language. The structure of a theory (or the form of equations in which phenomena are expressed) explains in an abstract way the phenomenon in question. This again was not only an exploration of the nature of physical theories, but also one of the language of physics. And indeed Hertz himself made some remarks indicating an understanding of this problem when he wrote:

> Ideas and conceptions which are akin and yet different may be symbolised in the same way by different modes of representation. Hence for a proper comprehension of any one of these, the first essential is that we should endeavour to understand each representation by itself without introducing into it the ideas which belong to another.[10]

Thus nineteenth-century physics was realizing Lavoisier's earlier idea that science cannot progress without improving and developing its language, and that *vice versa* an improvement of the language of a science is bound to further the development of this science. Since Lavoisier is always up to the point in his formulations, I shall quote him again:

> The impossibility of separating the nomenclature of a science from the science itself is owing to this, that every branch of physical science must consist of three things: the series of facts which are the objects of the science, the ideas which represent these facts, and the words by which these ideas are expressed. Like three

[9] H. R. Hertz, *Electric Waves* (London, 1899), p. 21. [10] Ibid., p. 21.

impressions of the same seal, the word ought to produce the idea and the idea to be a picture of the fact. And, as ideas are preserved and communicated by means of words, it necessarily follows that we cannot improve the language of any science without at the same time improving the science itself; neither can we, on the other hand, improve a science without improving the nomenclature which belongs to it.[11]

Of all the sciences, however, it was modern logic (now called mathematical logic) which contributed most to our full understanding of the rôle of language in intellectual endeavours; therefore, it more than any other science promoted the emergence of analytical philosophy. Mathematical logic has given our conceptual apparatus the precision which is required for the analysis and description of those concepts and problems with which analytical philosophy is preoccupied.

Many have seen Leibniz as the father of modern logic. Certainly his 'characteristica universalis' together with the 'calculus ratiocinator', anticipated the symbolic language of mathematical logic by more than a century. But his ideas remained unnoticed and undervalued until the twentieth century when they were rediscovered.

The transition from Aristotelian to modern logic was initiated by Augustus De Morgan. He made the first breach in the smooth wall of Aristotelian logic and contributed significantly towards ending the subject's long stagnation. It is rather paradoxical that the stagnation of logic was largely due to its relative perfection. Aristotle created a very neat and rounded system and formulated it with great clarity and definiteness. His successors did not think that there was room for further improvement. Even Kant thought that Aristotelian logic was 'the last word' in logic. Yet De Morgan enlarged and enriched Aristotelian logic, introduced new forms of syllogisms, for example the so-called oblique syllogism. Above all he introduced and developed a theory of relations.

And here the general idea of relation emerges, and for the first time in the history of knowledge, the notions of relation and *relation* of *relation* are symbolized. And here again is seen the scale of graduation of forms, the manner in which what is difference of form at one step of the ascent is difference of *matter* at the next.[12]

[11] Lavoisier, *Traité élémentaire de chimie*, Preface, p. 1.
[12] A. De Morgan, 'On the Syllogism', *Cambridge Phil. Trans.*, X (1858), p. 358.

A further development and turning-point in the new logic was due to George Boole and Gottlob Frege. The publication of Boole's *The Mathematical Analysis of Logic* in 1847 may be considered as the beginning of the new era of logic, that of mathematical logic. The break-through consisted in treating formal logic as a sort of algebra. Boole's algebra, of which one interpretation was formal logic, has since 1854 been improved in many respects, i.e. it has been axiomatized and interpreted in a variety of ways. At first interpretations were rather algebraic, and the algebra was treated as a class calculus. It was agreed afterwards that in essence Boole's algebra is a purely formal system, a set of inscriptions of a certain structure composed of symbols and intersymbols of specified shapes which allow new inscriptions to be constructed from those already accepted. The interpretations of Boole's algebra were, in the twentieth century, prolific beyond expectation. These enormous potentialities, however, were not very clear to Boole's contemporaries, who treated his algebra of logic as a mathematical invention unrelated to 'real' logic. But Boole himself seems to have been fully aware of the universality of his algebra. In *The Mathematical Analysis of Logic* he wrote:

> They who are acquainted with the present state of the theory of Symbolical Algebra, are aware that the validity of the processes of analysis does not depend upon the interpretation of the symbols which are employed, but solely upon laws of their combination.[13]

The insistence upon 'laws of combination' or, in other words, on the *form* of expressions and not on their content was to become the most characteristic feature of modern symbolic logic. Boole seems to have been aware also of the significance of language in the development of his algebra. However, he was involved in psychologism and contended that the laws of thought are to be interpreted psychologically. In the same study he wrote:

> ... The theory of Logic is thus intimately connected with that of Language. A successful attempt to express logical propositions ... should be founded upon the laws of the mental processes which they represent and would, so far, be a step toward a philosophical language.[14]

A further advance in logic was made independently by two mathematicians, Frege and Peano. Each arrived at his results by

[13] G. Boole, *The Mathematical Analysis of Logic* (Cambridge, 1847), p. 3.
[14] Ibid., p. 5.

the logical analysis of mathematics. The great contribution they made was to introduce a mathematical symbolism for deducing consequences from premises. This new symbolic language and the new method of drawing inferences swept aside Aristotle's logic, which is now considered but a limited collection of technical terms and a small set of rules of restricted power of inference. The syllogism constitutes only a small part of the subject-matter of contemporary textbooks of logic.

By the application of the symbolic language, Frege and Peano showed that such propositions as 'Socrates is mortal' and 'All men are mortal', regarded by Aristotelian logic as having the same form, are in fact different in form. An insistence on the *form* of the proposition, which appeared in a new light after the employment of symbolic language, made logic a science of logical forms. It became clear that in all inference, form alone is essential; the factual content is not important except to secure the truth of the premise. Further development of the technique of symbolism by Schröder and Russell made mathematical logic a precise and adequate instrument for reasoning in philosophy, science, and even in everyday life.

When suddenly the antinomies emerged in connection with Frege's *Die Grundgesetze der Arithmetik* (Vol. I, 1893) and shook the foundations of science, the conceptual apparatus was precise enough to deal with them. The necessity of solving these antinomies forced mathematicians, logicians, and philosophers to consider the structure of language more seriously and more thoroughly than ever before. Various theories of types, constructed after the appearance of the antinomies, can be thought of as homage paid to language.

Thus modern logic has supplied tools for enlarging the scope of and giving clarity to abstract thought, and has provided a countless number of possible hypotheses to be applied in the analysis of any complex problem. In this way it is the reverse of traditional logic or, as Russell expressed it, 'The old logic put thought in fetters, while the new logic gives it wings'.

The advancement of modern logic, with its highly specialized problems—e.g. axiomatization of mathematics in terms of logical constants or, in other words, a reduction of mathematics to logic seems at first sight rather irrelevant to the problem of language and science. But in fact it is of vital importance. By abstracting from incidental subject-matter, by purifying the form, and by introducing mathematical symbolism, the place of language has been refined and given its proper rank.

The development of science over the last two centuries provides many more instances supporting the thesis that scientific progress was linked to 'linguistic reforms' of the sciences. However, it is not our aim to trace all the instances or to write the 'linguistic history' of the sciences, but rather to examine the nature of these linguistic reforms and their consequences for analytical philosophy.

The process of acquiring a hyper-conscious attitude towards language, although covering many fields—e.g. botany, chemistry, geometry, physics, and logic—and evolving along sometimes very narrow and even devious paths, should be seen as one and the same thing. Once the process started to evolve in some sciences, other sciences came under the spell and, after a time, philosophy as well. Analytical philosophy is the final embodiment of this new attitude towards language.

The full recognition of the significance of language for philosophy does not, of course, imply a knowledge of *how* this came about. Neither does it mean that, because this attitude crystallized in science, analytical philosophy is to be intimately connected with science. We do not have to be historians of science in order to appreciate the achievements of science. We do not have to trace the interplay of various economic forces to experience the economic crisis when it comes. Whether analytical philosophers are aware of it or not, their attitude towards language is a reflection and, in a way, an inevitable heritage of an attitude developed substantially in the sciences. This was not the first time that changes in science or in society were reflected in philosophy in a seemingly unrelated way. It could be observed in eighteenth-century social philosophy with its prolonged discussions of such concepts as 'individual freedom', 'democracy', or 'the laws of nature'. These discussions, carried on in an apparently detached manner, were given impetus by social ferment and had vital implications for a new social order. Another example is the English idealism of the nineteenth century, which came as a reaction against the triumphs and threats of the natural sciences but did not itself try to be scientific, or to deal with the sciences.

On the Origins of Analytical Philosophy

RÉSUMÉ

Language is not all-important *in* philosophy, but it is of crucial importance *for* analytical philosophy. It is through the logical 'dissection' of language that analytical philosophy has acquired its distinctive characteristics. What is specific and new in analytical philosophy and what is common to various analytical movements is a contemplation of philosophy within the structure of language dissected in manifold ways. This anatomizing of language was accomplished through a long-drawn-out process occurring partly outside philosophy and partly within it. Other characteristics of analytical philosophy, such as its cognitive orientation, its piecemeal attitude towards philosophical problems, or even its scientific aspirations, are recurring features of many philosophical schools or attitudes, therefore they may be considered of secondary importance. From the point of view of the distinctiveness and novelty of analytical philosophy, its hyper-conscious attitude towards language is the factor of first importance. There would be no analytical movement if this attitude had not crystallized.

II

KAZIMIERZ TWARDOWSKI AND THE RISE OF THE ANALYTICAL MOVEMENT IN POLAND

I BACKGROUND

A genuine philosophical school is a phenomenon with many layers and many profiles; its sources and its influences are also numerous. No one is able to reconstruct it in all its aspects. In this chapter we shall attempt to sketch very broadly the background against which the school of Polish analytical philosophy emerged. Needless to say, the roots of this philosophy reach deeper and are more complex than depicted here. We have to start from one point chosen more or less arbitrarily; otherwise the *regressus* would lead us to antiquity.

In outlining the emergence of Polish analytical philosophy, various related philosophical trends will be mentioned. But no claim is made that all trends of this period are examined. We are not here concerned with the complete history of Polish philosophy in the twentieth century; even less so with its history in the nineteenth. Consequently, various cursory remarks about pre-analytical philosophy should be taken simply as points of reference, defining more clearly the realm of analytical philosophy proper.

Until the twentieth century Polish thinkers did not play an important or influential rôle in the history of European philosophy. In the period of the Renaissance (fifteenth and sixteenth centuries), it is true, they were quite accomplished in their own way. During the next two centuries, however, the Jesuits

24

gradually gained control over the entire Polish system of education with the result that thought became excessively rigid and
intellectual life stagnated. The middle of the eighteenth century
saw the beginnings of a period of educational reform. Intellectual
life awakened, but only briefly, for at the end of that century
Poland was to lose her independence for one hundred and thirty
years.

Nevertheless, in the nineteenth century quite a few novel ideas
were generated by Polish philosophical thought. Idealistic-
messianic philosophy, as represented by J. M. Hoene-Wroński and
particularly A. I. Cieszkowski was undoubtedly highly original;
its influence on Herzen and indirectly on Marx was appreciable.
Both Wroński and Cieszkowski produced their philosophical
systems abroad, mainly in France. On the other hand, in Poland
the most accomplished were J. Śniadecki and Hugo Kołłątaj
whose ideas in many respects anticipated Comte and the whole
positivist philosophy. But it would be an exaggeration to say that
any of them had a large influence or permeated philosophical
centres in Europe. Had it not been for the fact that Poland was
occupied in the nineteenth century, the renaissance of Polish
philosophy might have occurred earlier. This was to happen only
in the twentieth century, after Poland regained her independence
in 1918. Then a regeneration of Polish intellectual life and of
philosophy began in earnest. Before then Polish philosophers had
taken an active part in international congresses, but their efforts
lacked unity of direction. In occupied Poland conditions as a
whole were unfavourable for the development of philosophical
ideas and even less so for the creation of schools of philosophy,
with the exception of Galicia, which was under Austrian rule.

The first Polish philosophical school was founded by Brentano's pupil, Kazimierz Twardowski.[1] Brentano himself, as a
priest, was thoroughly trained in scholasticism and in Aristotle;
he later left the priesthood to become professor of philosophy in
Vienna. The legacy of Aristotle was therefore bequeathed by
Brentano to Twardowski. The elements Twardowski inherited
from his master were realism, objectivity, and the correspondence
theory of truth, in addition to a judicious attitude towards philosophical doctrines, and these elements he transmitted in turn to
his pupils. Thus the main characteristics of Polish analytical

[1] Twardowski was born in Vienna in 1866 and received his formal
education there. He died in Lwów in 1938.

philosophy became realism and the tendency towards objectivity inherited from Brentano, together with caution, minimalism, extensive employment of mathematical logic, and a sharpened sensitivity towards language.

British analytical philosophy derived inspiration from the same source. The realism of Moore and Russell was a decisive break-through leading to analytical philosophy; both were influenced and inspired by Meinong who, like Twardowski, was Brentano's pupil. Thus in both Britain and Poland, before the analytical movements proper started, realism and the tendency towards objectivity (both to a large degree inherited from Brentano) cleared the ground.

Twardowski established his headquarters at Lwów, but his school was called the Lwów–Warsaw school because most of his pupils made their contributions to analytical philosophy in Warsaw. The Lwów–Warsaw school, subsequently the core of Polish analytical philosophy, was the most important philosophical movement in Poland, both because of its influence on the country's intellectual life and because of its original philosophical achievements. Before the Second World War, Twardowski's disciples held most of the chairs of philosophy in Polish universities and in the 1930s the school gained an international reputation. This was probably the first time that Polish philosophy became known in Europe, and it is interesting to consider the factors which contributed to this recognition. Although not all sources can be traced when we attempt to explain so complex a phenomenon as the emergence of a philosophical school in a country without an established philosophical tradition, in the present case the seven major factors seem to be the following:

1. Born in Vienna and educated under Brentano, Twardowski brought to Poland philosophical maturity, high competence and an Aristotelian background.

2. The philosophy originating from Twardowski, given the name of 'small philosophy' by T. Kotarbiński,[2] showed the utmost care for semantic analyses. This was to become a leading tendency in European philosophical thought. In this the Polish analytical movement was in harmony with the philosophical mood of the time.

[2] The name was introduced by Kotarbiński in his inaugural lecture, 'Small and Great Philosophy', given at Warsaw University in 1918.

3. Twardowski's method of teaching, based on a somewhat Spartan drill, was thorough and systematic, but at the same time preserved broadness of horizon. Character was trained as well as intellect. An appreciation of the originality of ideas was instilled as of equal importance with wide philosophical knowledge. Many were unable to 'survive' that kind of school, but those who did were exceptionally well prepared for undertaking original research.

4. Twardowski's pupils, the generation which produced original ideas, matured philosophically in a free country. There was great enthusiasm, and even a renaissance in every field of scholarship, after Poland regained her independence in 1918.

5. Philosophers of the Lwów–Warsaw school worked in cooperation with mathematicians; the kinds of problems with which they dealt required a thorough knowledge of mathematical logic, which was developed by both philosophers and mathematicians. This was particularly noticeable in relation to certain antinomies, which were a matter of concern and even a source of annoyance to both. The Polish mathematical school was firmly established and well known at the time and stimulated those philosophers who were working in the field of mathematical logic. Indeed, many philosophers of the Lwów–Warsaw School—Leśniewski, Łukasiewicz, Ajdukiewicz, Tarski—studied mathematics, and the cooperation between philosophers and mathematicians was close and continuous.

6. A number of scholars with original minds also appeared on the scene; if this had not happened, Polish philosophy would probably have been limited to the understanding and interpreting of other philosophers' ideas.

7. The Poles, as is often claimed on the basis of their achievements in mathematics, theoretical physics, and mathematical logic, are gifted in analysis; they do not seem, however, to be so successful in creating syntheses.

The above seven factors concern Polish analytical philosophy 'proper', a philosophy which satisfies the criteria given in Chapter I. In addition to this logical-methodological-linguistic trend, some people would like to distinguish another as deriving from Twardowski, namely the psychological trend. Twardowski educated quite a number of psychologists. But since psychology became an independent science in the twentieth century, there is really no reason why psychologists in the strict sense of the word should be identified with philosophers. There is even less reason to treat them as if they were analytical philosophers. Thus, not all that originated from Twardowski is here given equal attention.

Though analytical philosophy was the prevailing and most significant trend in Poland between the two wars, it was not the only one. When Twardowski was beginning to teach in Lwów, the most important centre of philosophical activity in Poland was Cracow. The leading personalities there were Father S. Pawlicki (1839–1917) and M. Straszewski (1848–1921). In the nineteenth century, Cracow University established its reputation in the study of the history of philosophy and preserved it even after the First World War. Cracow was influenced very little by Twardowski's idea of philosophy. From the very beginning, Cracow philosophers showed a certain reluctance towards and a sense of separation from the approach of the Lwów–Warsaw School. The separation still remained after W. Heinrich (1869–1957) received a chair in 1905 and became a leading figure in Cracow. Heinrich studied under Avenarius and attempted to treat philosophy in a scientific way. In spite of this, he did not follow the trend initiated by Twardowski, nor did he even try to find a common ground with Twardowski's school.

At the time of Twardowski's appearance, the dominant position in Warsaw was held by H. Struve (1840–1912), a prolific writer, who delved into the history of philosophy, logic, epistemology, ethics, aesthetics, and psychology. His attempts to integrate new achievements of science with the traditional concepts of philosophy resulted, however, in a certain eclecticism. Another outstanding personality at that time was W. Lutosławski (1863–1952). He was associated with many places but did not settle in any particular one. He gained an international reputation with *The Origin and Growth of Plato's Logic* (London, 1897). Lutosławski was a colourful personality. At one time he advocated and practised yoga, at another he tried to establish an experimental community (in Algeria) for the sole purpose of producing geniuses. He was one of the most striking examples of Polish messianistic philosophers, believing that Poland was created in order to suffer and thus to save the world. His multifarious activities were not limited to the academic sphere. From time to time he had a number of enthusiastic followers, but he did not create a school of philosophy as did Twardowski.

Background

The only philosopher outside the analytical movement who developed philosophy in the grand, traditional manner and achieved results acknowledged outside Poland was Roman Ingarden, the phenomenologist. Born in 1893, he studied under Husserl at Göttingen and returned to Poland in 1924. Ingarden's philosophy is a fusion of two different traditions: German speculative metaphysics (of Brentano's rather than Hegel's kind) and restrained and painstaking Polish analytical philosophy. Although educated in Germany, he spent the rest of his life in Poland at the time when ruthlessly analytical orientation prevailed. Under pressure of the environment, he did not cease to weave grand philosophical designs, but wove them with excessive care and clarity. While opposing the onesidedness and narrowness of the analytical trend, Ingarden acquired the skills and techniques of analytical philosophers. This is why Ingarden's phenomenology distinguishes itself by intelligibility and clarity rather rare among metaphysicians and ontologists. In opposing the tenets of logical empiricism, Ingarden was probably the first to point out (in 1934) that the verification principle of meaning, being a meta-language proposition, is either meaningless or nonsensical since, like all meta-language propositions, it is in principle unverifiable.[3] This criticism was later followed by many others.

Ingarden was undoubtedly one of the most able pupils of Husserl, but in the sense in which Aristotle was the ablest pupil of Plato—as the one who starts from the position of the master to depart considerably from it later. Ingarden accepted Husserl's main analytical results and above all the phenomenological method, but rejected transcendental idealism as the inevitable solution. Instead, he showed the way to realism.

Ingarden's principal concern was with ontology. However, his way to ontology led through epistemology and aesthetics. It is aesthetics which as yet is the best known part of Ingarden's philosophy. Ingarden's extensive preoccupation with aesthetics and the original and significant results he achieved was but a station in his journey towards solving the controversy between idealism and realism. Ingarden's chief works in the philosophy of art are: *Das literarische Kunstwerk. Eine Untersuchung aus dem*

---

[3] Roman Ingarden, 'Logistyczna próba nowego ukształtowania filozofii' [A Logistic Attempt of a New Reform of Philosophy], *Przeg. Filoz.*, XXXVII, 1934. Also in French—'L'Essai logistique d'une refonte de la philosophie,' *Revue Philosophique* 120, 1935.

Grenzgebiet der Ontologie, Logik und Literaturwissenschaft (Halle, 1931); *O poznawaniu dzieła literackiego* [On Comprehending the Work of Literature] (Lwów, 1937); and *Studia z estetyki* [Studies in Aesthetics] (Warsaw, Vol. I, 1957; Vol. 2, 1958). In these volumes he was preparing the ground for the realistic solution in the controversy over the existence of the world.

Husserl had maintained that objects are either ideal or real. Ingarden pointed out that, apart from the two, there is the third kind of object—purely intentional objects. Real objects can be juxtaposed against ideal objects, but they can also be contrasted with intentional ones. These purely intentional objects are first and foremost objects of art. Works of art, as contrasted with spatio-temporal objects, depend for their existence on the conscious act of the artist. But they, nevertheless, transcend this act and continue to exist in their material shape afterwards. What makes them works of art is the intention of the artist to endow them with significance. It requires another intentional act on the part of the receiver to decipher this significance expressed by physically perceptible signs. Consequently, the work of art possesses many strata. In a literary work of art, for example, the following can be distinguished: (1) the visual or phonic stratum; (2) the stratum of the meanings of words and sentences; (3) the stratum of objects described; (4) the stratum of the appearances of these objects. All these strata are polyphonically orchestrated to compose one work of art. In a poem it is not the printed marks in the shape of letters, nor even the actual meanings of particular words that matter, but the 'poetic significance' achieved through these printed marks and through the meanings of particular words. The intentional act of the artist and another intentional act of the receiver are necessary for the existence of the work of art. And because of this works of art are called purely intentional objects.

Ingarden's main ontological work *per se* was his *Controversy over the Existence of the World*.⁴ It is impossible here even to begin to give an account of this treatise. It is an extraordinarily rich and ·complex work with problems of its own and a terminology of its own.

⁴ Roman Ingarden, *Spór o istnienie świata* [Controversy over the Existence of the World] (Cracow, Vol. I, 1947; Vol. II, 1948). The English translation of a substantial part of the first volume appeared in 1964 under the title *Time and Modes of Being*.

It would perhaps be premature now to attempt to give an appraisal of the full significance of Ingarden. It is sometimes claimed that his is the second phenomenology; the phenomenology freed from transcendental idealism and rooted in realism. It is also claimed that once his ideas are comprehended and absorbed, they will exercise a considerable impact and not only on the phenomenological school.

The only large group dealing with ontology and advocating a full philosophical system in the traditional sense were the neo-Thomists. The main centre of this school after 1918 was the Catholic University at Lublin. Among Catholic philosophers, the most outstanding were Father J. Woroniecki (1879–1949); Father K. Michalski (1879–1947), a renowned historian of medieval philosophy; Father J. Salamucha (1903–1944); and Father I. M. Bocheński (1902–   ). In recent years Bocheński has gained an international recognition. His works successfully combine scholastic subtlety, logical rigour (which no doubt he inherited from pre-war Poland), and a firm grasp of significant philosophical problems, usually rooted in traditional philosophy.

To return to Twardowski, he was a 'Brentanist' on the one hand and the founder of the Polish analytical movement on the other. He had an original and creative mind, but devoted himself almost entirely to teaching. He initiated a defence of the classical theory of truth, and his successors achieved important results in this field.

In the following pages of this chapter various aspects of his thought will be discussed. We shall first survey his contribution to the philosophy of mind, worked out in his early period in Vienna and not developed further in Poland. It is of relevance in understanding the transition from Brentano and his Aristotelian background to Polish analytical philosophy. Twardowski's theories on the philosophy of mind are now of historical value; Meinong improved upon them and transmitted them to the philosophical world at large.

In the next section the classical theory of truth is discussed in relation not only to Twardowski, but also in relation to his followers. The unshakability of Twardowski's belief in the Aristotelian concept of truth so influenced his pupils that even in the period when semantic notions were avoided as 'inconvenient' or even dangerous, the preoccupation with the theory of truth in Poland continued.

In the final section, Twardowski is presented as a teacher, because he contributed to Polish philosophy even more in that capacity than by his original writings.

2 TWARDOWSKI'S CONTRIBUTION TO THE PHILOSOPHY OF MIND

At the University of Vienna, Twardowski studied under Brentano and quite naturally followed Brentano's line of inquiry. At that time Brentano was interested in 'descriptive psychology' which was, broadly speaking, an investigation in the field of the philosophy of mind.

In the second half of the nineteenth century the philosophy of mind was dominated by a species of subjective idealism. It was contended that the existence of objects depends upon the operations of the mind. If there were no minds there would be no objects nor facts concerning these objects. Although this assumption was quite commonly held, heated discussions were centred around the question: What really lies behind those objects and facts which are being created by the mind? Is it a stream of consciousness, or is it sensation, or something else?

Franz Brentano was mainly responsible for the rejection of this approach, and for advancing the view that things and facts are not constructed by the mind but are simply recognized by it. It was under the influence of Aristotle's realism and partly under that of Fechner's inquiries in psychology that he developed his philosophy under the label of 'descriptive psychology'.

Brentano was not only responsible for the advancement of the philosophy of mind, but also initiated a new trend running counter to the prevailing speculative metaphysics, particularly German metaphysics. He considered Kant's philosophy a 'mistake which had led to grievous faults and to chaos in philosophy'. Philosophy, for Brentano, if it was to be a genuine science, needed to be grounded in psychology, that is to say inner experience or introspection. Thus, descriptive psychology, the very essence of Brentano's philosophy, was meant to be an empirical discipline, though in a different sense from the natural sciences. It was not based on experiment and observation but on direct apprehension of that which is before our minds. It was claimed that we can perceive our mental acts even though we cannot observe them.

The concern of descriptive psychology was with mental acts; the content of these acts, being non-mental, was outside the scope of psychology. From Descartes and Locke to Brentano's contemporaries, mental acts were considered to be inaccessible to systematic investigation because they cannot be observed. They cannot be observed, Brentano argued, but they can be perceived in inner experience. Consequently, consciousness for Brentano was not a complex of contents but a complex of acts. While observing, we trace the external appearances of things, using our sight; while perceiving, we examine the inner content of things, employing mainly our intellect. Thus the fundamental difference between science and psychology is that in science we 'observe' and in psychology, or descriptive psychology, we 'perceive'. It follows then that what is directly available to the scientist are not the objects themselves, but only their 'appearances'. Whatever he asserts about the objects of his science is a conjecture based upon his professional experience. The philosopher engaged in descriptive psychology has immediately before his mind the factual material of his inquiry. By examining mental acts he does not have to infer anything from something else, or to rely on the 'appearances' of things, but can describe directly that which is before his mind. Furthermore, in any science the apprehension of the objects of the science is a psychical process and is performed by our minds. Thus psychology provides the fundamental knowledge for all science—this was the thesis of psychologism. It was claimed that all the sciences, logic included, are, in the final analysis, to be reduced to psychology. The reason was the following: logic is concerned with the laws of thought. Thoughts are mental entities; their nature is a reflection and manifestation of the workings of the mind. Consequently, the laws of thought are the laws concerning the psychological mechanism of our thinking.

Psychologism had already been advocated by others, notably J. S. Mill, and it was not so important for Brentano and subsequently Twardowski as was the *practice* of descriptive psychology and the results achieved. Attempting to discover some characteristics which would be peculiar to mental acts, Brentano revived a property which in the Middle Ages was called the 'intentional inexistence' of an object 'which', wrote Brentano, 'we should describe as the relation to a content, or the direction to an object. . . . Every mental state possesses in itself something which serves as object, though not all possess their object in the same way.'[5]

The inquiry into the properties of mental phenomena was carried on by Brentano himself and by his pupils, of whom Twardowski was one. Brentano was an epistemological realist. Objects such as chairs and tables existed for him in the primary sense, and it is a special characteristic of mental acts that they have an ability to direct themselves towards something which is different from themselves. This is a fact *sui generis* without analogies in the external world and as such must simply be accepted. Thus Brentano's realism was based on the distinction between the mental act and the object towards which the mental act is directed. The 'intentional' relation, or ability to direct itself to something different from itself, is a peculiarity of the mental act.

This distinction, however, did not satisfactorily counterbalance the arguments of subjective idealists against realistic epistemology, because the question was still open as to *why* the object is perceived in this and no other way and what makes it be perceived at all. In short, Brentano himself did not discriminate between *content* and *object* (of the mental act) while resurrecting 'intentional inexistence'. Both the content of an act and its object were identified as the object of an act.

The analysis of the process of perception in terms of a mental act, its object and its content is usually attributed to Meinong. In fact, Twardowski was the first to distinguish clearly and sharply the third element: the content of a mental act. Meinong improved Twardowski's theory to some extent and wrote lengthy treatises on what he called 'the theory of objects'.[6] Twardowski produced only a single short treatise on descriptive psychology about which Professor J. N. Findlay has written: 'This is unquestionably one of the most interesting treatises in the whole range of modern philosophy; it is clear, concentrated, and amazingly rich in ideas. It represents a transitional phase between the image-theory of

[5] Franz Brentano, *Psychologie vom empirischen Standpunkte* (Vienna: 1874), II, p. 5.
[6] John Passmore observed this plainly: 'Meinong came to distinguish sharply between content and object with the help of the Polish philosopher, K. Twardowski, who in his *Towards a Theory of the Content and Object of Presentations* (1894) had distinguished three distinct elements in a "psychical phenomenon"—the mental act, its content and its object.' *A Hundred Years of Philosophy* (London, 1957), p. 182.

knowledge ... and the fully developed content theory of Meinong.'[7]

The treatise in question is *Zur Lehre vom Inhalt und Gegenstand der Vorstellungen* (1894), Twardowski's major philosophical contribution, for which he obtained a readership (a 'dozent' degree) at the University of Vienna. Perhaps the most important outcome of this investigation is a clear argument against Berkeleian idealism. During the act of perception the relationship between subject and object consists, as Berkeley claimed, in the fact that object becomes itself 'the content of consciousness'.

According to epistemological realists, of whom Twardowski was one, this relationship is quite different. In the act of perception, the subject moves as if away from itself to something else. This is an act of passing from the internal to the external world. Brentano attempted to explain this by attributing to mental acts an ability to direct themselves to something outside themselves. However, he failed to explain *why* an object should be perceived in this or that way. It is exactly the *content* that makes us perceive the object in a particular way. Through its content, which is, as it were, an intermediary step, we perceive the object. There is a bird in the sky which we perceive; we perceive it and no other object in the sky, and we perceive it in a particular way. This is a characteristic of the content which directs or forces the act itself to its object and which presents the object to our mind in a specific way, this and no other. Twardowski himself explained the three components, the act, the content, and the object, by the example of a painted picture and the process of painting in the following way.

If we compare the idea as an act with the act of painting, the content with the picture, and the object with the subject, a landscape for instance, depicted on the canvas, we shall have expressed approximately the relation between the idea as an act, its content, and its object. For the painter the picture is a means by which he depicts the landscape; he wishes to represent, paint, a real or imaginary landscape, and he does so while he paints a picture. He paints a landscape while he paints a picture of this landscape. The landscape is the 'primary' object of his painting activity and the picture the 'secondary' object. The case of an idea is similar. The thinking subject has an idea of some object, e.g. a horse. In having this idea, he sets a mental content before his mind. The content is an image of the horse

[7] J. N. Findlay, *Meinong's Theory of Objects* (London, 1933), p. 8.

35

in much the same way as the picture is an image of the landscape. If the thinker has an idea of an object, he has at the same time an idea of a content which refers itself to that object. The object of the idea as an act is its primary object; the content through which we have an idea of the object is the secondary object of the idea as act.[8]

In the above text, Twardowski uses the word 'idea' as equivalent to 'act'. The content of an idea and the object of an idea stand exactly for the content of an act and the object of an act.

The need to differentiate the third element, the content, in the act of perception was justified by Twardowski in a number of ways. Perhaps the most important is the fact that the content of an act (idea) is necessarily mental, whereas the object of an act (idea) may possess properties which no mental state can conceivably possess. For example, if we consider a golden mountain, we must realize that it is an extended object, which possesses a certain size and mass; it is made of gold, therefore it is different from granite; it may be larger or smaller than other mountains, etc. None of those properties can conceivably be thought of as an ingredient of the content of the idea of a golden mountain. That which we bear in mind is something mental, non-dimensional, without definite size or weight; made neither of gold, nor of granite, nor of any other describable substance, and it is simply absurd to conjecture that the *object* becomes an ingredient of our consciousness.

Another argument for observing the distinction between the content of an act and its object is this. The content of an act is an inseparable part of that act, whereas the object is not—it may or may not exist. If we take once again the idea of a golden mountain, we cannot have this idea without a certain content; yet the object has no existence whatsoever.

The content of an idea as distinct from its object was the subject of a powerful attack by Bolzano (1781–1848). Bolzano attempted to prove the impossibility of having an idea of a contradictory object. If we think of a round square, there is certainly no object in reality to correspond to the thought. If we are to have the content of this idea in our mind, according to Bolzano's argument, it would have to have contradictory attributes, and in that case it could not possibly exist because that which is con-

---

[8] K. Twardowski, *Zur Lehre vom Inhalt und Gegenstand der Vorstellungen* (Vienna, 1894), pp. 17–18.

tradictory cannot exist. If there is no idea without a content and if contradictory content is non-existent, then if we think of a round square we do not think anything at all. Twardowski's reply was as follows: From the fact that the object is contradictory and therefore non-existent, it does not follow that the content of the idea of that object is contradictory. Quite the opposite; because the content undeniably exists (we have an idea and therefore we have the content of this idea) it is not contradictory. Non-existence of the object does not prevent us from having the idea of that object, and therefore from having the content concerning that idea.

Other arguments in favour of the distinction made are comparatively less fundamental. One still worth mentioning is connected with the fact that we can have a single object and two different ideas concerning this object; it is therefore the content of those ideas which differentiates them. For instance, if we think of Rome first as the place where the Olympic Games took place in 1960, and next as that where Julius Caesar was killed, we have a situation of this kind. And conversely, the same idea may have many objects. The idea of a triangle has certainly only one content but undoubtedly very many objects: those existing and those possible. As to the first of these arguments, it might be maintained that when we point out two or more contents of the same object, it is, strictly speaking, not the same object but different objects. Caesar's Rome and the Rome of the 1960 Olympic Games may be considered to be two different objects.

The arguments given by Twardowski for the justification of his distinction of the act, its content, and its object were later developed at length with some corrections and many expansions by Meinong, who was more persuasive, more argumentative, and therefore more influential in the philosophical world at large.

Research in the philosophy of mind ceased to be attractive in Europe and Poland in the twentieth century for at least three reasons.

1. The defeat of psychologism, primarily the result of Husserl's *Logische Untersuchungen*. After descriptive psychology was dethroned as a super-science, inquiries into philosophical psychology, the philosophy of mind in particular, lost their attractiveness. Twardowski himself was once under the spell of psychologism, but later freed himself from its influence. His essay,

'O czynnościach i wytworach' (On Actions and Products), provided a weapon against the claim of psychologism that all the sciences in the final resort are to be reduced to psychology.[9] This claim, Twardowski argued, was based on confusing psychical actions (acts) with the products of these actions. The fact had escaped notice that 'psychical products can possess such properties that certain relationships among them (e.g. relationships between judgements concerning their truth and falsehood) can be ascertained *a priori*, therefore independently of the empirical results of psychology'.[10] The business of psychology is to inquire into psychical phenomena. The results of mental activity are the subjects of inquiry of the other sciences.

2. In the twentieth century psychology definitely emancipated itself as a science, becoming separate and independent from philosophy. Because of this, Twardowski's pupils specialized in either subject. Psychologists were either concerned with experimental psychology in Wundt's and Fechner's manner, measuring the threshold of stimuli and other measurable phenomena, or were engaged in 'conceptual' psychology. The most outstanding among Polish psychologists were: W. Witwicki, S. Baley, and M. Kreutz; each was Twardowski's pupil.

Witwicki (1876–1948) was a leading figure in Polish psychology in the inter-war period. In Poland he anticipated Adler's theory of power. In 1900 he presented a theory which he called 'cratism', in which he formulated the thesis that the human being instinctively avoids humiliation and quite naturally seeks power. This drive for power he saw as one of the most fundamental motives of human existence. It seems that it was in a large degree under his influence that a conceptual rather than an empirical or physiological approach prevailed in Polish psychology.

3. In 1907 Łukasiewicz began to teach mathematical logic in Poland. This discipline was making remarkable advances at the time, and quite understandably it attracted the attention of many

[9] Otherwise this essay had no influence. The idealistic semantics advocated in it, claiming that there must be, roughly speaking, special entities to correspond with certain forms of speech, was neither developed nor followed by his pupils who, on the contrary, developed and adhered to distinctly nominalistic semantics carried to their fullest extent in the work of Kotarbiński.

[10] K. Twardowski, *O psychologii, jej przedmiocie, zadaniach, metodzie, stosunku do innych nauk i o jej rozwoju* (On Psychology, its Subject, its Tasks, its Method, its Development, and its Relationship to Other Sciences) (Warsaw, 1913).

scholars. Łukasiewicz, although by training a philosopher, had a definite mathematical bent and began to propagate mathematical logic on a large scale in his early years. In 1910 he published *On the Principle of Contradiction in Aristotle*,[11] which was an historical break-through. In an appendix to this study, Łukasiewicz discussed Russell's antinomy of the classes. This problem became the subject of persistent and even obsessive inquiries by other Polish philosophers, particularly Leśniewski. After this study appeared, a distinct logical orientation can be discerned in the Lwów–Warsaw school. This was initiated by Łukasiewicz's inquiries, reinforced by Leśniewski's work on the foundations of mathematics (free from antinomies), and further strengthened by Ajdukiewicz's *On the Methodology of Deductive Sciences*, published in 1921.

All these logical crusades were inspired by and related to Russell's *Principia Mathematica*, which was the object of burning controversy; Twardowski himself took no part in these.

3 THE CLASSICAL THEORY OF TRUTH

A. *Twardowski's position*

In this section we shall present not only Twardowski's opinion concerning the concept of truth but also contributions of other analytical philosophers who, starting from Twardowski's standpoint, went beyond him. The views of Polish Marxists concerning truth will also be considered. The Marxists, although nominally in opposition to Twardowski, were nevertheless influenced by him.

The paper, 'On the So-Called Relative Truths',[12] in which Twardowski argued against the relativity of truth, together with his spoken advocacy of the classical theory of truth (as formulated by Aristotle and bequeathed to Twardowski by Brentano), decisively established the classical theory in Poland. This view was later generally accepted in Polish analytical philosophy.

11 *O zasadzie sprzeczności u Arystotelesa* (Cracow, 1910); see Chap. III, p. 65 ff.
12 K. Twardowski, 'O tzw. prawdach względnych' (On the So-Called Relative Truths) in *Księga pamiątkowa Uniwersytetu Lwowskiego ku uczczeniu 500-ej rocznicy Uniwersytetu Jagiellońskiego* (a Book to Commemorate the 500th Anniversary of the Jagiellonian University) (Lwów, 1900). A German translation in Archiv für Systematische Philosophie (1902). 2nd Polish edn., Polskie Tow. Filoz. (Lwów, 1934).

Twardowski's paper on truth is neither highly original nor particularly revealing. It is discussed here at considerable length because of the subsequent preoccupation of Polish philosophers with the theory of truth, and because this paper set the direction for further development. Twardowski's aim was to disqualify the claims of those who tried to distinguish between unconditionally true judgements and those only relatively true. These claims were found to be based on an imprecise and ambiguous formulation. If the meaning of each judgement is stated clearly and unambiguously, the relativity of truth disappears.

> There are no judgements which would be true only in certain circumstances and under certain conditions, which, following the change of these conditions and circumstances, might become false; on the contrary, every judgement, if it is true, is everywhere and always true, and it therefore follows immediately that those that are not always and not everywhere true are not at all, never were, and never will be true.[13]

However, the relativist might argue that such judgements as 'This flower has a pleasant odour', are only relatively true. To prove this, one requirement would have to be met, that the very same judgement would be true in certain circumstances and become untrue when the circumstances are changed. This is definitely not the case, because the relativist does not perceive that the identity of the external shape (identical letters or even words) of two expressions does not guarantee identity of meaning.

Expressions of the same shape (composed of the same letters) can express different judgements, because the words in an expression may have many meanings or because the expression itself is elliptic. When we are asked, 'Have you read *Hamlet*?', we usually reply, 'Yes.' This one word stands for the proper reply, 'I have read *Hamlet*'. In reply to the question 'Was Nelson ever married?', we also say, 'Yes,' but these two affirmatives obviously stand for two different things. There is no ambiguity when they are considered in context. Such elliptic expressions are very useful, and indeed unavoidable in everyday speech, but the variety of their usage ought not to be considered as a valid proof of the relativity of truth.

[13] K. Twardowski. 'On the So-Called Relative Truths', 2nd edn., p. 7. This quotation, as well as almost all other quotations from the writings of Polish philosophers, has been translated by the author.

Let us suppose that I utter the expression 'It is raining' while I am standing in Trafalgar Square in London and it is indeed raining. According to relativists, this is only relatively true, because one would not be able to utter this judgement at a different time or at a different place where the weather was fine. Twardowski, on the other hand, claimed that the judgement 'It is raining' uttered in these specific conditions is unconditionally true and always will be true. The point of importance here is that I am not speaking of any rain falling at any time and in any place; I assert a judgement about the rain falling *here and now*. I ought perhaps to say, 'It is raining here and now'.

But this would not be enough because, according to relativists, the words 'here and now' make the judgement still only relatively true. The same judgement, when uttered tomorrow or in another place, can become untrue. Of course, the words 'here and now' are notoriously ambiguous. The astronomer never says that 'There is now an eclipse of the sun', but always scrupulously indicates the time. The geographer never uses the word 'here', but gives accurate co-ordinates. The same applies to the words 'here and now' in the above expression. If we want to avoid ambiguities and to state accurately what is meant by the expression 'It is raining here and now', we would have to say 'At 8 o'clock p.m. Greenwich mean time on 25 August 1963, according to the Gregorian Calendar, it is raining in Trafalgar Square in London, England.' This long and cumbersome sentence is replaced by the succinct expression 'It is raining'. If this is uttered by a person present in Trafalgar Square at a specified time, we can safely assume that the person will not be misunderstood.

When this reconstruction is completed, we see clearly that the claims of relativists concerning the relativity of truth of the sentence 'It is raining' are ill-founded. The same expression pronounced in Trafalgar Square, and again on the island of Capri in the blazing sun, has a different content, and consequently we are dealing with two quite different judgements. Their logical status in terms of truth and falsity is different.

In a similar kind of way, Twardowski dispensed with the claims of relativists with regard to such expressions as: 'A cold bath is healthy.' When properly formulated with the use of quantifiers (for every person and at any time or for some persons and at some times), these expressions cease to be only relatively true. Once they are true, they are always true.

Finally Twardowski challenged the tenents of epistemological relativism, which is often used by relativists to support their claim that our psychosomatic constitution is an irremediable hindrance to correct judgement and to the unconditional truth. If this is so, then no judgement can appear as truth, and consequently the judgement about the human condition is not to be considered as true either. In other words, the standpoint of epistemological relativism is self-defeating, because it is based on the assumption which it seeks to overthrow.

The distinction between unconditional and relative truths is, therefore, only a figurative one. 'As regards judgements themselves, we cannot talk about their unconditional or relative truth, because every judgement is either true at all times and in all places, or it is not true at all in any place or at any time.'[14]

B. *Further development of the theory of truth*

The acceptance of the classical theory of truth had an important influence on the whole course of the analytic trend in Poland. The thesis that truth consists in the conformity of thought with reality implied the existence of the external world, and hence realism in terms of ontological commitment. This ontological commitment could be expressed as materialistic monism (Kotarbiński and Leśniewski); as pluralism (Łukasiewicz and Tatarkiewicz); or objective idealism (Witwicki and pre-war Ajdukiewicz), but it never took the form of subjective idealism, which was mistrusted altogether.

A heated discussion on the nature of truth was already in progress in Poland during the first two decades of the twentieth century. Among the philosophers who took part in it were Leśniewski, Łukasiewicz, and Kotarbiński. The most significant results, however, came in the 1920s and in the first years of the 1930s, particularly as far as Tarski is concerned. In Kotarbiński's main epistemological treatise of 1929, it was claimed that a sentence which asserts that such and such is the state of affairs is true if and only if the state of affairs is such and such. More simply, the truth of a sentence consists in its conformity with reality. This conformity is not to be conceived as identity or similarity, and hence we should distinguish the classical Aristotelian notion of truth from the 'pictorial' theory of truth held by the atomists.

---

[14] K. Twardowski. 'On the So-called Relative Truths', 2nd edn., p. 43.

From Kotarbiński's formulation of the classical concept of truth, the way was not far to Tarski's rigorous treatment of this problem. But without a highly developed logical syntax and a heightened sensitivity to language as distinct from metalanguage, the semantic concept of truth could never have been satisfactorily defined. Thus Tarski's definition of truth was a crystallization of two processes: the long-lasting defence of the classical concept of truth, initiated by Twardowski and carried on by Leśniewski, Łukasiewicz, Ajdukiewicz and particularly Kotarbiński; and the rise and development of semantics in a narrower sense. The latter was to a very large extent due to Leśniewski.

Stanisław Leśniewski (1886–1939), Twardowski's pupil, was the first in Poland and probably in Europe[15] to initiate a systematic study of philosophical semantics, conceived as an inquiry into 'expressions of a language and the objects those expressions are concerned with'. Grappling for more than eleven years with the problem of the antinomy of the classes, he developed many concepts which were later of vital importance for the formulation of Tarski's definition of truth, in particular the distinction between logic and metalogic. Leśniewski himself published but little. His publications appeared at scattered intervals over several decades in different journals and in different languages. None appeared in English—the most important language for transmitting knowledge of mathematical logic. His incurably perfectionistic attitude accounts for the fact that his disciples sometimes published papers on topics initiated by him, before he himself decided to do so. Some of his results were never published and were never attributed to him because in the search for perfection he waited too long; similar results were achieved and reported by others. In the power and originality of his mind, he was second to none among Polish philosophers. He was influential, but in a very small group; his ideas fertilized the minds of only those who were around him. His informal discussions were a vital part of the oral

[15] In recent years the prominence of Polish philosophers in semantics has been acknowledged. John Passmore, in *A Hundred Years of Philosophy*, writes: 'Semantics of the more narrowly philosophical sort derives from Tarski rather than from Ogden and Richards. In strict historical justice we should describe the work of Leśniewski and T. Kotarbiński to which Tarski is greatly indebted. But this has been published only in Polish. For the world outside Poland, Polish semantics begins with the appearance in a German translation of Tarski's 1933 essay on the semantic conception of truth.' (London, 1959), p. 402.

tradition of the Warsaw School of logic. He had practically no influence in a formal or institutional setting.[16]

Tarski's definition of truth was constructed in his famous essay, 'Pojęcie prawdy w językach nauk dedukcyjnych' (Warsaw, 1933), and translated into English under the title 'The Concept of Truth in Formalized Languages'.[17] This paper is both too well known and too technical to discuss extensively here. (As was stated at the beginning, no attempt is here made to survey or evaluate the logical enterprises of Polish analytical philosophers.) In short, for the first time a formally correct and materially adequate definition of the classical concept of truth was provided. More specifically, the definition given was that of a true sentence in a language L. It was demonstrated that non-contradictory definitions can only be constructed for a given language L. In other words, Tarski's definition is relativized to a language. Such a definition, therefore, cannot be stretched to cover all languages. Moreover, it can only be applied to formalized languages, whose structure is exactly specified (primitive terms explicated, as well as rules of definition, criteria for distinguishing sentences, and rules of inference.) This definition does not apply to everyday language, which is too 'untidy' and too 'rich' for the correct construction of any semantic notion. In everyday language, which is semantically closed—that is to say, which contains expressions, names of these expressions, as well as semantic notions like 'true' which refer to the expressions of this language—the antinomy of the liar can be constructed. As an example of this antinomy can be given the following:

> The boxed statement is false.

Now is this statement true or false? Let us suppose that it is a true statement; then if it is true, what it asserts is the case and consequently it will have to be considered as a false statement. Let us assume on the other hand that it is a false statement; then being

---

[16] The work on the reconstruction of Leśniewski's logic has been carried on for many years. Scholars most devoted to this task are: J. Słupecki (in Poland), Cz. Lejewski (in England), B. Sobociński and E. Luschei (in the U.S.A.). In their respective publications various contributions of Leśniewski are examined. The most comprehensive study so far is Luschei's *Logical Systems of Leśniewski*.

[17] A. Tarski, *Logic, Semantics, Metamathematics* (collected papers) (London, 1956).

false, what it asserts is not the case. So, since what it asserts is not the case, then, considering what it asserts, it must be true. Hence the contradiction.

The price to be paid for the precise formulation of the classical concept of truth is high indeed. It can be applied only to artificial languages. At the time of its publication, Tarski saw his work as having an important philosophical significance. He conceived of the immensely complicated apparatus of mathematical logic as the 'necessary tools for the investigation of even purely philosophical problems'. Ten years later he qualified the confidence he had placed in semantics. He wrote: 'It is perhaps worth while saying that semantics . . . is a sober and modest discipline which has no pretensions of being a universal patent medicine for all the ills and diseases of mankind, whether imaginary or real.'[18]

The philosophical significance of Tarski's concept of truth is slightly ambiguous, as is the kernel of his achievement. That is not to say that his discourse is ambiguous or that there are flaws in the construction of the semantic concept of truth. Rather, there are philosophical aspects which can be assessed differently according to the point from which one views the theory. It suffices to examine divergent opinions about 'what Tarski's concept of truth is about' to realize at once that various, often incompatible interpretations result from various approaches. Max Black wrote that:

> . . . The neutrality of Tarski's definition with respect to the competing philosophical theories of truth is sufficient to demonstrate its lack of philosophical relevance [because] neither this, nor any formal definition of truth, goes to the heart of the difficulties which are at the root of the so-called philosophical problem of truth.[19]

Black does not quite say what is at 'the heart of the difficulties' and what is 'the root of the so-called philosophical problem of truth'. One may guess that the *epistemological* aspects of the concept of truth are meant here. If the issue is whether truth is possible or not; whether, providing it is possible, it is a correspondence between reality and its linguistic description or some form of coherence among linguistic descriptions, then indeed

[18] A. Tarski, 'The Semantic Concept of Truth', *Philosophy and Phenomenological Research*, No. 3 (March 1944), p. 345.

[19] Max Black, 'The Semantic Concept of Truth,' *Analysis* (March 1948), p. 61.

Tarski's treatise on truth has little to offer. The assumption being made there is that truth consists in a correspondence and the concern of the treatise is to define this correspondence clearly. This re-establishment of the correspondence theory of truth as a basis for our inquiry (but not an inquiry into the nature of truth) is viewed by some as being of paramount importance. Thus Karl Popper claimed:

> . . . Tarski's greatest achievement, and the real significance for the philosophy of the empirical sciences lies, I believe, in the fact that he re-established a correspondence theory of absolute or objective truth which showed that we are free to use the intuitive idea of truth as correspondence with the facts.[20]

In this context Tarski's definition may be thought of as solving no 'philosophical' problem of truth, but rather as serving to relieve the anxiety of many philosophers who suffered from adhering to the classical (correspondence) concept of truth and from being unable to formulate it satisfactorily. It should be clearly seen that what Tarski achieved was the (more exact) *formulation* of the old Aristotelian concept. In the 1930s, when *precision* was the watchword and 'metaphysics' a very bad term altogether, open adherence to the classical concept of truth, which seemed to imply an element of metaphysics if not mystery, resulted in embarrassment. Tarski brought relief when he showed that, retaining all the criteria of precision, the classical concept of truth could be used as a perfectly respectable, non-metaphysical concept. This was clearly expressed by Popper:

> . . . although I accepted, as almost everybody does, the objective or absolute or correspondence theory of truth—truth as correspondence with the facts—I preferred to avoid the topic. For it appeared to me hopeless to try to understand clearly this strangely elusive idea of a correspondence between a statement and a fact.[21]

This was also the position of other philosophers, notably Carnap and Ajdukiewicz. However, Tarski's formulation did more than end worries. As Popper and others admitted, the correspondence theory of truth is rather vital for the development of the philosophy of science, which assumes that scientific theories deal with reality and are to be assessed in terms of truth and falsity. In this context Tarski's formulation is a prerequisite for inquiries in the philosophy of science.

[20] K. R. Popper, *Conjectures and Refutations* (London, 1963), p. 223.
[21] Ibid.

On still another plane Tarski's definition was made the battle-ground in the controversy over the nature of language, that is whether ordinary language is consistent or inconsistent. Did Tarski ever attempt to show that ordinary language is inconsistent? It is doubtful. His concern was with formalized languages, and the perfunctory remarks he made about ordinary language were an expression of his regret that natural languages cannot be treated in a precisely formal fashion. Does it follow, however, from his conclusions about formalized languages that ordinary language is inconsistent? It does if we understand the meaning of the terms 'consistent' and 'inconsistent' as they are are understood in formalized systems. The critics of Tarski who insist that ordinary language is not inconsistent (characteristically, more of them say that ordinary language is not inconsistent than simply that it is consistent) use the terms 'consistent' and 'inconsistent' in a way which is different from that used in formalized languages. It is exactly clear what is meant by consistent and inconsistent statements in a formalized language. It is not exactly clear what we mean by inconsistent statements when we recognize that ordinary language is consistent. If we are able to recognize inconsistent statements in ordinary language, this means that they belong to it, and consequently that ordinary language is inconsistent. If there are only consistent statements in ordinary language, then we do not have a notion of inconsistent statements and consequently we cannot even talk meaningfully about the problem of inconsistency. This aspect of Tarski's theory which has to do with the controversy over the nature of language I shall call *linguistic*. It seems that, regardless of how profitable this discussion stemming from Tarski has been, it is not germane to the main tenor of Tarski's own considerations.

In addition to the aspects of the semantic concept of truth, already discussed, another view is offered by Alonzo Church, who wrote:

> ... Tarski has emphasized especially the possibility of finding, for a given formalized language, a purely syntactical property of the well formed formulas which coincides in extension with the semantical property of being a true sentence. And in Tarski's *Wahrheitsbegriff* the problem of finding such a syntactical property is solved for various particular formalized languages.[22]

[22] Alonzo Church, *Introduction to Mathematical Logic* (Princeton, 1956), p. 65.

Church's is perhaps the most accurate and most proper interpretation. Tarski's definition of truth, considered as finding a purely syntactical property of the sort specified by Church, is without question the task which he set for himself.

Whether, and in what sense, we perceive the philosophical significance of the semantic concept of truth, the fact is that Tarski's essay was a landmark in the history of modern semantics. It was, as R. M. Martin put it, 'a fountainhead whence almost all subsequent work on the subject sprang'. Thus Tarski's essay was significant in a more general sense—as the beginning of an era in which semantics was recognized as a philosophical discipline. Furthermore, semantics contributed, in the course of time, towards overcoming some of the limitations of analytical philosophy when the latter was dominated by syntax.

After the semantic definition had been provided, the interest of Polish philosophers in the theory of truth did not diminish. On the contrary, some philosophers who had previously adhered to this theory, but were unwilling to tackle it explicitly, as it seemed to be overshadowed by the antinomy of the liar, began to discuss it.

Further inquiry into the concept of truth was carried on after the war by Mme Maria Kokoszyńska,[23] who published two papers in English concerned with the theory of truth: 'What Means the "Relativity of Truth"?' and 'A Refutation of Relativism of Truth'.[24] The first is a continuation and refinement, with the help of mathematical logic, of the arguments put forward by Twardowski in his essay 'On So-Called Relative Truths'. The second paper is an exposition of Tarski's achievements in the theory of truth.

More important, however, is the work of Roman Suszko.[25] He accepts the classical concept of truth, and particularly Tarski's formulation according to which truth is relativized to language. But he goes a step further and relativizes truth to language and to a model. His important contribution is the introduction of the

---

[23] Mme. Kokoszyńska was Ajdukiewicz's pupil, who in turn was Twardowski's pupil.

[24] These papers appeared in *Studia Philos.*, Vol. 3 (1946) and Vol. 4 (1948) respectively.

[25] R. Suszko, 'Logika formalna a zagadnienia teorii poznania' (Formal Logic and the Problems of the Theory of Knowledge), *Myśl Filoz.*, Part I, 2/28 (1957); Part II, 3/29 (1957).

second relativization, that to a model. Tarski relativized truth only to language.

Truth, in Suszko's understanding, is a general relationship between 'a sentence of a language' and a certain 'model M' attributed to this language. The traditional formulation of the classical concept of truth refers to the conformity of thought with reality (object). In Suszko's theory, the reference to reality (object) is generalized and replaced by 'model M'. The relativity of truth in the sense above specified is connected with the problems of the development of cognition.

Sentences true in one epoch (in a model corresponding to an epoch) and false in another are called *partly true*, in contrast to *eternal truths* which are true for an epoch and remain true in every following epoch (models corresponding to following epochs). The *picture of the world* is defined as a set of assertions approved of by science in a given epoch; the *perspective of the world* is a deductive system of these assertions; and the actual *knowledge about the world* is the picture of the world in a given epoch.

The absolute concept of truth can be introduced relatively—separately for each epoch; it can be introduced in particular for $t = t_0$; that means that the absolute concept of truth is relativized to the language of the actual epoch t_0.

Suszko's arguments are expressed in a highly technical language of mathematical logic and abstract algebra. The philosophy of every age is derived from and based upon the achievements of the sciences of that age, and the philosophy of our age should be based, according to Suszko and many mathematically minded philosophers, on the new achievements of the mathematical sciences. Suszko himself goes so far as to assert that 'formal logic is . . . an abstract and highly specialized . . . part of the theory of knowledge'.[26] He argues that the specific problems of the theory of knowledge are centred around the relationship between thinking and the objects of thought. These relationships, from the point of view of formal logic, are semantic relationships between language and models. Hence he is prompted to assert that 'formal logic is a part of the theory of knowledge'.

Suszko reiterates his position in the essay, 'Formal Logic and the Evolution of Human Cognition,' delivered to the International Colloquium of the Philosophy of Science held in London,

[26] Op. cit., 3/29, p. 45.

July 1965. (This essay can be found in the volume containing papers of the colloquium.) Labouring over the concept of *diachronic* logic, Suszko argues for the usefulness of formal logic in the analysis of human cognition. It seems, in general, that he is under the spell of the idea, now almost entirely abandoned, that mathematical logic can cure all philosophy.

Perhaps it might be added that no suggestion is made here that Twardowski and Suszko are discussed on the same pages because they share intrinsically the same manner of treating the problem of truth; far from it. The link is only historical; once Twardowski gave the impetus to the discussion of truth, this problem remained obstinately in focus for decades, even after Marxism came to dominate Polish philosophy. Thus in Poland the classical definition of truth continued to hold the attention of philosophers, and furthermore was extended beyond the analytical school, although disguised in different terminology.

It was not mere chance that the first extensive monograph on the Marxist concept of truth ever written in the Marxist world was produced in Poland. The treatise in question was Adam Schaff's *Some Problems of the Marxist Theory of Truth*[27] (1951). True, Schaff clearly wished to advocate and defend the Marxist position, and particularly its Leninist interpretation. However, a substantial part of his work consists in a polemic against the theory of truth held by Polish analytical philosophers—Twardowski, Kotarbiński, Ajdukiewicz, Tarski. Throughout the treatise Schaff emphasizes in an exaggerated form the differences between the Marxist and the classical standpoints. Nonetheless, his indebtedness to the philosophers criticized and the extent to which he incorporated their learning into his theory are far greater than he would wish to admit.[28] Moreover, in Schaff's study, we can perceive the influence of analytical philosophy in terms of method; many fine distinctions had been made which were later 'substantiated' by relevant quotations taken from the 'classics' (of Marxist philosophy). Schaff's treatise was recognized

---

[27] Adam Schaff, *Z zagadnień marksistowskiej teorii prawdy* (Some Problems of the Marxist Theory of Truth) (Warsaw: K. i. W., 1951); 2nd enlarged edn., 1959.
[28] A more extensive discussion of the problem of truth in Marxist philosophy, particularly in Poland, is to be found in *Philosophy and Ideology—The Development of Philosophy and Marxism–Leninism in Poland since the Second World War* (Dordrecht., 1963) by Z. Jordan.

as a standard work on the Marxist theory of truth. This 'analytic' and to a certain extent 'linguistic' approach was a novelty in the Marxist philosophy which was to crystallize more distinctly in the time to come.[29]

Another important contribution to the Marxist theory of truth was made by a young Polish Marxist, Leszek Kołakowski. It should be remembered that before he declared himself a Marxist, Kołakowski studied under T. Kotarbiński and Mme J. Kotarbińska, and therefore his essay, under the title: 'Karl Marx and the Classical Definition of Truth',[30] ought not to be considered as entirely surprising. In his essay Kołakowski is concerned with the epistemological standpoint of the young Marx as radically opposed to the 'Marxist' epistemology which was formulated by Engels and particularly by Lenin.

Kołakowski examines two theories which claim that the practical activity of man has an epistemological bearing: positivistic Marxism, 'which refers to the effectiveness of activity as a criterion by which we can test our knowledge', and Jamesian pragmatism, 'which introduces practical utility as a component of the definition of truth.'[31] Kołakowski shows that the first theory can be compatible with the classical definition of truth, but also points out that in its later development by Engels and Lenin, Marx's theory involved some fundamental revision. Instead of holding that judgement is to conform with reality, Lenin stated that our theories were nothing but the best possible copy of the world at any given time. Although, according to Marx, we live in a reality which is man's reality, explored by man and, in a sense, created by man, 'there is an unchanging reality common to us all'. Because of this, Kołakowski claims, we can apply the Aristotelian concept of truth so successfully.

> The conformity of the judgement with reality is not a relation between the judgements and the world itself; it is used in that world to which the human being has already given a substantial form.[32]

The discussion of the concept of truth continued in Poland, chiefly among Marxists, in the early 1960s. Needless to say, the

[29] This problem will be discussed further in Chapter VII where analytical-linguistic Marxism, a specifically Polish phenomenon, is analysed.

[30] L. Kołakowski, 'Karol Marx i klasyczna definicja prawdy' (Karl Marx and the Classical Definition of Truth), *Studia Filoz.*, 2(2), 1959.

[31] Ibid., p. 43.

[32] Ibid., p. 59.

tradition of the analytical school weighed very heavily in this discussion.[33]

After this excursion, let us return to Twardowski.

4 THE FORMATION OF THE POLISH ANALYTICAL MOVEMENT

A. *Twardowski as a teacher*

In 1895 Twardowski moved to Lwów, where he was appointed to the chair of Philosophy at the University. He still continued his research, but the results, although abundant, were not so original. He did not stop writing, but his work after 1895 was of a different calibre. However, a few of his later works are of some theoretical importance, such as 'Wyobrażenia i pojęcia' (Images and Concepts) of 1898; 'Über Begriffliche Vorstellungen' of 1913; 'O istocie pojęć' (On the Nature of Concepts) of 1924. In these works he minutely and thoroughly analysed images and concepts, and was probably the first to introduce the concept of intentional judgement into modern philosophy. Intentional judgement is judgement which is entertained but not believed, e.g. in 'Napoleon was a Russian general', we comprehend the idea but do not believe the statement.

On arrival in Lwów, Twardowski found philosophy in a far from flourishing state. He was thus faced with the dilemma of whether to continue his previous line of inquiry, or to sow the seeds of future development. Although he had said in the past that the goal of his life was to build philosophy, he chose the second alternative and became a teacher. For thirty-five years he devoted himself with undivided attention to the creation of the Polish philosophical school.

Twardowski was an exceptionally gifted teacher with great pedagogical intuition and an unusual organizing ability. Although these qualities are not uncommon among teaching philosophers, their combination in Twardowski and their forceful utilization brought about uncommon results. In teaching his students, he

[33] See papers by A. Wiegner, Mme H. Eilstein and W. Krajewski in *Studia Filoz.* It is interesting to observe that Kołakowski's essay on the subject, although very relevant to the discussion, was completely disregarded by such orthodox Marxists as Mme Eilstein, owing, as it appears, to Kołakowski's unorthodox approach to Marxist philosophy.

distinguished the knowledge of philosophical problems (the understanding of their different solutions with the arguments pro and con) from a philosophical outlook on the world.

As to the first point, his virtuosity in instilling knowledge of philosophical problems was universally acknowledged. He was one of those pedagogues who teach and influence students through personal example. It can fairly be said that Twardowski's life and work were perhaps the most important components of his educational method.[34]

In turn he was very demanding, and his school was a hard one. Lectures began at six o'clock in the morning. Nevertheless, it was not military drill which was the outstanding feature of his school, but rather the way of philosophizing which he imposed upon his students. He developed to an unusual degree their ability to interpret texts.[35] The student was compelled to put into his own words the content of a given philosophical paragraph. Moore's question 'What on earth did he [the philosopher] mean?' was very often employed. Two goals were set in this way: first, an understanding of the author's thoughts; second, developing the author's ideas through clarifying and expressing in a lucid form what the author merely suggested, expressed vaguely or ambiguously. Particular emphasis was laid on the ability to criticize each philosophical doctrine by discovering all gaps, shortcomings, and inaccuracies in reasoning. In this activity Twardowski encouraged the student to be plain but precise. As a result, a rather unusual stringency of thought was developed. Reasoning was always under the firm control of logic. There was no place for bombast or tortuous argument. What was to be said had to be said clearly and accurately. Twardowski's main concern was to nourish the critical faculties of the student. The question of converting students to any particular doctrine was immaterial to his teaching. Twardowski himself was very reticent about his own

[34] He was a kind of sage to whom not only his students could come at any time to discuss philosophy, but also the townspeople of Lwów to seek help on their personal problems. His unbending character, highly developed sense of justice, exceptional devotion to the university and to teaching led to his being elected Rector three times. He made no discrimination, whether of race, religion, or nationality—Poles, Ukrainians, and Jews were all treated alike. It was also to a great extent due to him that women were admitted to the University of Lwów.

[35] His favourite philosophical readings were those of the English empiricists, Hume's *Treatise* in particular.

philosophical credo.[36] Perhaps it is true that in the course of time he became exceedingly sceptical and that this killed his creativeness. What is most striking about his standpoint is sobriety, caution, and moderation. He fought against logistics when he thought that it had become a danger to philosophy;[37] but we ought not to forget that in 1898 he himself lectured on new achievements in mathematical logic for the first time in Poland.

The main significance of his work, however, lies not in his crusade against other philosophical doctrines, nor in developing his own theories, but in establishing a philosophical school. In this he was entirely successful. His non-committal attitude undoubtedly helped his pupils to form a school of 'small philosophy' where the nucleus of philosophical activity consisted in meticulous analyses.

B. *Homogeneity of the analytical movement in Poland*

It is sometimes held that we cannot speak of Twardowski's school as the only one or, in other words, about the homogeneity of analytical philosophy in Poland. It is claimed that, apart from the Lwów school, which was concerned with philosophical psychology, there was in fact another school, the Warsaw School of Logic, influenced by Twardowski but quite separate.

True, we would not be able to find a body of beliefs shared by master and followers, the usual criterion of a 'school of thought'; but we would be able to find a body of disbeliefs. And above all the same principles of methodological procedure were advocated by all adherents of the school. Through all the stages of its development there was an unvarying conviction of the way in which philosophy should be treated. Traditionally, in the history of philosophy, a school of thought is defined by the ideas of a group of thinkers. But often a turning-point in philosophy has been made by a new approach, by introducing new methods of philosophizing. It seems quite legitimate, therefore to apply the term 'philosophical school' to movements whose main accomplishments sprang from the soil of a methodological unity. The Lwów–Warsaw school is a case in point.

---

[36] Some people claim that in later years he secretly adhered to the philosophical doctrine of Fechner. However, there is no evidence for this in his writings.

[37] See K. Twardowski, 'O symbolomanii i pragmatofobii' (On Symbolmania and Pragmatophobia), *Ruch Filoz.*, Lwów, VI, 1921.

The significance of Twardowski's school should also be measured by its importance to the intellectual life of the country. Practically everyone in the Polish philosophical world came under its spell. In determining the intellectual atmosphere of the country, this school had no rivals. Its influence on all other philosophies in terms of asserting the need for rigour in philosophical argument was unquestioned; its significance for other humanistic disciplines in terms of providing suitable categories was repeatedly admitted; its success in the rehabilitation of philosophy as a 'respectable' inquiry in the layman's eyes was striking.

RÉSUMÉ

It is not easy to characterize Twardowski's place in the history of Polish philosophy. This is always difficult with regard to those persons who sacrifice their own creativeness to initiate a school or a movement which may reach a culminating point in the next generation. Twardowski was not so original a thinker, or at any rate not so accomplished as some of his pupils. He gave rise to the analytical movement in Poland, but himself belonged to the period of transition. His original contributions were in the philosophy of mind, which later was developed by Meinong as the theory of object, and which inspired Husserl to create a new branch of philosophy—phenomenology. Twardowski's merit was to advocate effectively the classical (correspondence) concept of truth, the extensive discussion of which accelerated the emergence of semantics in the narrower sense as contrasted with syntax. His greatness lay in his teaching, which led to the creation of a school of philosophy of international reputation. His importance for Poland goes beyond philosophy. One might say about him what John Stuart Mill said about his father: 'He did not revolutionize or create one of the great departments of human thought. But in the power of influencing by mere force of mind and character the convictions and purposes of others, he left few equals among men.'

III

JAN ŁUKASIEWICZ AND THE DILEMMA

OF MODERN SCIENTIFIC PHILOSOPHY

I EARLY DEVELOPMENT

Jan Łukasiewicz was born in 1878 in Lwów, then part of the Austro-Hungarian monarchy, and completed his primary and secondary education there. He started his philosophical training under Twardowski, who was already a professor of philosophy at Jan Kazimierz University at Lwów. In 1902 he received his doctor's degree with distinction, and in the next four years visited various philosophical centres in Europe. In 1906 he returned to Poland and received the degree of a 'Privat Dozent'. In the next year he began to teach philosophy and mathematical logic as a Reader in Lwów University, and continued to teach there as a professor until 1915.

In 1915 Łukasiewicz moved to Warsaw, where he was appointed a professor of philosophy at the University. He was elected its Rector for the academic year 1922–1923 and re-elected for 1931–1932. For a short time in 1918 he was secretary of the department of higher education at the Ministry of Religious Affairs and Public Education and was a member of Ignacy Paderewski's cabinet. Łukasiewicz was awarded the degree of doctor *honoris causa* by the University of Münster in Westphalia in 1938, and by Trinity College, Dublin, in 1955.

During the Second World War Łukasiewicz remained in Warsaw. His unpublished manuscripts were burnt in the siege of 1939. After the war he moved to Brussels for a short time and finally in 1946 he was invited to Dublin where he was appointed a professor of mathematical logic by the Royal Irish Academy. From 1946 until 1956 he lectured, mostly on symbolic logic, at the Academy in Dublin; occasionally at University College, Dublin; Queen's University, Belfast; and the University of Manchester. In spite of his considerably advanced age and serious heart trouble, a legacy of the war, his Dublin period was one of the most prolific of his academic career. He died in Dublin in 1956.

To the world outside Poland Jan Łukasiewicz is known as a logician and a historian of logic. His philosophical views are unknown, because none of his philosophical papers has been translated into English. In this chapter Łukasiewicz will be presented as a philosopher, although his logical profile will also be sketched. At the beginning of his career he considered logic basically as an auxiliary means of securing the soundness of philosophical inquiry. But, in the course of time, Łukasiewicz the philosopher was eclipsed by Łukasiewicz the logician. Logic became all-important. Against traditional philosophy with its ambiguity, vagueness, and amorphousness he contrasted the systems of formal logic in which he found a paradigm for philosophical inquiry. His own logical systems, unique in precision and formulated in the succinct language of mathematical symbols, were conceived as models for *the* system of philosophy. This was his idea of scientific philosophy. Thus he demanded that philosophy should be as precise and definite as logical systems can be. His attempt to make philosophy scientific was not unique; many philosophers in the twentieth century have had the same intention, but his venture was perhaps bolder than others.

Łukasiewicz's desire to make philosophy scientific had two main sources: the teaching of Twardowski, who often claimed that philosophy should be treated in a scientific manner; and Łukasiewicz's own preoccupation with mathematical logic.

At first Łukasiewicz had no clear idea of what scientific philosophy should look like. However, as early as in 1907[1] he demanded that philosophical argument, to be recognized as valid, must fulfil the requirement of scientific precision. Criticizing an argument of Sigwart he said: 'To appeal to undefined and intangible feeling, or to explain the concept of action as ambiguously

---

[1] J. Łukasiewicz, 'Analiza i konstrukcja pojęcia przyczyny' (Analysis and Construction of the Concept of Cause), in *Z Zagadnień logiki i filozofii, pisma wybrane* (On Problems of Logic and Philosophy—Selected Papers), (Warsaw, 1961).

57

as Sigwart did, would not do in critical scholarship.'[2] In the same paper, referring to empiriocriticism, he wrote: '. . . this theory could not be consistently carried on; it does not fulfil the requirement set for scientific research.' At the end of the paper Łukasiewicz formulated for the first time his philosophical credo:

> The systems of the theory of knowledge that have been created are, in fact, beautiful but fantastic and unscientific. And when I search for the reasons for what seems to me the downfall of philosophy, I find always one and the same: the lack of historical education in the great representatives of modern philosophy, the lack of scientific tradition.[3]

Moreover, in the same paper he said:

> Neither Kant nor Hume knew what metaphysics is . . . Hume's and Kant's struggles against metaphysics were not real struggles; their treatises do not indicate that they ever looked into Aristotle.[4]

It is clear that Łukasiewicz at that time did not condemn metaphysics or traditional philosophy, nor did he think that its study would be useless. What he recommended was a different approach based on logical analysis as opposed to the prevailing psychological one. His study of the concept of cause is an example of his early idea of the scientific treatment of philosophy. It is a logical analysis of one chosen problem which is first properly formulated, next purified of irrelevancies and metaphysical muddle, reconstructed with the help of logic, and completed with a body of conclusions expressed in simple and unambiguous language. Finishing his essay he wrote: 'I have attempted to explain every assertion so clearly and unequivocally that no one could doubt what I thought. I hope that if there are any mistakes in my work they will be easily found.'[5]

The results achieved by Łukasiewicz were, for his time, new, original, and interesting. His Platonic bent at this stage was quite obvious. The logical analysis and construction of the concept of cause meant for him 'to find out the characteristics of the abstract object called cause and examine the relationships which occur among them [these characteristics].'[6] By the application of the inductive method, he came to the conclusion that the 'objects' which are called *causes* are only those which 'are correlate with

[2] Op. cit., p. 20.   [3] Ibid., p. 53.   [4] Ibid., p. 53.
[5] Ibid., p. 56.   [6] Ibid., p. 50.

regard to the *effect* and which remain to the effect in such a necessary relationship that the object, being a cause, brings forth
necessarily the object which is the effect.'[7] From this it follows
that the effect does not necessarily have to bring forth the cause.
Among those characteristics which define the abstract object
called cause, the *time relationship* does not have to be included.
Łukasiewicz's formulation of the causal relationship was significantly different from empiricist and other theories of causality at
that time which claimed that the causal relationship could be
reduced to the relationship of antecedent and consequent.
Logically then the cause implies the effect; if cause, then effect;
$p \rightarrow q$. However, q does not imply p.

The characteristics (of the abstract object called cause) obtained
by the application of the inductive method were next tested by the
deductive method. At this stage the author claimed to prove that
non-occurrence of the effect implies necessarily non-occurrence of
the cause'; from this it logically follows that non-occurrence of the
cause is not to be necessarily tied to non-occurrence of the effect.
At this stage *modus tollens* is in action: $(p < q) < (- q < -p)$
That is: from the negation of q (non-occurrence of the effect)
follows non-p (non-occurrence of the cause), but not conversely.

Łukasiewicz also claimed that the universally accepted conviction that nature is governed by causal necessity is 'only a
premature and unscientific formulation of the data of experience'.
The indeterministic conviction so strongly expressed in this essay
resulted perhaps from his scrutiny of the concept of cause. But
it is equally feasible that his indeterministic outlook preceded the
essay and gave rise to it. He defended his conviction with unswerving determination for the rest of his life. As we shall see
later, the origin of the three-valued logic was in a way a by-product of his defence.

Before we go any further, two points should be brought into
focus regarding Łukasiewicz's early philosophy; the first concerns
his attitude towards traditional philosophy. He wrote: 'My
opinions were formed in opposition to the great philosophical
systems of modern philosophy such as Hume's and Kant's, and
out of this attitude grew this essay.'[8] This theme will occur
repeatedly in his later philosophy. The second point has to do
with his attitude to logic. Throughout the essay on cause Łukasiewicz made great use of logic (at that time ordinary, not

[7] Op. cit., pp. 50, 51.   [8] Ibid., p. 53.

symbolic) and very much pursued accuracy and definiteness of thought and expression. A concern for logicality, precision, and clarity eventually came to dominate his thinking.

In his later work on mathematical logic, when he arrived at original and important results, this attitude to philosophy became extreme. Let us first briefly trace his contributions to logic in order to understand better his wholesale condemnation of metaphysics and his prophetic call for a new, scientific philosophy.

2 CREATIVE ACHIEVEMENTS IN THE FIELD OF MATHEMATICAL LOGIC AND PIONEER WORK IN THE HISTORY OF LOGIC

Although, as already said, this book does not attempt to examine and evaluate the achievements of Polish logic, a brief review of the logical accomplishments of a thinker will sometimes be given in order to provide a key to the understanding of his philosophy. Such is the case with Łukasiewicz. It is only in conjunction with his work and achievements in formal logic that we can understand his philosophical evolution, his later condemnation of all traditional philosophy and his stringent programme for a new scientific philosophy.

Łukasiewicz's inquiries in mathematical logic were focused on two main problems: the classical calculus of propositions, and many-valued logics. He thought of the propositional calculus as a laboratory in which the properties of formal systems can be analysed. His work on deductive systems has a more than merely technical value. By investigating the properties of these systems and thereby the properties of mathematical cognition, he enlarged our comprehension of the deductive method and deepened our understanding of the essence of mathematical cognition. It is in these terms that the philosophical significance of his work on the propositional calculus should be assessed. As the result of these investigations, he felt entitled to assert on behalf of the Warsaw school of logic: 'We have probably understood better than others the nature of formal systems and how they should be built.'

In the course of his inquiry, Łukasiewicz invented a special notation which replaced the traditional one which uses parentheses. In his symbolism he used the signs C, N, A, K, D, E—to stand respectively for: implication, negation, alternation, conjunction, alternative denial, equivalence. In this symbolism, the connectives are written before the arguments. This notation has been accepted by other logicians and is known in Europe as the Łukasiewicz notation, and in the United States as the Polish notation. Compared with the traditional one, it is more economical, more easily manipulated, but perhaps less obvious. Investigating and constructing deductive systems on the basis of the propositional calculus, he strove for the maximum of simplicity and elegance.

In 1879 Frege formulated a simple axiomatic system for the propositional calculus as follows:

$$
\begin{aligned}
&\text{I. } CpCqp &&\ldots\ldots\ldots\ldots\quad p < (q < p) \\
&\text{II. } CCpCqrCCpqCpr &&[p < (q < r)] < [(p < q) < (p < r)] \\
&\text{III. } CCpCqrCqCpr &&\ldots\quad [p < (q < r)] < [q < (p < r)] \\
&\text{IV. } CCpqCNqNp &&\ldots\ldots\quad (p < q) < (-q < -p) \\
&\text{V. } CNNpp &&\ldots\ldots\ldots\quad -(-p) < p \\
&\text{VI. } CpNNp &&\ldots\ldots\ldots\quad p < -(-p)
\end{aligned}
$$

Łukasiewicz discovered that the third axiom is superfluous because it follows from axioms I and II. Soon after, he also proved that the axioms IV, V, and VI can be replaced by a single one. He formulated a system of axioms of his own, preserving the same primitive terms of implication and negation:

$$
\begin{aligned}
&\text{I. } CCpqCCqrCpr &&\ldots\quad (p < q) < [(q < r) < (p < r)] \\
&\text{II. } CCNppp &&\ldots\ldots\quad (-p < p) < p \\
&\text{III. } CpCNpq &&\ldots\ldots\quad p < (-p < q)
\end{aligned}
$$

For many years the problem of the 'single, sufficient and shortest axiom' of the propositional calculus was eagerly investigated by Łukasiewicz and his followers. In 1925 Alfred Tarski provided such an axiom containing fifty-three letters. Owing to the work of Łukasiewicz and B. Sobociński, other such axioms were found, each shorter than the last.[9]

It was, however, the creation of many-valued logics that

[9] In 1933, Sobociński provided the following twenty-seven letter axiom:
$$CCCpqCCCNpNrsCrtCuCCtpCvCrp$$
which was shortened soon afterwards by Łukasiewicz to twenty-five letters:
$$CCCpqCCCNpNrsCrtCuCCtpCrp$$
and shortened again by Łukasiewicz in 1936 to twenty-three letters:
$$CCCpqCCCNrNstrCuCCrpCsp.$$
The shortest one as yet proposed containing twenty-one letters was given by C. A. Meredith, Łukasiewicz's Irish associate, in 1955:
$$CCCCCpqCNrNsrtCCtpCsp.$$

brought Łukasiewicz his fame and assured him a permanent place in the history of logic, and therefore in the history of philosophy.

Łukasiewicz's paper 'On the Three-Valued Logic'[10] was published in 1920. In the next year, E. L. Post presented his three-valued logic, but the two were created independently. In actual fact, we have definite evidence that Łukasiewicz's three-valued logic had already been constructed in 1917, because in 1918 he mentioned it for the first time in a farewell lecture delivered at Warsaw University on 7 March 1918.[11] 'I proved that, apart from true and false statements, there exist possible statements which have to do with something else besides being or non-being. So the three-valued logic which I worked out in detail last summer has emerged.[12] The system in itself is as solid and consistent as Aristotle's logic, but much superior to it with regard to the wealth of laws and formulae.'

In 1922, in his paper 'Numerical Interpretation of the Theory of Propositions', he constructed the first many-valued system of the propositional calculus. In relation to this he wrote:

> The system explained is the *first* system which differs from the normal system of propositional calculus and is founded on *intuition*.

[10] J. Łukasiewicz, 'O logice trójwartościowej' (On the Three-Valued Logic), *Ruch Filoz.*, V, 1919, 1920.

[11] The address was published as a single-page leaflet and as such can be found in various libraries in Poland.

[12] An interesting exchange of arguments took place in 1961 between Professor Greniewski and Professor Kotarbiński, both of Warsaw University, as regards the priority in creating the three-valued logic. Professor Greniewski asserted that Jan Łukasiewicz was not the only creator of the three-valued logic. In fact, according to Greniewski, the first outline of the three-valued logic can be traced in Kotarbiński's paper, 'The Problem of Existence of the Future' of 1913. In reply, Kotarbiński said: 'It is undoubtedly true that ideas expressed in the specified paper were concerned with the possibility of prescribing a third logical value to at least some sentences. However, no attempt was made to build an axiomatic system of the three-valued logic, and, as a whole, this paper was apart from considerations of mathematical logic.' In reply to this, Professor Greniewski made the following distinction: the creator of the first three-valued logic was Tadeusz Kotarbiński; Jan Łukasiewicz, on the other hand, was the creator of the first three-valued system of propositional calculus. Next, Greniewski went on to say, referring to Kotarbiński's book, *Lectures in the History of Logic*: 'The historian of logic, Tadeusz Kotarbiński, should be accused of neglecting Tadeusz Kotarbiński, the logician.' (This discussion took place in the weekly *Przegląd Kulturalny* (*The Cultural Review*), 21–31 December 1961; and 25 January 1962.)

Although Post (1921) has already investigated a many-valued system of propositional calculus from a purely formal point of view, he failed to interpret it logically.[13]

Łukasiewicz always emphasized that his systems of many-valued logic evolved from philosophical investigation, whereas Post's were the result of a formal game. In fact, the emergence of the three-valued logic was prompted by Łukasiewicz's defence of indeterminism—the only philosophical issue to which he was committed and which he defended with unabating conviction even after having withdrawn from the field of philosophy. Łukasiewicz thought that the deterministic outlook which, according to his own words, regards facts happening in the world as parts of a monstrous movie-drama prepared somewhere in the workshop of the universe, is not obvious at all and is in fact, rather incredible. But he admitted that there are two powerful arguments to support determinism. One, descending from Aristotle, refers to the law of excluded middle; the other, already known to the Stoics, refers to the principle of causality.

Two sentences, e.g. 'There will be a sea battle tomorrow' and 'There will not be a sea battle tomorrow,' are contradictory. They cannot both be true. There is another logical law, the law of excluded middle, which asserts that of two statements composing one compound sentence like the following: 'Either there will be a sea battle tomorrow or there will not be a sea battle tomorrow' —both cannot be false. Therefore, one has to be true. This is the conclusion following from ordinary logic. Łukasiewicz objected to this and claimed that statements about the future are neither true nor false, but have a certain *intermediary* value which he called the third value apart from the accepted two: truth and falsehood. This was not an admission of any kind of relativism in the theory of truth, but an admission of the third logical value; something between truth and falsehood. Hence sprang the system of the three-valued logic as consistent and legitimate as the traditional, bivalent one.

The difference between the two-valued logic and many-valued ones could be perhaps best illustrated with the aid of a geometrical diagram. If we take a true statement p, then its negation not-p will be false. We can symbolize truth by 1 and falsity by 0. Geometrically we may say that truth will be at the beginning of

[13] J. Łukasiewicz, 'Interpretacja liczbowa teorii zdań' (Numerical Interpretation of the Theory of Propositions), *Ruch Filoz.*, VII, 1922/23, p. 92.

our diagram and falsity at the opposite pole, after we have turned 180°. Thus a change in the logical value from truth to falsity or vice versa is always a turn of 180°.

If we negate our statement twice, then as in geometry we arrive at the original point; we then turn 360°. In the two-valued logic we can only turn 180°—from one pole to another. The introduction of the third logical value is, in geometrical terms, an admission of turns of 90°. So that we can be at neither of the poles but between them. Numerically, if true statements are symbolized by 1, false statements by 0, then the in-between, that is the intermediary statements, will have the value of $\frac{1}{2}$.

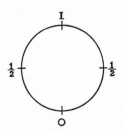

The geometrical diagram suits us admirably for infinitely many-valued logic. Then we can move from one pole to another through infinitely many stages—as indeed is the case in geometry.

The philosophical significance of the concept of a many-valued logic was assessed differently by different people. Łukasiewicz himself thought that his creation was comparable with the creation of non-Euclidian geometries. Some people, notably Reichenbach, saw in it a solution to difficulties in which modern physics found itself after Heisenberg stated the principle of uncertainty. Irrespective of the philosophical assessment, many-valued logic became an invaluable instrument for inquiries concerned with the two-valued logic and especially with the problem of the logical independence of sentences and axioms. The concept of a many-valued logic proved to be comprehensive enough to embrace other non-classical logics created independently, as for example Lewis' logic of strict implication or Heyting's intuitionistic logic. The researches of Łukasiewicz's pupil Wajsberg showed that these logics can be interpreted as different species of many-valued logic.

Apart from mathematical logic, another field which Łukasiewicz pioneered was the history of logic. His work on Aristotle's logic was partly prompted by his indeterministic outlook. In order to preserve his indeterminism he had to remould a part of Aristotelian logic. But this was not the only source of his interest. He was struck also by the absence of innovation in formal logic for so many centuries. From Aristotle until the nineteenth century, there had been no progress in logic. Kant himself thought that logic, as presented by Aristotle, was the last word which could be said in this field. This illusion, as it now appears, was due to the fact that Aristotle produced a very neat and rounded system; when faced with this seemingly finished creation, his successors saw no possibility of further development. In order to find the reason for this state of affairs, Łukasiewicz decided to analyse, from the point of view of mathematical logic, what had been written on logic in the past. He was the first to apply the method of mathematical logic systematically in all his historical research. His publications in this field marked the beginning of an era which turned out to be fruitful beyond expectation.[14] His first explorations resulted in *O zasadzie sprzeczności u Arystotelesa, studium krytyczne* (On the Principle of Contradiction in Aristotle) of 1910, already mentioned (Chap. II, p. 39). This study is a good example of the clarity, lucidity and elegance of Łukasiewicz's style. Through a creative interpretation (this method was par-

---

[14] Łukasiewicz's studies in the history of logic stimulated other Polish logicians: Adam Krokiewicz continued research in Stoic logic; Konstanty Michalski investigated medieval logic; J. Salamucha dealt with Ockham's propositional calculus; Z. Jordan with Plato's logic; Father J. M. Bocheński devoted a great deal of attention to the history of logic in his *Formale Logik* in addition to his main studies in the field (*La Logique de Theophraste*, Fribourg, 1947 and *Ancient Formal Logic*, Amsterdam, 1951); and finally Tadeusz Kotarbiński published in 1957 his *Lectures in the History of Logic* in which he examined the problems of the history of logic since Aristotle from the standpoint of formal logic.

ticularly cultivated in Twardowski's school), Łukasiewicz shed a new light on Aristotle's logic. On the basis of Aristotle's original writings, he formulated three principles of contradiction:

1. *Ontological*—'No object can possess and simultaneously not possess the same property.'

2. *Logical*—'Two sentences, one of which attributes a property to an object, and another which denies it, cannot both be true.'

3. *Psychological*—'Two beliefs which are expressed by two contradictory statements cannot exist in one mind.'

Łukasiewicz claimed that the ontological and logical principles are equivalent to one another, but not equi-significant, whereas the psychological principle which at best can be regarded as an empirical law of a high degree of probability is, as a matter of fact, not equivalent to the former, nor is it equi-significant.

Of course, strictly speaking, the psychological formulation of the law of contradiction is not the law of contradiction. Being a sort of empirical law, it is often valid, but it has so many exceptions that one cannot really say that 'Two beliefs which are expressed by two contradictory statements cannot exist in one mind.' Much depends on whether we mean that two beliefs instantly follow one another and are explicitly contradictory, or whether we mean two beliefs which occur in the same mind but (*a*) at different times or (*b*) at the same time but in an implicit form (i.e. when one is not a flat contradiction of the other, but leads to a contradiction after a few logical steps).

The philosophical tenor of this work, in Łukasiewicz's view, is that the principle of contradiction, in its ontological formulation, is *not* the 'first principle' nor a 'fundamental law of thought'. It is a logical theorem, the validity of which may be questioned and therefore must be proved. Such a proof, however, is not to be found in Aristotle or anywhere else. Łukasiewicz argued that this principle is accepted for important extra-logical reasons which are of a practical or moral nature so as to guard against fallacy and error. This contention is disputable and has been much discussed in Poland.

Łukasiewicz's investigation of Aristotle's logic continued over a period of more than forty years and was finally crowned by the publication in 1951 of *Aristotle's Syllogistic from the Standpoint of*

Modern Formal Logic,[15] which was written in English. (Łukasiewicz had gone to the Royal Irish Academy in Dublin in 1946
where he remained until his death in 1956.) This book has been
recognized as a classical work on Aristotle.

But perhaps most important in the field of the history of logic
was Łukasiewicz's rediscovery of the logic of the Stoics which,
until his time, was underestimated and almost unknown. He
showed that Stoic logic was independent of Aristotelian logic
and, in fact, was 'logically' prior—in Aristotelian logic some
assertions of Stoic logic must be assumed, while in Stoic logic
no assumptions of Aristotelian logic are made. Łukasiewicz
demonstrated that Stoic logic was a certain kind of propositional
calculus.[16]

Łukasiewicz's inquiries into Stoic as well as Aristotelian logic
also led to other discoveries. In many instances false interpretations and erroneous evaluations of ancient logic—resulting from
the superficial knowledge of previous scholars—were rectified.
Łukasiewicz's paper, 'On the History of the Propositional Calculus',[17] in which he summarized his work on Stoic logic, was
said by an eminent German logician, H. Scholz, to be the most
interesting twenty-five pages he had ever read on the history of
logic. Evaluating Łukasiewicz's achievements in the field of
mathematical logic, A. N. Prior wrote: 'No logician since the
Stoics has done more than Łukasiewicz to develop the propositional calculus; and without him we might not have been aware of
the Stoic achievement either.'[18]

3 THE SCIENTIFIC METHOD IN PHILOSOPHY AND THE SYSTEM OF SCIENTIFIC PHILOSOPHY

In the light of his work in mathematical logic, we can better
understand Łukasiewicz's later, highly condemnatory attitude

[15] J. Łukasiewicz, *Aristotle's Syllogistic from the Standpoint of Modern
Formal Logic* (London, 1951); 2nd edn., 1957.
[16] Thirty years later Benson Mates in *Stoic Logic* (Berkeley and Los Angeles,
1961) admitted: 'The aim of this study is to present a true description of the
logic of the old Stoa. It repeats most of Łukasiewicz's published conclusions
on the subject and offers additional evidence for them.' p. 1.
[17] This paper was delivered at an international philosophical congress in
Prague in 1934; it was reprinted in his *Selected Papers*.
[18] A. Prior, 'Łukasiewicz's Contributions to Logic', in *Philosophy in the
Mid-Century* (Florence, 1958), II, p. 53.

towards traditional philosophy. He was quite outspoken about the motives which led him to this position. His confession is a rare document in the history of philosophy.

> My critical judgement of philosophy to the present day is the reaction of a man who, having studied philosophy, and having read exhaustively various philosophical works, at last alighted upon the scientific method—not only in theory, but in vivid and creative personal practice. This is the reaction of a man who personally experienced this particular delight which gives a correct solution of an unequivocally formulated problem. The solution can be checked at any time with the help of an accurate, scientific method, about which one simply knows that this must be such and such, that it cannot be otherwise, and that it will remain forever as a permanent result of methodical research. This seems to be the normal reaction of each scholar in the face of philosophical speculation.

Why is this reaction hardly ever openly expressed?

> But the trouble is that the mathematician or the physicist who does not know philosophy and who comes across it by chance usually does not have enough courage to express his opinion about philosophy openly.
>
> He who has been a philosopher, and subsequently became a logician, and has mastered the most exact and subtle methods of reasoning which we have today at our disposal; he has no such scruples, because he knows how much philosophical speculation is worth; he also knows the value of reasoning carried on, as usually happens, in the vague, ambiguous terms of everyday language— reasoning which is not supported by experience or by the solid scaffolding of a symbolic language.[19]

Łukasiewicz gave up the teaching of philosophy in 1925 after delivering a course of devastatingly critical lectures on Kant.

> When we approach Kantian philosophy with the criteria of scientific criticism, its constructions fall to pieces like a house of cards. At each step there are vague notions, incomprehensible statements, baseless assertions, contradictions, and logical errors. Nothing is left but a few ideas, possibly those of a genius, raw material waiting for scientific elaboration. Therefore this philosophy did not fulfil its promise, although it exercised a tremendous influence. Philosophizing after Kant did not become more critical, rational and careful. From Kant grew the German idealistic philosophy, as fantastic and unscientific as any. There remained metaphysical questions, unsolved, but not insoluble. But they should be approached

[19] 'Logistics and Philosophy,' in *Selected Papers*, p. 202.

with the scientific method, the same well-proved method which is used by the mathematician or the physicist. And above all, one has to learn to think clearly, logically and with discipline.[20]

This judgement was not limited to Kant nor to past philosophy alone; it was extended to contemporary philosophy as well. In Łukasiewicz's opinion 'all modern philosophy suffers from unclear, imprecise and unscientific thinking'. It was, of course, mathematical logic which was to provide the basis for the new scientific philosophy. Łukasiewicz's great satisfaction with the achievements of this logic led him to assign to it a great rôle, and even a mission.

> ... in spite of the fact that twenty-five centuries have passed from the moment when logic was generated, we are not able to think logically; we are not able to think accurately, consistently, or conscientiously—either in philosophy or in other sciences; neither in public life nor in private. I believe that only mathematical logic will teach us precise thinking, and in this I see its greatest significance, I would even say its *social mission*.[21]

The programme of Łukasiewicz's new philosophy was formulated and pronounced in 1927 in a short and very condensed speech delivered during the Second Congress of Polish Philosophy. This congress was a turning-point after which Polish analytical philosophy produced its finest achievements and became recognized in Europe. The successful development of mathematical logic in Poland by Łukasiewicz, Leśniewski, Tarski, Chwistek, and partly by Ajdukiewicz and Kotarbiński, led to an uncritical trust in and even undue glorification of mathematical logic. These tendencies found their strongest expression in Łukasiewicz's paper 'On Method in Philosophy'. This paper is quoted here at some length because it beautifully expresses Łukasiewicz's position and because it has never been republished or translated.

> The scientific philosophy of the future must build its structure from new beginnings, from new foundations. This means first of all the reviewing of philosophical problems and the choosing of only those which can be comprehensibly formulated; the rest should be

---

[20] Logistics and Philosophy,' in *Selected Papers* p. 202.
[21] J. Łukasiewicz, 'O znaczeniu i potrzebach logiki matematycznej' (On the Significance and Needs of Mathematical Logic), *Nauka Polska* (1929), 10, p. 615.

rejected. Mathematical logic can be useful even at this pre-intro-ductory stage by helping us to establish the meanings of expressions which belong to philosophy. Next, we should try to answer those questions which can be comprehensibly formulated. The most suitable method for this purpose seems to be that of mathematical logic, deductive and axiomatic. We should build upon only those propositions which are intuitively clear and accept such propositions as axioms. In regard to primitive terms, that is to say, undefined terms, those expressions should be chosen whose meanings can be explained completely by means of examples. We should only attempt to work with a small number of axioms and primitive terms. All of them should be exactly specified. All other terms must be unconditionally defined on the basis of the primitive terms, and all other theorems proved on the basis of the axioms with the help of the rules of inference accepted in logic.

After explaining the method, Łukasiewicz went on to discuss the outcome of his method.

Results obtained in this way should be constantly checked with the data of intuition and experience, and also with findings in other sciences, particularly the natural sciences. In case of discrepancy, the system should be rectified by means of new axioms and new primitive terms. We should uninterruptedly maintain contact with reality in order not to create mythical beings like Platonic ideas or the things-in-themselves, but to try to comprehend the essence and the structure of the real world in which we live, in which we act, and which we want to transform into a better and more perfect one.

In this work we should behave as if nothing had been done in philosophy. Any return to Aristotle, or Leibniz, or Kant will be of no use; it will rather be a drawback because we become influenced by these great names and acquire bad mental habits.[22] When the axiomatic method as applied to philosophy bears results, then will be the time to return to the past and to search for the beginnings and traces of new achievements of thought in the history of philosophy. The work which is waiting for future scientific philosophers is gigantic and will be done by minds much more powerful than any which have ever existed before on earth.[23]

[22] It is worth observing here that this attitude of 'let us forget about the past philosophy in order not to acquire bad mental habits' was equally strongly expressed by Austin in the 1950s. In both cases it was the insistence on a new method of philosophizing (admittedly different in Łukasiewicz and Austin) that was to cure philosophy.

[23] J. Łukasiewicz, 'O metodę w filozofii' (On Method in Philosophy), *Przegl. Filoz.*, 31 (1928), pp. 4, 5.

Łukasiewicz conceived of scientific philosophy as a system, but a system of a strictly inferential nature. In 1946, about thirty years after his paper, 'On Method in Philosophy', he still insisted that 'The synthesis of philosophical inquiry is a philosophical system, an all-embracing outlook on the world and life.'[24] He admitted humbly in the same address:

> I cannot provide such a system. I do not believe that it is possible today to construct a philosophical system which would fulfil the requirements of scientific method.[25]

There remained the general prescription that it should be an edifice resembling formal logic, and 'we should build upon only those propositions which are intuitively clear,' that 'terms should be unconditionally defined on the basis of primitive terms, that theorems should be proved on the basis of the axioms and with the help of rules of inference accepted in logic', and that 'we should constantly maintain contact with reality in order not to create mythical beings like Platonic ideas and things in themselves.' Given this, 'The work which is waiting for future scientific philosophers is gigantic and will be done by minds much more powerful than any which ever existed before on earth.' As yet no such minds seem to have appeared.

Being unable to provide a system which would meet his high demands and, on the other hand, by no means prepared to be satisfied with any *ersatz*, Łukasiewicz left the construction of scientific philosophy to future generations. Such an attitude of critical restraint is not unreasonable. From the fact that we are unable to achieve something, it does not follow that future generations will not succeed either. However, Łukasiewicz's conception of a system of scientific philosophy seems to indicate that future generations also will fail. The all-embracing system is to be achieved from single axioms by means of rules of inference, that is, in a deductive way. To accomplish this would be a formidable achievement. But, alas, it seems to be beyond the possible.

Applying strictly deductive procedures, no new knowledge, apart from formal, can be obtained. If new knowledge is arrived at, it means that the axioms were of a peculiar nature; not ordinary axioms but axioms invested in a pre-axiomatic stage with hidden characteristics. So either we shall have the whole system

24 J. Łukasiewicz, *Selected Papers*, p. 114.   25 Ibid., p. 114.

71

of scientific philosophy implicit in our 'axioms' (in this case application of the deductive method will result in an expansion of the given theme into a complete musical composition), or we shall not have the entire system in our 'axioms' and then no deductive procedure can help us to arrive at an 'all-embracing system'. If the 'axioms' do not contain the complete outline of the system, and such a system is achieved by means of inferences, these inferences cannot be of a strictly deductive nature, but 'looser' in their logical structure. In this event the postulated method will be violated. Consequently, in either case, the construction of scientific philosophy will not meet Łukasiewicz's requirements.

The whole matter could be summarized by the pertinent statement of Waismann: 'The failure to establish a sort of Euclidean system of philosophy based on some suitable "axioms" is, I submit, neither a mere accident nor a scandal, but deeply founded in the nature of philosophy.'[26] It should also be observed that when philosophy is really forced to acquire the shape of science, according to the design of the formal sciences, as for example in Carnap's *The Logical Syntax of Language*, then genuine philosophical problems are caricatured.

4 ŁUKASIEWICZ'S ATTITUDE TOWARDS THE VIENNA CIRCLE

Łukasiewicz's paper 'On Method in Philosophy' contained a number of points which were later emphasized by the philosophers of the Vienna Circle, who independently enunciated a similar programme of philosophy. The recommendation of a scientific philosophy, with an axiomatic and deductive method, a use of mathematical logic and a rejection of those problems which we cannot formulate comprehensibly, became an integral part of the programme of the Circle.

However, in spite of many similarities between them and members of the Circle, Łukasiewicz and other Polish philosophers were rather more sensitive to differences. The Poles did not go to the extremes the Viennese did and consequently did not have to withdraw later. As a whole, Polish philosophers had a very thorough philosophical training in Twardowski's school. Philoso-

---

[26] F. Waismann, 'How I see Philosophy', in *Logical Positivism*, ed. A. J. Ayer (London, 1960), p. 346.

phers of the Vienna Circle were, by and large, scientists without a thorough philosophical training; hence their extremeness and onesidedness. Łukasiewicz particularly objected to the reduction of all philosophical questions to syntactical questions, that is questions about the structure of language. It appears that Carnap was led to this reduction (of all philosophical questions to those of syntax) in order to preserve verifiability as the criterion of meaning. Questions concerning, for example, space and time, were reduced to questions about the structure of formation and transformation rules concerning space and time coordinates. Such reductions and oversimplifications were particularly objectionable to Łukasiewicz, whose position in this matter was representative of the majority of Polish analytical philosophers. The verifiability principle and syntactical reductions were met with reserve and incredulity in Warsaw, even in their heyday. In the paper 'Logistics and Philosophy', after expressing his enormous appreciation of the precision in Carnap's works on the syntax of language, Łukasiewicz went on to say:

> Among questions which can be determined on the basis of language, I would include only questions of this type, whether all bodies are extended, under the assumption that by a 'body' I mean something which is extended. Only such statements are analytical and only such statements are, according to my opinion, capable of being discussed on the basis of language. I cannot comprehend, however, how the question, whether the world is finite or infinite, can be discussed on this basis. By the 'world' I mean neither something which is finite nor which is infinite, so I am concerned here not with an analytic statement, but with a synthetic one. Furthermore, I know that being finite is something different from being infinite, and that only one or the other can be the case, and which is really the case does not depend at all on us, nor does it depend on our linguistic rules. The same refers to the questions of causality and determinism. Either causal necessity rules supremely in the world, or not, and everything is either determined *a priori*, or not, and this once again cannot depend on any of our rules of syntax of language. These questions I regard as questions of facts; these are 'subject matter' questions and are objective and have to do with more than formal linguistics. I have strong and unyielding objections to the way in which Carnap attempts to reduce objective questions to linguistic ones.[27]

[27] J. Łukasiewicz, 'Logistyka i filozofia' (Logistics and Philosophy), *Przegl. Filoz.*, XXXIX, 1936; also in *Selected Papers*, pp. 126, 127.

He concluded in the following way:

> ... Carnap's consideration of this matter I regard as hazardous philosophical speculation which will pass away as all similar speculations have done.[28]

There is not much to be added to the above comment. One point, however, perhaps needs some elucidation. Carnap, in his radical phase, and many of his followers claimed to have cultivated scientific philosophy. And indeed their inquiry undeniably had an intersubjective character, was rigorous in procedure, and was not to be identified with any of the existing sciences. It was, in a word, a strictly scientific inquiry. In the sense that this inquiry aspired to be philosophy as well, it was a scientific philosophy.

However, 'scientific philosophy', the label attached to the inquiries conducted by Carnap in the 1930s, and 'scientific philosophy' meaning 'philosophy elevated to a scientific level' are two quite different things. Carnap never attempted to make or—more precisely—to transform philosophy into a science. What he did was to *replace* philosophy by something else. This is stated quite explicitly in *The Logical Syntax of Language* in the section entitled 'Philosophy Replaced by the Logical Syntax'. There he said that 'according to traditional usage, the name "philosophy" serves as a collective designation for inquiries of very different kinds.'[29] However, he arbitrarily decided that '. . . the logic of science takes the place of the inextricable tangle of problems which is known as philosophy'.[30] There is a difference between providing a new branch of science and transforming philosophy into a scientific discipline. In the latter, Carnap failed entirely. He succeeded, however, in enriching formal science with another branch, logical syntax. Carnap's undertaking which aimed at improving philosophy was in fact an attempt to liquidate it: philosophical problems were replaced by problems of his favourite branch of research—logical syntax.

In other words, Carnap was simply mistaken in believing that philosophy can be reduced to or be replaced by logical syntax. Only insofar as all questions are transformed to syntactical questions can philosophy be named scientific according to Carnap's usage of the term. Then philosophy becomes a sort of

---

[28] Op. cit., p. 129.
[29] R. Carnap, *The Logical Syntax of Language* (London, 1951), p. 277.
[30] Ibid., p. 279.

formal discipline not too clearly distinguishable from logic and mathematics. And consequently, it either drastically narrows the scope of philosophical inquiry, and leaves behind quite a large corpus of philosophical problems; or, in an attempt to embrace a large volume of problems, it 'purifies' these problems[31] to such an extent that their content is changed out of recognition.

These limitations and oversimplifications were observed not only by Łukasiewicz, but by other Polish philosophers as well. Mme Maria Kokoszyńska, for example, in the paper 'Syntax, Semantik and Wissenschaftslogik' (1935)[32] argued against Carnap's idea of scientific philosophy limited to syntax by pointing out the validity and indispensability of semantics. Owing to the works of Leśniewski, Tarski, Ajdukiewicz, and Kotarbiński, semantics conceived as an inquiry into 'expressions of a language and the objects those expressions are concerned with' was, in Poland, considered as a quite legitimate and, in fact, indispensable part of philosophical inquiry.

The concept of scientific philosophy, as concerned solely with the investigation of the logical syntax, is now outdated. Carnap himself seems to have recovered from the 'syntactical spell' in the United States, and made semantics the main object of his studies.

It is characteristic that those philosophers in Poland who advocated scientific philosophy, Łukasiewicz in particular, did not arrive at philosophically interesting results. Others, notably Kotarbiński and Ajdukiewicz, hardly ever used the adjective 'scientific' together with the term 'philosophy', but tried their utmost to make philosophy a 'respectable' discipline—clear in expression, stringent in argument and significant in content. Philosophy has to do with problems which are by no means merely formal problems to be solved by logic alone. This seems to have been a tacit assumption of most Polish analytical philosophers (logicians apart) who, although they sought exactitude and definiteness, did not go to oversimplifications and extremes.

The general attitude of Polish analytical philosophers towards the Vienna group was characterized by Ajdukiewicz during the Congress of Scientific Philosophy held in Paris in 1936. 'In Poland

---

[31] At one point, Carnap literally says: 'Once philosophy is purified of all unscientific elements, only the logic of science remains.' (Ibid., p. 279.) Then, of course, philosophy is a science in virtue of tautology.

[32] M. Kokoszyńska, 'Syntax, Semantik und Wissenschaftslogik', *Actes du Congrès International de Philosophie Scientifique*, Vols. 1–8 (Paris, 1935).

there are no close followers of the Vienna Circle; I personally do not know any Polish philosopher who would accept as his own the "subject matter" theses of the Vienna Circle.'[33] And Łukasiewicz added to this his own comment: 'We are too sober for that.' Carnap himself wished to understand the term *logic of science* 'in a very wide sense' so as to include 'the works of Warsaw logicians'. However, Polish philosophers transcended the boundaries established by Carnap.

Łukasiewicz stated a wider conception of philosophy in the paper 'Logistics and Philosophy', discussed above. Tarski provided the semantic concept of truth. Ajdukiewicz advocated a theory of meaning in which empirical (that is to say, by definition extra-syntactical) rules of meaning were recognized, and upon his theory of meaning he built other philosophical constructions. Kotarbiński developed concretism, an ontological edifice.

RÉSUMÉ

Łukasiewicz the philosopher was led astray by mathematical logic. He became over-absorbed by it in his search for the method which would make philosophy scientific. His scholarship in mathematical logic, particularly in the propositional calculus and the history of logic, won him world recognition. A fascination for the precision and neatness of formal logic prompted him to design for philosophy a structure impossible to achieve. Because of this he was called in Poland an 'anti-philosopher'. His programme of scientific philosophy, to be fashioned according to the structure and the language of formal logical systems, although never fulfilled, was one of the boldest among various programmes of the twentieth century aiming at curing traditional philosophy of its traditional illnesses. Łukasiewicz did not take part in 'making' philosophy, but talked *about* philosophy. In the minute analyses characteristic of the Polish analytical movement he had no share; instead he prescribed what philosophy should look like. His philosophical influence in Poland was undeniably great and his authority fully recognized.

[33] K. Ajdukiewicz, 'Der Logistische Antirationalismus in Polen', *Actes du 8ᵉ Congrès Internat. de Philosophie* (Paris, 1936).

IV

TADEUSZ KOTARBIŃSKI—CONCRETISM

AND PRAXIOLOGY

A. *Kotarbiński—the man*

Tadeusz Kotarbiński was born on 31 March 1886 in Warsaw. At first he studied architecture at Darmstadt, Germany; but after two years he gave it up and enrolled at the University of Lwów to read philosophy with Twardowski. Between 1907 and 1912 he studied philosophy and the classical languages. In 1912 he produced his doctoral thesis entitled: 'Utilitarianism in the Ethics of Mill and Spencer', which was subsequently published in 1915. For the next few years he taught classical languages in high schools.

From 1918 until 1957 Kotarbiński taught at Warsaw University, first as a dozent, then as a professor. His formal teaching was interrupted only during the Second World War. In 1957 he ceased to teach at the university on being elected the President of the Polish Academy of Sciences. He held this office for six years.

In the years 1957–1960 he was Vice-President of the Institut International de Philosophie and became its President, for the years 1960–1963.

After 1956 he was a visiting professor at the following universities and academic centres: Belgrade, Brussels, Cambridge (England), London, Manchester, Paris, Stockholm, Vienna; and in the United States—Pennsylvania State College and Berkeley.

The two most prominent philosophers of the Polish analytical movement were Kotarbiński and Ajdukiewicz. The former was

77

known throughout Poland and often considered *the* philosopher; the latter enjoyed a high esteem, but only among a relatively small circle of experts. Kotarbiński gained his recognition through:

1. The establishment of a school of 'exact' thinking which continued Twardowski's tradition.
2. His original philosophical contributions,
    (*a*) concretism, a philosophical system which was a kind of materialistic monism and which resulted, roughly speaking, from a semantic analysis of traditional philosophical concepts, and
    (*b*) praxiology, a new branch of scholarship concerned with the efficiency of action whatever the activity, claimed to be the first systematic attempt to formulate theoretically success and failure in our individual and social activities.
3. His active part in social life, including
    (*a*) a keen interest and continuous participation in social affairs, and a sharp sensitivity to all forms of injustice, and
    (*b*) a fulfilment of the philosopher's rôle as conceived in Antiquity, when a philosopher not only created and propagated philosophical doctrines, but also himself set an example of a worth-while life.

Kotarbiński became almost as well known in Poland as Russell in Britain. The two men, indeed, had much in common. Both appreciated mathematical logic but did not allow themselves to be tyrannized by its formal requirements. Instead they both developed philosophies, and in so doing attempted to be as exact as the subject allowed. Both were endowed with a gift for words[1] and expressed their ideas on a wide range of topics in articles intelligible to the layman. Both stood firm in defence of their opinions on important issues of social and individual life.

[1] Kotarbiński did not confine his gift for words to philosophy alone. In 1957 he published a book of verse entitled *Joyous Sorrows*. And his aphorisms occasionally appear in weeklies. Here are a few examples:

You have to make order, but disorder makes itself.

People are reluctant to get rid of their vices; they would rather acquire new virtues.

Philosophy itself has no priceless results, but its study brings priceless results.

Let us remember that among nations Poland is a big mouse, not a small elephant.

B. *Kotarbiński—the teacher*

Kotarbiński started to teach at the University of Warsaw in 1918. His inaugural lecture: 'On Great and Small Philosophy' became well known and widely discussed. It was a programme for a new philosophy, but formulated in a very modest way (in contrast with the programme of the Vienna Circle which was strenuously proclaimed): 'Let us give up the construction of great systems; let us cultivate small philosophy which will lead to a reform of all intellectual pursuits.' Thus, the laborious and time-consuming work of elucidating the meaning of terms used in philosophy and outside it was initiated. But out of minute analyses there soon began to appear the framework of a new edifice which was recognized, somewhat to the surprise of the author himself, as being a philosophical system. The doctrine which emerged from these analyses was first called reism, next pansomatism, and finally, after the war, concretism. The main outline of Kotarbiński's doctrine is to be found in his *Elementy teorii poznania, logiki formalnej i metodologii nauk*,[2] to be referred to in further discussion as *The Elements*. This was meant to be a textbook, but its scope and importance far exceeded the calibre of ordinary textbooks. It was, in fact, the most important and most influential Polish philosophical book published between the two wars.

Kotarbiński was primarily a teacher and secondly a thinker, if such a distinction is to be recognized; for him, at any rate, the two were inseparably linked. Clarity was the principle he taught his pupils, and clarity the principle which served as the leitmotif in the construction of concretism. Philosophers can be divided into two classes: those whose writing is full of imaginative and

[2] *Elementy teorii poznania, logiki formalnej i metodologii nauk* (The Elements of the Theory of Knowledge, Formal Logic and Methodology of the Sciences), 1st edn. (Lwów, 1929); 2nd edn. (Wrocław–Warsaw–Cracow, 1961). The second edition has been enlarged by thirteen papers written in the years 1947–1958, and centred around problems dealt with in *The Elements*. The second edition appeared in English under the (rather unfortunate) title *Gnosiology* in 1966 by the Pergamon Press.

After the early 1930s *The Elements* became the official textbook at the University of Warsaw; for students of philosophy it was a condition *sine qua non*. Students of other disciplines in the humanities and sciences were also trained in the intellectual rigour of *The Elements*, as they were obliged to take a course in logic and the methodology of science which was based on *The Elements*.

suggestive associations and, because of this, is rather imprecise; and those who write in a clear and straightforward fashion. The discourse of the members of the latter class is not so stimulating, but that is compensated for by definiteness. Kotarbiński contended that only the latter method can be adopted for creating a school of thought.

This approach was successful, particularly because Kotarbiński possessed an extraordinary 'maieutic' gift: in helping his pupils to express their ideas sharply and clearly, he often perceived more significant implications in a student's statement than the student himself had conceived. Thus, the student was led (sometimes forced) to excavate the entire content and to draw all of the implications that were contained in his original and sometimes misty statement. As a result, his pupils felt a strong sense of 'belonging'. This is more than evident by the publication of two volumes of essays in honour of Kotarbiński, the first in 1934 and the second in 1959.[3] Both publications have fundamentally the same tenor: the essays consist of meticulous analyses, precise formulations of problems, and sometimes solutions of partial and detailed problems, but no attempt was made to solve large grandiose problems in a vague, general way. The important difference between the two collections of essays is that the first is primarily concerned with problems of the methodology of the deductive sciences, while the second is mainly devoted to problems of methodology in the empirical and social sciences and in the humanities. One might say that the first book is focused on

[3] *Fragmenty filozoficzne*, Księgą Pamiątkowa ku uczczeniu 15-lecia pracy nauczycielskiej w Uniwersytecie Warszawskim profesora Tadeusza Kotarbińskiego (Philosophical Fragments, Studies in Honour of Tadeusz Kotarbiński, to Celebrate the 15th Anniversary of his Teaching at Warsaw University) (Warsaw, 1934). This book was printed at the expense of fifty-one of Kotarbiński's pupils and contained essays by nine of them. In the introduction, the pupils wrote that, although it is 25th anniversaries that are traditionally celebrated, they did not wish to wait a further ten years to express their feelings. Had they done so, this book would never have appeared because of the war. They pointed out in the Introduction that Kotarbiński's school 'connected people of different theoretical interests, of different scientific outlooks and different social attitudes'.

In 1959 to celebrate the 40th anniversary of Kotarbiński's professorship at Warsaw University, another volume of studies in honour of Kotarbiński, Philosophical Fragments (second series), appeared. It contained fifteen essays by his former students.

The third series of *Fragmenty filozoficzne*, celebrating Kotarbiński's eightieth birthday, is to appear in 1967.

logic, the second on the philosophy of science. This indicates a general change of interest.

C. *Ethics*

Kotarbiński's moral principles very often were given expression in action. Although his maxim was 'practical realism', that is to say, not to demand more than can be achieved, but at the same time to demand consistently all that can be achieved; and although he did not go to such extremes as Russell did in his pacifism, Kotarbiński through his judicious, quiet, but firm insistence on the rights of the individual contributed significantly towards reducing the measure of intolerance and oppression exerted by reactionary forces in Poland. Poland in modern times has had no liberal and democratic tradition, and 'non-progressive' elements, to put it euphemistically, were constantly at work; consequently, voices of protest had real significance, and Kotarbiński's was one of them. A left-wing liberal and an incorrigible individualist with the courage to express his opinions and the ability to do so convincingly, Kotarbiński very often antagonized 'non-progressively' minded people, who bitterly attacked and insulted him. He was always heard when the voice of a humanist was needed. At the time when racism was rampant, when pro-fascist political bodies organized anti-Jewish riots, Kotarbiński spoke out in defence of the persecuted. Inkpots were thrown at him in the university as he spoke in defence of the Jews. He also fought actively for intellectual freedom, before the war and after; for social equality and independent ethics, against the tyranny of religious and non-religious orthodoxies.

In the early fifties, when he was accused by the Marxists of not having changed his attitude although the times and the situation had altered, he replied: 'In the face of historic perturbations, one can behave like the needle of a barometer, changing according to changes in the atmospheric pressure; on the other hand, one can behave like the needle of a compass, pointing always in the same constant direction.' Regardless of how awkward it was for the ruling authorities, he continued to express the views he considered right and true.

Kotarbiński's interest in non-theoretical issues, i.e. in the conditions of individual happiness and ways of achieving a harmonious life, led him to the province of ethics. Considerations outside the scope of philosophy in the strict sense composed a significant part of all his writings. His *Selected Papers*,[4] published in two volumes in 1957–1958, contained: I—*Thoughts About Acting*; II—*Thoughts About Thinking*. In the introduction to the first volume he said that his *Thoughts About Acting* arose from a desire for 'something more real and more concrete than the scholastic problems of formal logic'. It should be kept in mind that Kotarbiński's moral writings did not derive from nor were they connected with his philosophical doctrines. He considered them to be the reflections of an individual upon moral issues.

Kotarbiński's lay ethics, which he called *independent ethics*, was based on the principle of the 'brave, reliable guardian'. To be a brave guardian of those with whom we share good and bad fortune by our own choice or by chance is, in his opinion, the principal maxim which comprises all positive and negative directives of a noble life: active goodness, loyalty, courage, and their derivatives on the one hand; and on the other, condemnation of cruelty, cowardice, treason, and such like. The basic principle was explained thus: 'One should act according to the motives which characterize the emotional structure of the reliable guardian.'[5] The attitude of the reliable guardian should be adopted, not only towards those with whom our lot is naturally cast, but also towards those with whom we are in conflict. In the latter case, however, the supreme court of our behaviour is our conscience. As Kotarbiński said, we should not try to find in ethics exact instructions, inter-subjectively justified like mathematical theorems. 'Independent ethics is also independent in this sense that one's own conscience cannot be deputized for by another voice.'[6] This position coincides closely with the recent standpoint of British philosophy in which we may observe the revival of the Kantian idea that morality is essentially autonomous and a matter of self-legislation.[7]

In Kotarbiński's view, independent ethics were described as such because they were independent of religious belief and also

---

[4] T. Kotarbiński, *Wybór pism* (Selected Papers)—Vol. I, *Myśli o działaniu* (Thoughts about Acting) (Warsaw, 1957); Vol. II, *Myśli o myśleniu* (Thoughts about Thinking) (Warsaw, 1958).

[5] T. Kotarbiński, *Sprawy sumienia* (*Matters of Conscience*) (Warsaw, 1956), p. 15.

[6] T. Kotarbiński, *Matters of Conscience*, p. 24.

[7] This view is maintained in a representative book by R. M. Hare, *Freedom and Reason* (Oxford, 1963).

of philosophical outlooks. In order to behave honourably, honestly, and with integrity, he argued, one need not be motivated by a desire to gain the approval of the Omnipotent or the Noblest Being, or by an expectation of reward or punishment. One can be an atheist and, by observing the principles of 'independent ethics', behave as nobly as it is humanly possible for members of a religious community. Secondly, the principles of 'independent ethics' do not involve us in any explicit or implicit philosophical commitment. One may be a materialist or an idealist, a realist or a phenomenologist and still follow 'independent ethics'.

In arguing for an ethics independent of philosophy, Kotarbiński declared that 'ethics, in my opinion, in the same way as medical care and administration, requires no "Weltanschauung" justifications'.[8] What is really needed is a defence against phantasmagoria in a justification of ethics. In his booklet *Matters of Conscience*, where he formulated his own ethical views, he said: 'We are not in the least concerned with providing an appearance of a finished system of independent ethics. We only desire to suggest a possible outline of a set of opinions and directives.'[8] Therefore, we should not expect a rigorous treatment of these postulated ethical principles. It should be noted that 'independent ethics' was constructed to provide a guide for moral conduct in concrete, everyday life, not as a basis for theoretical disputations. From the examination of ethical systems, it appears that the more theoretically elaborated a system of ethics is, and the more rigorously its principles are developed, the less workable it is in practice. In other words, to be a real moral guide in everyday life, a system of ethics must be 'open', that is to say, not too rigorously nor too precisely defined.

Although Kotarbiński claimed to provide no *system* of ethics, he was aware that from his ideas a system could be developed, and possibly not one only. And indeed in *Matters of Conscience* all the elements characteristic of ethical systems are provided. Fundamental moral values are spelled out, and defended against possible criticism; rules for behaviour are formulated with reference to the fundamental values accepted; advice is given as to how to apply the rules to individual and social life.

'Independent ethics', which gained many followers in Poland, was developed on the (rather old-fashioned) assumptions that the

[8] T. Kotarbiński, *Matters of Conscience*, p. 12.

individual is endowed with 'the voice of conscience', and that there is also a sort of 'common conscience'. Therefore, to obtain a guide for moral conduct, we do not have to undertake any sociological or historical studies of morals to determine what other people at other times understood by a decent and honest life, but we have to examine our own 'voice of conscience', assuming, of course, that our conscience corresponds to the 'common conscience'. This 'common conscience', although it may have different verbal formulations in different ages, seems to comprise a more or less unchanged nucleus which has persisted throughout all these formulations. This nucleus is determined by certain ethical *constants*, as Kotarbiński called them, which can be perceived throughout the history of civilized man in various cultures and various religions.[9] The admission of these constants is, on the one hand, a weakness and, on the other, a strength of independent ethics. It is a weakness in that some objective elements, which are in a sense absolute, are dogmatically accepted (the dogmatic acceptance of absolute elements in religious ethics is usually regarded as their main weakness from logical and sociological points of view). It is a strength because independent ethics advocates, without appealing to religious motivation and religious justification, those patterns of behaviour and those moral ideals which are usually instilled by religious ethics (and basically accepted in most human societies). As a matter of fact, independent ethics strongly resembles the ethics based on the major religious systems and, in particular, Christian ethics. Of this Kotarbiński was perfectly aware. He did not think, however, that owing to this similarity his ethics was inferior or derivative. On the contrary, both attempted to grasp the essential nature of man and to offer a guide to a harmonious life. The fundamental difference was that of motivation and justification; principles of Christian ethics were constructed with reference to the Omnipotent and Perfect Being, whereas independent ethics was constructed with reference to man alone.

[9] Independent ethics was set out in a very condensed form, that is to say, only the main skeleton was given. Therefore, in many instances we must make inferences on the basis of its principles rather than expect to find the elaborated answer in Kotarbiński's writings. For example, how is the concept of the 'common conscience' understood in relation to the society of the Third Reich? Surely not by reference to the majority of Germans who happened to accept Nazi ideology.

2 THE PRINCIPLE OF CLEAR THINKING AND COMMON SENSE

Although they shared many common characteristics, Polish philosophers differed in emphasis; many of them had their own 'leitmotif', that is to say, a methodological device which played a decisive part in the formation of their ideas. For Łukasiewicz, this was the criterion of strictness provided by mathematical logic; for Ajdukiewicz, the principle of rationality; for Kotarbiński, clarity of thought in conjunction with common sense. Needless to say, the principle of clear thinking was observed by many Polish philosophers, but for none was it so essential as for Kotarbiński for whom it gives the clue to the form and the content of his philosophy.

It is rather unusual for philosophers to start with a methodological principle. The traditional procedure has been to start with a body of beliefs, and then to superimpose criteria of strictness and coherence to which these beliefs should conform. Sometimes, however, especially in the twentieth century, philosophers have started with methodological principles, setting out beforehand requirements for philosophy. By and large, this has been conceived as clarifying the meaning of concepts, which usually meant the sharpening of tools for further use. However, the tools were often sharpened for their own sake; 'methodological' philosophers often got no further than the clarification of concepts. Their philosophical activity was reduced to methodology, or logic, or semantics, and sometimes to linguistics only.

Kotarbiński started as a distinctly 'methodological' philosopher. But, after a few years of grappling with the elucidation of philosophical concepts, he rather unexpectedly arrived at a system of philosophy. In the beginning he had no philosophical system or body of philosophical beliefs at all, but only a wish to cultivate 'small' philosophy as a programme of intellectual reform. In his analysis of traditional philosophy, he found some categories meaningless and some used in ways different from those in which they were meant to be used. This led to the elimination of such categories. The remaining categories precipitated in the form of a philosophical system.

A point of comparison between Łukasiewicz and Kotarbiński is worth noticing here. They both wished to make philosophy a sound and respectable discipline, but their roads led in different directions. Łukasiewicz started with philosophy and, 'after having exhaustively read all sorts of books on philosophy', became thoroughly disenchanted and abandoned the subject, particularly because it could not measure up to the standards of precision established by mathematical logic. Kotarbiński did not become mesmerized by the advances of mathematical logic, but took as much advantage of its achievements as he could. He never supposed, however, that philosophy could become a formal system of the same degree of stringency as systems of formal logic.

True, Kotarbiński was dissatisfied with traditional philosophy, but not hostile to it. In his provocative article, 'On the Need to Abandon such Words as "Philosophy", "Philosophical", etc',[10] he objected to philosophy as traditionally conceived because it is an amalgam of various disciplines having little in common, either in method or in subject-matter. Each of these disciplines gravitates more towards something outside the scope of philosophy (traditionally conceived) than towards the remaining philosophical disciplines. In order to avoid confusion as the result of mixing up different things, Kotarbiński proposed to abandon the term 'philosophy' and its derivatives entirely. Instead of philosophy, there should be separate and distinct disciplines: logic, epistemology, ethics, aesthetics, the history of philosophy. Instead of philosophical congresses, there should be congresses devoted to particular problems of these disciplines. Instead of philosophical journals, there should be journals specifically concerned with achievements in these separate fields.

These ideas, at least to a large extent, were favourably received. There is a striking coincidence between the appearance of his articles and the radical partition of philosophy which took place in Poland at that time (the 1920s). First, at a number of universities philosophy was detached from the humanities and established as an independent faculty. Next, chairs for specialized subjects were established. Consequently, students read either the history of philosophy, or logic, or aesthetics, or ethics. It was unfashionable and simply 'not done' to study philosophy as such. So the analytical tendency was enhanced and fortified: in being limited to these special disciplines, students as well as lecturers had to concentrate on small, partial problems and elaborate them minutely and scrupulously. Students were encouraged to dig

[10] T. Kotarbiński, 'O potrzebie zaniechania wyrazów "filozofia", "filozof", "filozoficzny" itp.', *Ruch Filoz.*, Nos. VI–VII, 1921.

fairly deeply into a small field rather than to expand rather superficially over a large area.

This had many important consequences, some of which were not at all beneficial. In the first place it led to overspecialization and to exaggerated perfectionism, particularly in the field of logic. An undue emphasis was laid on precision. The unmitigated urge for precision was already, in the 1920s, perceived as a danger. Łukasiewicz, whom no one can accuse of underestimating the importance of precision, wrote in 1929:

> Many a valuable achievement has been irretrievably lost for Polish learning because the authors of these achievements, in striving for perfection, delayed the publication of their results.[11]

The emphasis on precision in the field of logic, although it was accompanied by some 'losses', was in some measure justified: a number of contributions were published (Tarski's definition of truth is an example) which in elegance, neatness, and consistency provided a paradigm for other scholars. In other disciplines, the insistence on formal strictness was less fortunate. By and large it resulted in a formal and highly technical, rather than in a conceptual treatment of philosophical problems. Moral philosophy, for example, was transformed into the historical and sociological study of morals, or else into the logical scrutiny of the structure of ethical systems; research in aesthetics took the form of the logical analysis of major aesthetic categories, or else the analysis of the structure of various forms of art. Of course, not everyone obeyed this formal drill, although most younger philosophers did. In general, overspecialization in the teaching of analytical philosophy in Poland has produced a certain narrowness of philosophical horizons and a kind of inhibition in tackling larger philosophical issues.

It is worth while pointing out that Twardowski's pupils, at any rate the more outstanding of them, had a broad philosophical and general education, and on top of this some specialized training, usually in mathematics. Their own pupils, however, were trained differently—in separate faculties of philosophy and in specialized subjects. This was not an illogical consequence. Because Kotarbiński and other philosophers were disgruntled with traditional

---

[11] J. Łukasiewicz, 'O znaczeniu i potrzebach logiki matematycznej' (On the Need and Significance of Mathematical Logic), *Nauka Polska*, 10, 1929, p. 607.

philosophy, and because one of the main sources of their dissatisfaction lay in the fact that traditional philosophy attempted to embrace an amalgam of diverse subjects indiscriminately, it appeared quite natural to discriminate major subjects and to treat each in a specialized manner. This consequence, although it seemed logical, led in practice to rather unfelicitious results.

Overspecialization in science produces narrowness, compensated for, however, by the thoroughness and meticulousness of the results achieved. But in the long run, even in science acute specialization leads, not to progress, but to stagnation. This seems to be even more true in philosophy. It appears that by its nature philosophy (whether more narrowly or more broadly conceived) must be more general than science, and therefore minute specialization is in philosophy even more detrimental. Philosophers ought to have some specialized knowledge, but only in addition to their general humanistic education. The two main arguments against specialization in philosophy are these:

1. If philosophy is divided into small compartments, and if these compartments exhaust its range, then there is no room for general philosophical problems (such as the problem of universals, of existence, of the necessary and the contingent, of the nature of truth, etc.), because within each compartment the problems dealt with are rather 'small' and detailed. If some large problems exceeding the boundaries of separate fields are to be left, this would mean that the division of philosophy into sections was in fact fictitious. It should be also added that the effective execution of 'small' problems requires the knowledge of and implies a commitment to more general issues.

2. It appears that in philosophy as well as in science new and fruitful doctrines or theories have emerged as the consequence either of a transplantation of certain methods or procedures from one branch of learning to others, or else have resulted from creating a common foundation for several disciplines. If specialization is consistently followed, then there will be little opportunity for these cross-fertilizations from one field to another. If trespassing is to be allowed, then again what is the point of the division of philosophy?

True enough, some really fine results have been achieved in modern philosophy, particularly in the field of semantics, by specialization and rigorism in research. However, when this specialization was consistently pursued, it invariably ended in a philosophical blind alley. This can be seen in the work of some philosophers of the Vienna Circle, some Polish philosophers, and some Oxford philosophers of ordinary language.

When philosophy was departmentalized in Poland, the consequence seems to be the following. The more seriously philosophers took the idea of specialization in philosophy, and the more conscientiously they tried to observe it, the more meticulous and 'solid' were their results, but the less interesting philosophically. In all fairness to these philosophers it should be added that there were some other reasons which impeded their philosophical expansion. When they were at the threshold of their philosophical maturity the war broke out; after the war when they started to compose themselves, another 'obstacle' arose—the invasion of Marxist philosophy.

Symptomatically enough, while educating their followers in the regime of 'sectionalized' philosophy, the older masters (e.g. Kotarbiński, Ajdukiewicz) did not confine themselves to the boundaries of particular sections. Those who did specialize (e.g. Łukasiewicz, Tarski), ceased after a time to be philosophers.

Whether Kotabriński, with his articles on the need for abandoning the term 'philosophy' and its derivatives, was mainly responsible for the departmentalization of philosophy in Poland, it is hard to say. At any rate, in the 1950s he no longer liked the idea that it might be so; he then openly regretted that philosophy was separated from the faculties of the humanities. All the same, there is little doubt that his initial dissection of philosophy into clearly defined compartments pushed many to follow the narrow path of specialized research.

Apart from the principle of clear thinking, Kotarbiński has always had much respect for common sense and has used it as another important methodological device when forming philosophical doctrines. Common sense was applied by Kotarbiński in at least three different ways.

First, in the direct way when he asserted that some opinions and theories disregarded common sense. For example, he found La Mettrie's mechanical materialism inspired by thoughts 'hostile to the spirit of common sense'.[12] When taking stock of idealistic

---

[12] T. Kotarbiński, 'O różnych znaczeniach słowa "materializm"' (On Different Meanings of the Word 'Materialism'), *Przeg. Filoz.*, XXXIV, 1931; also in *Selected Papers*, Vol. II, p. 72.

doctrines, he said in *The Elements*: 'Idealism, both objective and subjective, ontological as well as epistemological, is foreign to common sense which gives support to realism.'[13]

Second, by resting the *onus probandi* on advocates of idealism in disputes about the existence of non-corporeal objects. Like G. E. Moore, whose attitude towards common sense he shared, he thought that the existence of corporeal objects was obvious, whereas the existence of non-corporeal ones was not. Therefore, in the dispute the *onus probandi* rests on those who claim that non-corporeal objects exist. When the realist claims that corporeal objects exist (even when he is convinced that *only* corporeal objects exist), he at the same time does not have to give a proof that non-corporeal objects *do not* exist. There is no reason to accept the existence of the latter, and until a proof is provided by the idealist that they *do* exist, the realist need not feel uncomfortable. The appeal to common sense in this respect was expressed for example in the paper, 'The Problem of the Existence of Ideal Objects';[14] and particularly strongly in *The Elements*, where he wrote:

> The person writing these words subscribes to materialism understood as a doctrine which claims that those objects which I see, hear, enjoy, desire in general are identical with certain bodies. This doctrine is thrust upon him with a compulsion; all that he heard against it did not stand critical examination.[15]

Third, by adhering to the principle of contradiction and consistency in ontological argument. Often Kotarbiński emphasized that opinions and doctrines violating common sense are phantasms, idle fancies, or are contradictory or seriously inconsistent. In 'On the Reistic or Concretistic Attitude' he wrote:

> Assuming the existence of anything other than Aristotelian substances in the first sense is regarded by the concretist as committing a hypostasis, that is, as making idle fancies which are the result of an illusion caused by the existence of certain nouns.[16]

In *The Elements* he said that he felt '... an absurdity in the assumption that there are tastes which are not experienced by

[13] T. Kotarbiński, *The Elements*, 2nd edn., p. 90.
[14] T. Kotarbiński, 'Sprawa istnienia przedmiotów idealnych', *Przeg. Filoz.*, 1920; also in *Selected Papers*, Vol. II, p. 7.
[15] T. Kotarbiński, *The Elements*, 2nd edn., p. 392.
[16] T. Kotarbiński, 'O postawie reistycznej', *Myśl Współczesna*, 1949; also in *Selected Papers*, Vol. II, p. 150; similar arguments on pp. 139, 144.

anybody, scents which cannot be smelled, patches of colour imperceptible to the eye, etc.'[17] In 'The Problem of the Existence of Ideal Objects' he claimed: 'Contradictory objects, even ideal, do not exist because they are contradictory.'[18]

The opinion is often held that Moore's importance for philosophy lies not so much in the novelty of his views, but rather in his new standards of practising philosophy—unswerving sobriety, boldness in being plain, and resilience against the bafflement of philosophical argument. All this is attributed to his tough common sense. Kotarbiński possessed the same quality to a high degree, but, somewhat unlike Moore, he also had a philosophical doctrine of his own which he defended all his life against the vicissitudes of criticism. This doctrine was concretism.

3 REISM—PANSOMATISM—CONCRETISM

A. *The formative stage of reism*

Kotarbiński was Twardowski's pupil; Twardowski in turn had been a pupil of Brentano. Some of the doctrines held by Brentano were bequeathed via Twardowski to Kotarbiński. This was the case with the classical (Aristotelian) theory of truth,[19] but not with Kotarbiński's reism.

In the introduction to *Realism and the Background of Phenomenology*, Chisholm rightly said:

> The only 'genuine objects' according to the later doctrine of Brentano are concrete individual things. . . . On learning that there are horses, a philosopher may say: 'The being of horses exists', or 'The property of being a horse is manifested in reality'. But in these cases the fictional subject terms, according to Brentano, do not have even the advantage of being abbreviations. The linguistic theory of fiction is quite in the spirit of later positivistic philosophy and of one phase of twentieth-century realism.[20]

Chisholm further asserted:

> The Polish philosopher Tadeusz Kotarbiński developed his reism or concretism under the influence of Brentano's writings.[20]

[17] T. Kotarbiński, *The Elements*, 2nd edn., p. 92.

[18] See footnote 14.

[19] See Chap. II, section 3.

[20] R. M. Chisholm, ed., *Realism and the Background of Phenomenonology* (New York, 1961), p. 5.

Here, however, Chisholm seems to be mistaken. It is sufficient to examine the development of the two reisms to realize that they were created independently. Brentano's reism was a product of his classification of mental phenomena (1911). Kotarbiński at the beginning was not concerned at all with the philosophical problems of psychology. Only when the main body of the reistic doctrine was formulated was he compelled, for the sake of consistency, to interpret mental phenomena in terms of his concretistic language. The differences between Brentano's and Kotarbiński's reisms will be discussed in due course.

There is another piece of historical evidence to demonstrate that Kotarbiński's reism was developed independently. Dr George Katkov, a zealous devotee of Brentano, noticed in 1931 the striking similarity between Brentano's late doctrine and Kotarbiński's reism. By that time the doctrine of reism had been fully formulated in *The Elements* (1929). From the time when the Brentano Society was founded, Kotarbiński was in close touch with some of its members.[21] In actual fact, Kotarbiński's reism had some influence on the Brentanists, not the other way round. This was openly admitted in *Die Werttheorien, Geschichte und Kritik* which was a kind of official organ of the Bretanists. Then the word 'reism' was adopted by the Brentanists and at the same time a marked dissemination of the philosophy of late Brentano took place. Years later, Dr. Katkov said: 'We have adopted the word; we have been encouraged by Kotarbiński's attempt.'[22]

I shall now examine the development of Kotarbiński's concretism, the doctrine which he improved and modified throughout his entire life. The central focus of the doctrine was ontology and the main issue: What there is. The epistemological issues, 'How do we know?' and 'What do we know?', were on the periphery.

As was mentioned before, Kotarbiński started with a rather

[21] The Brentano Society was officially founded in Prague in 1932 with Thomas Masaryk as honorary president, and Oskar Kraus as the chairman. The Society functioned until the war of 1939. In 1939 there was a project of transferring it from Prague to Oxford, but this did not materialize. After the war broke out, some members of the Society found refuge in Britain: Oskar Kraus in Edinburgh, and George Katkov at Oxford. Dr. Katkov has been a pillar of the society from its beginnings. From him the author of this work has obtained most of the valuable information concerning the Brentano Society and its relation to reism.

[22] From interview at Oxford in May 1963.

modest methodological programme: to elucidate to the maximum the content of philosophical propositions. This requirement—to think clearly and to formulate thoughts precisely—may seem banal. When followed with absolute rigidity and consistence it led to results which were far from banal.

Consider statements like

'Whiteness is a property of snow'
'Roundness is a property of the orange or the ball'
'Magnanimity characterizes noble people'[23]

in which are mentioned the properties of 'whiteness', 'roundness', 'magnanimity'; and also statements like

'Between John and his son, Peter, there is the relation of age'
'Between Mount Everest and Mont Blanc there is the relation of size'[23]

in which appear the comparative relationships: 'age' and 'size'. Kotarbiński came to the conclusion that these statements, referring to properties and relationships, cannot be understood literally, but must be understood somewhat figuratively. When we talk about 'roundness' or 'age' in the above sentences, we do not mean to make assertions about these alleged entities, but we mean to say something about things, i.e. that 'balls are round' or 'John is older than his son'. Although the nouns 'roundness' and 'age' stand as subjects or predicates in subject–predicate sentences when used in the above way, they do not commit us ontologically, but should be regarded as *façons de parler*, as surrogates for sentences exclusively about things, that is about concrete objects located in space and time. Because we happen to possess such nouns, we do not have to assert that such entities exist. In other words, certain nouns, although they may refer to objects, are not to be recognized as names unless objects to which they apparently refer are concrete things located in space and time. Briefly, expressions which do not refer to concrete objects are not names, but pseudo-names or apparent names or onomatoids. Though they may stand as subjects or predicates in subject–predicate sentences, they ought not to be treated in the same way as the words 'table' and 'Saturn' in the sentences 'A table is a piece of furniture' and 'Saturn is a planet'. In the previous sentences

[23] Kotarbiński, *The Elements*, 2nd edn., pp. 72–4.

93

(involving 'magnanimity' and 'roundness'), expressions functioning as subjects were formed from adjectives, and although we can
form such abstract nouns from adjectives, there is no reason to
regard them as equal to nouns which have referents (designates)
and are genuine names, e.g. a 'table' and the planet 'Saturn'.

Thus for Kotarbiński, to be a name is to denote; but to denote
(a given object in a given language) is equivalent to 'being suitable
in that language as a predicate in a true sentence of the type "A is
B" about that object when the copula *is* functions in its fundamental sense'.[24] The fundamental or *existential* sense of the copula
is distinguished from other, derivative senses of the word. The
copula *is* may be used in many different senses. Various usages and
therefore various meanings of this term were penetratingly
analysed by Leśniewski, who found about twenty meanings of the
term (in Polish).[25]

B. *The principles of reistic semantics*

Kotarbiński worked out his own semantics while clarifying the
muddles of philosophical disputes. This is why his materialism
can be called *semantic materialism*, to be distinguished from all
other materialisms. The distinction between genuine names and
pseudo-names (i.e. apparent names) is of vital importance for
Kotarbiński's semantics. Names (i.e. genuine names) are:

> *Individual* (the planet Saturn, Lord Nelson), when the number
> of referents (designates) is one;
> *Common* (tree, table, man) when the number of referents is more
> than one;
> *Empty* or vacuous (buildings whose height is 1,500 feet) when
> there are, as yet, no referents, but we can conceive such re-
> ferents.

From the above should be sharply distinguished:
> *Apparent names* (pseudo-names) or onomatoids, i.e. expres-
> sions which appear to be names but in fact are not, because they

[24] T. Kotarbiński, *The Elements*, 2nd edn., p. 18.
[25] S. Leśniewski, 'O podstawach matematyki' (On the Foundations of
Mathematics), *Przeg. Filoz.*, 34 (11), 1931. Incidentally, this section is a
beautiful piece of analysis in the style of Oxford philosophy of ordinary
language. However, the main difference is that the analysis was not undertaken for its own sake, but was a by-product of Leśniewski's logical constructions.

have no referents and cannot conceivably have any (in the world of concrete physical objects). Examples of such apparent names are 'roundness', 'age', etc., all so-called names of properties and relationships.

The criticism first directed against properties and relationships was next applied to such further categories as events and processes. Sentences in which these apparent names appear as subjects cannot be interpreted literally, but only figuratively as abbreviations of expressions which, if properly formulated, express the intended meaning without any recourse to onomatoids. By emphasizing that apparent names could and should be eliminated if we wish to use accurate, non-figurative language, reism pronounces that pseudo-objects, appearing to be referents of these apparent names, neither exist in the world of concrete material things nor in any other sense. Kotarbiński argued that these ideal objects are either contradictory and therefore cannot exist, or if they are not contradictory, we have no evidence whatsoever to assert that they do exist; therefore, why should we admit their existence?

This was the first stage of the development of concretism which at that time was called reism from the word 'res' (thing). The fundamental thesis of reism was that only names of things can be substituted as subjects or predicates in true subject–predicate sentences in which the copula 'is' stands in its fundamental *existential* meaning.

Concretism was further developed through the absorption of some aspects of Leśniewski's ontology.[26] As a matter of fact, reism had been created independently of Leśniewski's logical systems. Some of his concepts and theories, however, proved helpful. Kotarbiński wrote: 'Thus reism got its chance when an excellent invention in the shape of [Leśniewski's] ontology appeared. Reism did not need to find for itself formal logical tools; it received the apparatus from a superior functioning factory.'[27]

After rejecting the existence of properties, relationships, events, and other ideal objects, reism formulated its positive thesis in the

[26] Leśniewski gave the name of ontology to one of his logical systems. Although he has justified the use of the word, it is rather remote from what is usually conveyed by the term 'ontology'. See in particular Cz. Lejewski, 'On Leśniewski's Ontology', *Ratio*, 1, 1958.

[27] Kotarbiński, 'Fazy rozwojowe konkretyzmu' (The Development Phases of Concretism), *Studia Filoz.*, No. 1, 1957; also *The Elements*, 2nd edn., pp. 505–6.

following way: 'Only bodies exist', or 'Whatever exists is a body'. If by 'body' is understood a physical object located somewhere in space and time, perceived by the senses, then we have the somatic interpretation of reism.

Thus it is clear that Kotarbiński's programme was a kind of reductivism in which references to non-bodies have been eliminated in favour of assertions in which references are made only to bodies. Now the question may arise: What is so special about the reduction to bodies? After all, if non-bodies can be analysed out and reformulated in terms of bodies, it seems to be quite legitimate to try to analyse out bodies in terms of, for example:

1. *Space-time areas* (a body being the occurrence of relations and qualities in a space-time area), or
2. *Events* (a body being a spatially and qualitatively unbroken series of events).

However, the latter reductions (of bodies to non-bodies) seem to be less legitimate than the former of non-bodies to bodies.[28]

The reistic kind of reduction can be justified as more 'legitimate' because:

1. Whenever a reduction of a different kind is undertaken, the 'entities' in terms of which bodies are analyzed out have been previously (and usually implicitly) defined or described with reference to bodies. So we have here a hidden circularity. A clear, exact and exhaustive description of these 'entities' in terms of which bodies are to be analysed out can only be given with reference to and in terms of these bodies themselves.

2. [This argument supports 1.] It is in reference to bodies that language is initially taught.[29] Kotarbiński, when justifying concretism in general terms, touched upon the same point but in a slightly different way. He said:

> The basic justification for concretism is naîvely intuitional and inductive in the ordinary sense of the word. It is often the case that in order to explain to someone the proper sense of expressions

[28] It should be noticed at this point that uttering expressions like: 'non-bodies can be analysed out' or 'the reduction of bodies to non-bodies' is, granted that reistic semantics is accepted, uttering nonsense. If 'Whatever is, is a body', then 'non-bodies' is a contradiction in terms. This point will be further discussed in section D of this chapter.

[29] This argument was suggested to me by Mr. A. Quinton.

containing nouns, which are not nouns naming things [not real names], we skip to expressions which do not contain such nouns. Thus, for example, in order to explain the sense of the expression 'John is overwhelmed by happiness', we say 'John is extremely happy' and a conjecture occurs that this is always the case. This is the core of concretism—genetic and morphological in a sense.[30]

This statement is rather revealing and explains to a large degree Kotarbiński's staunch and unabating defence of his doctrine.

3. The existence of bodies is more intelligible to common sense than non-corporeal entities. This argument, of course, had a first-rate validity for Kotarbiński. In fact, one of his own arguments for the rejection of abstract entities was that common sense gives them no support. When talking about intelligibility, it appears that these philosophical doctrines or reductive programmes which attempted to constitute bodies in terms of non-body constituents succeeded in doing so only insofar as these constituents were first explained with reference to bodies. And the converse seems also to be valid. This, of course, brings us back to point (1).

C. *Imitationism and extraspectionism*

The somatic interpretation of reism is not the only possible one. It was only after Kotarbiński coined the terms 'reism' and 'pansomatism' (i.e. somatistic reism) that he discovered that a kind of reism was advocated by the late Brentano.[31] There was however an important ontological difference between Brentano's and Kotarbiński's reisms. Brentano's was *dualistic*, Kotarbiński's *monistic* (materialistic monism). Brentano accepted the duality of substances, Cartesian *res extensse* and *res cogitantes*, i.e. the division

[30] Kotarbiński, 'The Developmental Phases of Concretism', *The Elements*, 2nd edn., pp. 510–11.
[31] The history, in Kotarbiński's words, was the following: 'After I had delivered a paper to the philosophical congress at Oxford (1931) on radical realism, which is in fact a particular case of reism, I received a letter from Dr. Katkov, an expert on Brentano.'
In this letter Katkov pointed out the similarities between the late Brentano's and Kotarbiński's views. Kotarbiński continued: 'In order to reply to this letter, I read the relevant places [in Brentano] and this is what I can say about them. Brentano (16.1.1838–17.3.1917), under the influence of Leibniz as it appears, began to assert and repeat, at least from 1911 onwards, theses which would allow us to recognize Brentano as the initiator of reism, at any rate in the 20th century.' 'Uwagi na temat reizmu' (Some Remarks on Reism), in *Selected Papers*, Vol. II, p. 110.

into bodies and spirits; he did not try to reduce the latter to the former. The somatistic reism of Kotarbiński accepted only bodies —physical objects located in space and time. The experiencing subject (*res cogitans*) is regarded as a thing and is identified with a certain biological creature. The only difference between this thing (*res cogitans*) and other things is that, in addition to being a physical object, it is a thing which can undergo experiences: can feel, desire, perceive, think. In short, somatic reism identifies experiencing subjects with bodies.

Thus the thesis of *somatism* is that every soul is a body.[32] *Pansomatism* claims that whatever is, is a body. It does not claim that souls do not exist, as mechanical materialism of the past had claimed, but only (which is linguistically paradoxical) that every soul is a body.[33] Since qualities, properties, and other attributes of physical things are discarded, and since souls are bodies, therefore whatever is, is a body and nothing else exists but bodies. This was the thesis of pansomatism.

Now, if this is so, it must be shown how so-called mental phenomena, or alleged mental processes such as introspection, dreaming, or experiencing mental images can be understood and explained in the language of reism.

At this point it is perhaps worth noticing, as an introduction to further argument, that Kotarbiński's position is very close to that of Gilbert Ryle as formulated in *The Concept of Mind*.

> It must be noticed from the start that it is one thing to say that certain human actions and reactions exhibit qualities of character and intellect; it is, *by an unfortunate linguistic fashion*, quite another thing to say that there occur mental acts or mental processes [italics mine].[34]

However, it must be admitted that the interpretation of mental occurrences in the language of concretism has always been some-

[32] Kotarbiński, 'Zasadnicze myśli pansomatyzmu' (On Pansomatism), *Selected Papers*, Vol. II, p. 127.

[33] Kotarbiński objected very strongly to being identified with mechanical materialists. He said: 'I am not a mechanist because I do not reduce psychology to behaviourism as it is inconceivable to me to explain everything by means of the centimeter, gram and second.' ('Odpowiedź' (A Reply), *Myśl Filoz.*, 2 (4), 1952. Also *Selected Papers*, Vol. I, p. 195.)

[34] Gilbert Ryle, *The Concept of Mind* (London, 1962), p. 135. See an extensive comparison of Ryle's and Kotarbiński's views in the last section of Chap. IX.

thing of a problem. Kotarbiński returned to this question again and again but never felt that the solution was quite satisfactory.[35]

So-called mental acts or processes are described in psychological propositions which are statements about particular experiencing subjects, asserting that a given subject experiences this or that. Can an experiencing subject be reduced entirely to a body? There are some who claim that 'experiencing subjects' *ex definitione* are different from corporeal objects. This claim Kotarbiński found logically unconvincing; the difference between the contents of these two expressions—an 'experiencing subject' and a 'body'— does not imply a difference in their extensions because in general the difference in the meaning of two names does not necessarily imply a difference in their extensions.

Another argument against Kotarbiński's identification of a soul (that is, an experiencing subject) with a body is the following: If someone relates the content of his dream, it seems obvious that he does not speak about physical objects, but of what are popularly called mental images. The following narrative can be an example of this situation: 'I saw in my dream a snow-covered mountain and I dreamed that I was climbing it tied to my partner.' If this sort of statement does not describe mental images, how is it to be understood? The peculiarity of psychological propositions consists, according to Kotarbiński, in the fact that they have two layers; the first refers to various ways of experiencing and is expressed by phrases such as: 'John experiences that . . .' or 'John dreamed that . . .'; the second gives a description of the content of the experience, and this is entirely in terms of bodies. In other words, if we want to report on the mental images allegedly possessed by someone who reacted to certain stimuli, we usually do so by describing these stimuli, and we describe them *imitatively*

---

[35] As a historical curiosity it should be mentioned that at the beginning of the development of reism, when his opponents pressed him to show where are, for example, mental images if they do not possess existence independent from bodies, Kotarbiński used to answer that they are in the head. In the course of time he was led away from this position of mechanical materialism. The difficulties connected with his initial standpoint were: in which part of the head are mental images situated? How is the term 'in' (in the phrase 'in the head') to be understood? Is it at all possible to talk about a spatial location of something which is not spatial (because mental phenomena are not spatial in the sense that they are three- or two-dimensional)? These considerations led Kotarbiński to develop a new theory concerning mental phenomena which he called imitationism.

as if they were described by the person himself at the time of his reaction. Thus the thesis of imitationism is that mental images and other mental phenomena are imitatively expressed in psychological statements exclusively by means of names of physical objects.

To repeat, in the scheme of a psychological proposition, after the expression 'X experiences . . .' comes a colon, after which follows the description of things as if they were described by the narrator experiencing these things himself immediately and directly. In the case of the dream of climbing the snowy mountain, in the final resort we deal with a description of the mountain and the climbing. Consequently, we can now say that what was called a description of mental images cannot be distinguished from descriptions of corporeal objects: mountains and people. The person who relates his own dreams uses names corresponding to those he would have used when climbing a real mountain.

As has been stated, the imitative description of alleged mental images is, in the final resort, an ordinary description in terms of physical objects. However, in some complicated cases, the imitative description is psychological as well. When, for example, we analyse statements about 'experiences of psychologists', we deal with an imitation of an imitation. There are possible situations in which we can imagine an imitation of an imitation of an imitation as, for example, the description of a dream of experiencing 'the experience of a psychologist', or the description of a dream in which we experience a narrative of another dream of a person who had dreamt about mountains represented by a theatrical décor.

A psychological proposition does not cease to be psychological even if it is clearly false. For example, a dream of tetrahedral bright pink mountains will still be reduced to the imitative description of mountains by means of a statement which will be false.

It should be observed that the theory of imitationism differs markedly from behaviourism, at any rate from radical behaviourism. The behaviouristic description contains no imitation; there is no attempt to describe things in the way they appear to the experiencing person. The behaviourist describes these things in the way they occur to him. In other words, the behaviourist identifies the psychological statements concerning the person X with descriptions of the movements of the person X as observed by other persons. For the concretist, the description of the behaviour of a person is the description—in an imitative idiom—of the experiences of the person as they occur to him; for the behaviourist, the description of the behaviour of a person is the description of the outward movements of the person as they appear to others.

In the same way as the alleged mental occurrences of other people are reduced to the description of physical bodies, introspection is reduced by means of imitation to *extraspection* or auto-imitation. If all psychological propositions could be analysed in extraspective terms then there would be left only one source of experience, extraspection. This was the thesis of *extraspectionism* which Kotarbiński hypothetically formulated in 1935[36] with this characteristic qualification: 'quod autem potest esse totaliter aliter'.[37]

Kotarbiński returned to this problem again in the late 1950s.[38] Then he admitted that the only non-extraspective element in psychological propositions is contained in the first layer of the psychological proposition 'John wishes that . . .' The difficulty remains in showing that this element can be reduced to extraspection as well.

Before considering the further development of concretism, a few words should be said about Kotarbiński's interpretation of so-called names of sense data. Kotarbiński argued that 'X has in his field of vision a green patch' probably means 'X experiences, here and now, something green'. However, this 'something' is not a name of an immanent coloured patch, but the name of a green object, for instance grass. And analogically 'X smells the scent of jasmine' means 'X experiences something that smells like jasmine'. 'X hears rhythmical knocking' means 'X experiences something knocking rhythmically'. The 'something' which smells or knocks is not a mental content, but a certain physical object. In relation to experiencing a sense datum of 'greenness' when there is no green physical thing nearby, first the imitative description should take place, and next the interpretation as in the above cases. 'After

[36] Kotarbiński, 'Zasadnicze myśli pansomatyzmu', *Prze̜g. Filoz.*, No. 4, 1935; also published in *Mind* under the English title 'On Pansomatism', Vol. LXIV, No. 256, 1955.

[37] Ibid., the final sentence.

[38] Kotarbiński, 'Próba redukcji poznania psychologicznego do ekstraspekcji,' *Stud. Filoz.*, No. 5, 1958; also published in *Atti del XII Congresso Internazionale di Filosofia*, Vol. 5 (Florence, 1960) under the title 'Essai de reduire la connaissance psychologique à l'extraspection'.

such reductions,' Kotarbiński said 'concretism is, so to say, at home.'

D. *A critique of 'The Elements'*

Reism in its somatic interpretation was completely formulated in *The Elements* of 1929. This is Kotarbiński's main philosophical treatise. Undeniably, the core of *The Elements* consists of clarifying the meanings of terms. The purpose of these clarifications, however, was not to make as many distinctions as possible and to introduce battery after battery of concepts for the sake of analysis. The underlying concern was with actual problems and their formulation in a comprehensive, unequivocal language; this language was based on Kotarbiński's semantics.

In attempting to define his doctrine sharply, Kotarbiński not only asserted that only bodies, that is to say, physical objects exist, but also emphasized these propositions: 'properties do not exist', 'relationships do not exist', 'no object is an event', 'thoughts do not exist'. These contentions met with severe criticism by Ajdukiewicz in his incisive review of *The Elements*;[39] the treatise was shown to contain discrepancies between the negative statements such as: 'properties do not exist' and the principles of reistic semantics.

According to reistic semantics, only names (genuine names) can be admitted in subject–predicate statements, with the fundamental sense of the copula *is*. In other words, the semantic category of things includes only those names whose referents exist in space and time.

A semantic category (according to Leśniewski whom Kotarbiński and other Polish philosophers followed) is a class of expressions which possesses the property that in a given proposition two expressions of the same class can be replaced without destroying the meaningful structure of the proposition, that is without committing nonsense.[40] If, in the proposition 'The Duke of Wellington was a man', instead of 'man' we put the word 'be-

[39] It is rather characteristic that this review, which is a kind of polemical booklet, has been incorporated (in the Appendix) in the second edition of *The Elements* of 1961. This indicates a healthy cooperation among Polish analytical philosophers. This highly critical review can in fact be considered as complementary to *The Elements*.

[40] At this point it should be noted that it is not implied here that Kotarbiński's and Leśniewski's categories were alike; and that consequently Leśniewski observed the distinction between genuine and apparent names. This is not so. Leśniewski made no distinction of the kind. His categories were syntactical rather than semantic in the strict sense. In the 1920s there

cause' (which is of a different semantic category), we obtain a nonsensical expression: 'The Duke of Wellington was because.' The expression is neither true nor false; it is meaningless, or simply nonsense. If, however, instead of 'man' we put 'chair' (which is of the same semantic category as the word 'man'), we obtain a false but meaningful sentence: 'The Duke of Wellington was a chair.' So semantic disorder or nonsense occurs only when instead of a word of a given category, a word of a different, category is used.

A few more words should be said about semantic categories before a criticism of *The Elements* is presented. Leśniewski (and after him Kotarbiński and others) distinguished two basic semantic categories: *propositional* and *name* categories. Apart from these, there are derivative categories which include the connectives (or so-called functors); for quantifiers and parentheses no special categories were prescribed.

We shall now give an example of a proposition analysed in terms of these categories. Ajdukiewicz's notation, somewhat simplified, will be used here:

n—symbolizes a name

p—symbolizes a proposition

$\dfrac{n}{n}$—stands for a name composing functor (connective); 'n' in the numerator indicates what kind of functor we are dealing with (name or propositional).

'n' in the denominator denotes the number and kind of argument.

In the expression 'a good poet', which itself is a name, the word 'good' is a name composing functor of a one name argument: $\dfrac{n}{n}$.

$\dfrac{n}{nn}$ —stands for a name composing functor of two name arguments. In the expression 'a very good poet' (which is again a name), the word 'very' is such a functor.

$\dfrac{p}{nn}$ —stands for a propositional functor of two name arguments.

In the proposition 'John is a poet,' the word 'is' functions as such

was no sharp distinction between syntactical and semantic categories, and both were treated equally as semantic. It was the idea, the concept of the category (in the sense explained in the text) that was introduced by Leśniewski and followed by others.

a proposition-composing-functor by means of connecting two names: $\frac{p}{nn}$.

$\frac{p}{p}$ —stands for a propositional functor of one propositional argument. In the proposition 'It is not true that John is a poet', the expression 'it is not true that' is the above-mentioned functor.

$\frac{p}{pp}$ —stands as a propositional functor connecting two proposi-

tions which together form another proposition. Examples of such functors are: 'if . . . then . . .' in implication; 'and' when connecting two propositions; 'or' as an alternative of two propositions.

Let us now take a more complex sentence and analyse it according to the above characterized categories. In the proposition 'If John is a good poet then John is an artist and creator,'

$$1 \quad 2 \quad 3 \; 4 \quad 5 \quad 6 \quad 7 \quad 8 \; 9 \; 10 \; 11 \quad 12 \quad 13$$

after enumerating all words, we shall have semantic categories as follows:

   n—categories: (2), (6), (8), (11), (13), (4–6), (10–13);
   p—categories: (1–13), (2–6), (8–13);

and we shall have functors (connectives) as follows:

$\frac{n}{n}$: 5

$\frac{n}{nn}$: 12

$\frac{p}{nn}$: 3, 9

$\frac{p}{pp}$: 1, 7.

Summing up: the semantic categories are of propositions, names (in Kotarbiński's semantics there is only one category of name), and functors, which are characterized in the above way.

The criticism of the ontological theses of reism, initiated by Ajdukiewicz and more or less repeated by others, was as follows. Reism claims that only genuine names (i.e. names of the fundamental existential category) can be admitted. Let us see therefore what happens if this principle is applied to some statements of reism, i.e. 'properties do not exist', or 'relationships do not exist'.

If these statements are interpreted literally, they must be considered as nonsense. The semantic order has been violated because the subjects 'properties', 'relationships' are not genuine names, but pseudo-names. In reistic semantics we can say that 'Mount Everest does not exist'. The sentence is false but meaningful. But the phrase 'Mount Everest' as a name of a physical object cannot legitimately be replaced by the word 'relationship' if the sentence is to preserve its meaningfulness, because 'relationship' is not the name of a thing. To say that 'relationship does not exist' is to fall into semantic disorder or simply nonsense. From this it follows that the ontological interpretation of reism will not do. If reism is to be consistent and is to observe the rules recommended by its reistic semantics, it cannot assert very much about the external world. It can only assert that bodies exist, but this is nothing specific for reism, because every dualistic system and every pluralistic system contains this assertion. Reism in particular cannot assert its main negative ontological thesis because to assert that abstract entities of a given kind do not exist would be to violate the rules, to talk nonsense. So, what is left of reism is its semantic version, that is to say, the thesis that in the final analysis all statements should be formulated in sentences in which apparent names do not appear.

This was, as Kotarbiński described it, the dramatic phase of the development of concretism.[41] It had to withdraw from the ontological to the semantic position, from assertions about the world to assertions about language.

As the result of this criticism, Kotarbiński tried to reinforce his doctrine and preserve its ontological interpretation. He then explained that so far as the affirmative statements such as 'properties exist', 'a certain object is a property', or 'relationships exist' are concerned, they should be considered as semantically incoherent, as nonsense, and not be regarded as sentences at all. However, with negative statements such as: 'properties do not exist', 'no object is a property', the phrases *'do not exist'* and *'is not'* should not be understood as logically negative statements expressing the existence of properties, relationships, etc., but should be understood as phrases expressing rejection, as signs of total repudiation of the existence of these pseudo-entities. This was the main correction of the system formulated in *The Elements*.

[41] Kotarbiński, 'On the Reistic or Concretistic Standpoint', *The Elements*, 2nd edn., pp. 495, 496.

E. *Concretism as the final stage of the development of reism*

Reism in the further phases of its development, when it bore the name concretism, tended to be a semantic doctrine rather than an ontological one. '. . . The principal rule of reism may be formulated as follows: We should attempt to reduce every statement to a form which contains only concrete names.'[42]

Although more cautious in its later years, concretism never gave up the idea of being an ontological doctrine, in spite of the logical difficulties discussed above. Referring to the recent phase of development, Kotarbiński himself expressed his uncertainty as to 'whether the main thesis of concretism is ontological or semantic'.[43]

Another serious difficulty which concretism has had to contend with was objections raised by mathematicians, particularly by set theorists. Since concretism aspires to be a consistent materialistic monism, it has to embrace all spheres of reality and interpret them in its concretistic language. Mathematicians insist, however, that there exist classes, among them an empty class, and these classes are not to be interpreted as bodies. The mereological interpretation of classes provided by Leśniewski[44] did not satisfy many mathematicians because it apparently did not convey the intended meaning of the term 'class'. So concretism had to find a remedy. When existence is taken in the fundamental sense, existential expressions about classes must be rejected. However, it is possible to give a concretistic interpretation of classes, where the word 'existence' is not understood in its fundamental sense, but which according to Kotarbiński should satisfy set theorists.

Let us understand the statement, 'There exists a class of M', as 'Something is an M or something is a non-M'. Therefore, Kotar-

---

[42] Kotarbiński, 'On the Reistic or Concretistic Standpoint', in *Selected Papers*, Vol. II, p. 142.

[43] Kotarbiński, 'The Developmental Phases of Concretism', in *The Elements*, 2nd edn., p. 510.

[44] Leśniewski elaborated his own interpretation of the term 'class' which is to be distinguished from the sense in which mathematicians use the term. In set theory, mathematicians, by a part of a set M, understand any set of N which is either a proper part of a set N, or the set itself. In mereology the word 'part' is given the meaning it has in everyday usage, i.e. by a 'part' is understood a section of a given object, and such a section as is not identical with the object itself. The term 'class' is defined in mereology by reference to the term 'part'. A class denotes a certain object composed of sections in the sense specified above.

biński argued, even if we start with the assumptions that there are no 'somethings' but things, we may and ought to acknowledge the existence of classes; moreover, we may and ought to accept the existence of empty classes. If, Kotarbiński continued, something is an M and something is a non-M (e.g. something is a man and something is a non-man), therefore there exists a class of M and there exists a class of non-M, and neither of the two is complete or empty. If something is an M and it is not true that something is a non-M (e.g. something is a body, and it is not true that something is a non-body), then there exists a class of M and there exists a class of non-M. The first class is complete whereas the second is empty. In the third and last case, if it is not true that something is an M and it is true that something is a non-M, therefore there exists a class of M and a class of non-M (e.g. for $M =$ wooden iron). But the class of non-M is complete, while the class of M is empty. Such is the concretistic interpretation of the problem of classes.[45]

However, this is not the end of the difficulties. There is the problem of interpretation of the class of classes, and next the class of classes of classes, and so on. There is also the problem of the concretistic interpretation of arithmetical theorems (cardinal numbers, for example, are defined in terms of classes of classes). Exponents of concretism have been acutely aware of these difficulties.

> Fully mature concretism announces with firmness only the programme. It declares that with the maximum of persistence, it will attempt to free itself from apparent names. Its hopes are built on partial but undoubted successes. These hopes are far-reaching, the hopes of complete success in the future. Hope is neither an assertion nor a certainty. One can hope in spite of unfavourable omens.[46]

F. *Final discussion of concretism* [47]

The last point to be discussed in relation to concretism is of a more general nature. Concretism is a monistic doctrine. Only one kind of entity (physical objects placed in space and time) is

---

[45] Kotarbiński, 'The Developmental Phases of Concretism', in *The Elements*, 2nd edn., pp. 511–12.   [46] Ibid., p. 511.

[47] A more technical discussion of the semantic aspects of concretism can be found in the illuminating and lucid essays of Vito Sinisi: (1) 'Kotarbiński's Theory of Genuine Names', *Theoria*, Vol. XXX, 2, 1964; and (2) 'Kotarbiński's Theory of Pseudo-Names', *Theoria*, Vol. XXXI, 3, 1965. Although presenting admirably the logical and semantic facets of Kotarbiński, Sinisi somewhat neglects and underestimates the ontological aspects of concretism.

accepted. Owing to this many philosophical problems which baffled philosophers for centuries have been discarded as spurious. The remaining problems, although some unsolved, have been at least formulated clearly. All this only brings credit to concretism. But the question is whether the ontological simplicity and clarity of concretism has not been achieved at too high a price, at the expense perhaps of impoverishing reality.

When we use a language corresponding to a given philosophical system, a language which adequately expresses the content of this system, it is rather difficult to express the content belonging to a different system. The more adequate are the languages corresponding to two philosophical systems, and the more divergent are the basic philosophical assumptions of the two systems, the more difficult it is to express the ideas of one system in the language of the other.

The richness of language matters here as well. If we disregard for the moment the content of philosophical systems, then we realize that one language is richer than the other, that is to say, in one we can express more than in the other. As a rule, languages of pluralistic systems are richer than monistic ones.

In monistic systems, when we wish to say something about objects which are not objects of the first order (for concretism, objects of the first order are physical objects located in space and time; for spiritualism they are spiritual substances), then we must say that either they exist in a secondary sense, or they can be reduced to objects of the first order, or that in a correctly and consistently constructed language we cannot talk about them at all. In regard to the last case, statements which assert anything about these objects must be considered as nonsense and consequently rejected.

Now, the question is whether concretism has constructed a language adequate for describing and expressing all of reality, or whether reality has been oversimplified and possibly impoverished in order to conform to the language? Have strictness, simplicity, and neatness been achieved at such a price that not only badly formulated metaphysical problems disappear, but also some genuine philosophical problems, which can be legitimately discussed in a different language but not in the concretistic language. Ajdukiewicz, an indefatigable critic of reism, indicated[48] that if

[48] K. Ajdukiewicz, 'W sprawie "uniwersaliów"' (On Universals), *Przeg. Filoz.*, 37, 1934.

names are interpreted in (what he considered to be) the spirit of Aristotle, we have two semantic categories of names, general and singular,[49] instead of one as accepted by concretism; therefore, we have two legitimate uses of the term 'is' (instead of one in concretistic semantics, where 'is' is a propositional functor of two names—$\frac{p}{nn}$. In such constructed language the problem of *universals*, which is dissolved in Kotarbiński's language, must be considered as valid.

Kotarbiński developed, tidied, and perfected his doctrine for forty years. The final picture is clear and homogeneous.[50] However, in spite of all the ingenuity of concretistic reductivism, there remain some problems, that of psychological propositions, or particularly problems of set theory, which do not lend themselves to concretistic interpretation. Psychology and mathematics resist total absorption into concretism.

To summarize: concretism is basically an ontological doctrine; it appears to be a contemporary formulation of the old doctrine of materialism. This is materialism formulated and defended in the age of semantics; hence in this study it is called semantic materialism. As an ontological doctrine, concretism did not have much influence; it does not appear to have convinced those who

[49] In his distinction between *general* and *singular* names, Ajdukiewicz closely follows W. E. Johnson's line as explained in Johnson's *Logic* (London, 1921), Part I.

. . . we may point out that a universal characteristic of the general name is its connection with the article—the use of the grammatical term 'article' being extended to include this, that, some, every, any, etc. All terms of this kind . . . might more properly be called applicatives or selectives. Now a general name is distinguished as that to which any applicatives can be significantly prefixed (p. 97). The consideration that to the general name any applicative can be prefixed distinguishes it from the singular name. . . . (Ibid., p. 99.)

General names ought not to be mixed up with common names, and singular names ought not to be mixed up with individual names. The difference between common and individual consists in the number of designates. The criterion of distinguishing the general from individual names is different. The extensions of the two divisions are different.

[50] Homogeneity and stylistic purity seem to have been very important for Kotarbiński. He objected to being called a materialist because the meaning of the term has become somewhat debased and because, in spite of the basic agreement about the structure of the world, concretism and traditional materialism share very little.

were allergic to materialism. Those who were materialistically inclined, however, found in concretism a more precise, more elegant, and more consistent formulation of their convictions than in any other materialist system. And they accepted the theses of concretism as theirs. However, hardly any of Kotarbiński's pupils (although he had many) attempted to develop the ontological line of concretism. Nevertheless, concretism was influential as a semantic doctrine; as such it was widely spread and inspired much research. Also, as a nominalistic programme in the reconstruction of the foundations of logic and mathematics, concretism cannot be easily disregarded.

4 ATTITUDE TOWARDS CONTEMPORARIES

A. *Towards logistics*

Kotarbiński was recognized as a member of the Warsaw School of Logic, although in actual fact he did not make any formal contribution to mathematical logic. True, he was acquainted with the discipline sufficiently well to herald and to propagate it; however, he did not devote his life to its development as others did. The important difference between him and the triumvirate of 'anti-philosophers'—Łukasiewicz, Leśniewski, and Tarski—was that while they sharpened tools and developed logical concepts, Kotarbiński applied them, particularly the concepts of Leśniewski's ontology. Although not a logician in the strict sense, Kotarbiński seems to have done more to popularize and further mathematical logic in Poland than the others. They worked on particular problems, usually of a very sophisticated and highly specialized nature, but the scope of their activity was limited. Kotarbiński attempted to cover the whole field. For this reason his lectures and his publications, particularly *The Elements*, established his reputation as a champion of mathematical logic.

After the war, when mathematical logic had achieved a very high level of abstraction, Kotarbiński no longer followed its course of development as its philosophical relevance appeared to be questionable. Yet his position as an authority on formal logic did not seem to diminish. In 1957 he published his *Lectures on the History of Logic*.[51] This was an attempt to survey the history of

[51] Kotarbiński, *Wykłady z dziejów logiki* (Lectures on the History of Logic) Łódź, 1957). The French translation: *Leçons sur l'histoire de la logique* (Paris, 1964).

logic from the standpoint of modern formal logic. Kotarbiński once admitted[52] that in actual fact he disliked mathematical logic, particularly because of its sterilizing effects on philosophical imagination; however, one cannot really conceive what his concretism would look like without the achievements of modern logic.

B. *Towards Marxism*

The encounter of Marxism with concretism, and generally speaking with Kotarbiński's philosophy, is one of the most interesting and at the same time one of the most paradoxical phenomena in contemporary philosophy. The crux of the matter lay, curiously enough, not in the divergencies but in the convergencies between concretism and Marxist philosophy. The fundamental ontological theses of the two philosophical systems were almost identical. In addition, Kotarbiński's participation in public affairs and his firm stand for social justice were, in the inter-war period, as manifestly progressive as that of the most progressive Marxists at that time. However, after the war Kotarbiński would make no concessions to Marxism and no attempt to fit his philosophy into the Marxist framework. On the contrary, he was always keen to emphasize the distinctiveness of his own position. Because of the convergence of basic philosophical views, and because Kotarbiński's system was logically more consistent and coherent, Marxists were aware that a reconciliation of the two might result in a schism within Marxism. So, instead of recognizing the similarities, they concentrated on emphasizing the differences. This situation is not uncommon. In the history of philosophy, and particularly in the history of religious doctrines, the most violent objections have often been made not to views entirely foreign to the orthodoxy in question, but to views differing little from it. This was the case with Marxism *versus* concretism.

Because no arguments could be launched against Kotarbiński in the usual Marxist manner when non-Marxist philosophers are criticized for the 'idealistic, fideistic, and obscurantist' character of their philosophy, a great deal of ingenuity had been employed to make Kotarbiński's philosophy really appear to be antagonistic to Marxism. The main line of attack was the following.[53] Because

[52] In a private conversation in May 1962.

[53] B. Baczko, *O poglądach filozoficznych i społeczno-politycznych Tadeusza Kotarbińskiego* (On Philosophical and Socio-Political Opinions of Tadeusz Kotarbiński) (Warsaw, 1951).

Kotarbiński was thoroughly submerged in semantics and because semantics was the centre of attention of 'reactionary' philosophers of the West, Kotarbiński's philosophy could not be of any value. More specifically, the charges indicated that semantic materialism, as represented by concretism, appeared to be:

1. Old-fashioned as against modern materialism—dialectical materialism.

2. Mechanistic (because it did not include the laws of dialectics) as against the 'dynamic' and 'vivid' form of materialism apparently represented by dialectical materialism.

3. Conventionalist and subjective (owing to its semantic attire and a hypothetical formulation of the fundamental ontological theses) as against the objective and irrefutable theses of dialectical materialism.

4. Ecletic as against the 'homogeneous' system of dialectical materialism.[54]

Almost all these 'accusations' were retracted after 1956.

Kotarbiński himself contended that what separated him most from the Marxists was the fact that the latter did not recognize (in the 1950s) the universal validity of the law of contradiction. When in the course of time Marxists changed their opinion and began to respect the law of contradiction and formal logic in general, he came to the conclusion that the basic conflict had ceased to exist.[55]

This does not mean that after 1956 Kotarbiński was prepared to let his concretism be dissolved in Marxism. Generally speaking, he considered Marxism too crude to be capable of improving upon his doctrine. Not that he was hostile towards Marxism; he saw many positive and promising aspects in Marxist philosophy. However, the whole doctrine, as it was represented by Marxist philosophers in the Socialist camp, appeared too little sophisticated for his taste. As a matter of fact, he brought the same charge —crudity—against behaviourism in its interpretation of mental life.

In the early 1960s an attempt was made to reconcile concretism with dialectical materialism. It has been pointed out that there are no basic differences, and that concretism can be interpreted in the

[54] More information about the struggle between Marxism and other philosophies in Poland is to be found in Z. Jordan's *Philosophy and Ideology*.
[55] A further discussion of this development is to be found in Chap. VIII.

philosophical framework and language of dialectical material-ism.[56] It can be granted that the basic ontological assumptions are the same. However, in epistemology, for example, owing to the peculiarity of the process of 'abstraction' by means of which, according to the Marxists, theoretical knowledge is acquired, and in the theory of truth, the differences are still quite apparent.

C. *Towards the Vienna Circle*

Kotarbiński's attitude towards the Vienna Circle has never been clearly defined. He admired the thorough and scientific education of the philosophers of the Vienna Circle, which was based on new physics and modern logic, and he appreciated their method of philosophizing, particularly their attempt to dissolve spurious prob-lems, but he was never excited about the philosophical assumptions underlying their teaching. There is a striking similarity between Kotarbiński and the Vienna Circle in the emphasis placed on the elimination of pseudo-problems and pseudo-entities. Reism, in its somatic interpretation—'Whatever exists is a body', a physical ob-ject—is in a way a predecessor of the more recent physicalism. The Reistic language could very well be used as a general framework for the unified science (*Einheitswissenschaft*). The physical language was chosen by the Vienna Circle as a homogeneous language in which all scientific statements were to be formulated. Physicalism, con-ceived as a syntactical doctrine, was to provide a basis for the reduc-tion of all scientific statements to physicalistic statements, that is to say, statements in which only specific physical terms appear and the spatio-temporal coordinates as non-logical constants. As Mme Kotarbińska wrote: '. . . the language of things, proposed by Carnap, is almost identical with the reistic language which has been for years advocated by Professor Kotarbiński, or more precisely, is almost identical with the somatic aspect of that language.'[57] Carnap admitted in 1965 in *The Philosophy of Rudolf Carnap* that " 'reistic language' . . . derived from Kotarbiński's term 'reism' " fits best the programme of physicalism (p. 869).

[56] In 1962 a doctoral thesis was written at the Philosophical Department of Warsaw University by T. Sokołowski under the title: 'Concretism and Dialectical Materialism in their Methods and Semantics' in which the author tried to integrate concretism into the doctrine of dialectical materialism. The attempt was only partially successful. See also Adam Schaff's *Intro-duction to Semantics* (Oxford, 1962).

[57] J. Kotarbińska, 'Le Physicalisme et les étapes de son évolution', *Library of the Tenth International Congress of Philosophy* (Amsterdam, 1948), p. 695.

In spite of apparent similarities, Kotarbiński was not enthusiastic about identifying the language of concretism with that of physicalism. After all, concretism (called at that time reism) was definitely formulated in about 1928; *The Elements* appeared in 1929. In the same year the Vienna Circle was first formed as an organized group. What is important, however, is not so much chronological priority, but differences in the content and vocabulary of the two languages. For the philosophers of the Vienna Circle, the physicalistic language was required for an empiricistic reconstruction of knowledge. Kotarbiński was not actively concerned with the problem of empiricism; the language of concretism resulted from a consideration of 'what there is'. In other words, Kotarbiński sought for answers to ontological questions, whereas the physicalists looked for answers to epistemological questions. Different interests resulted in different vocabularies. The identification of the language of concretism with that of physicalism would mean the reduction, or at any rate the replacement, of the ontological discourse by the epistemological one.

D. *Towards Twardowski*

A few words should be said about Kotarbiński's relationship to Twardowski. Needless to say, there were some obvious influences. Perhaps the most important inheritance was the idea of how a philosophical school should be formed. *Claret distincte* was of course not peculiar to Twardowski; it was cultivated by the Greeks and passed on to modern philosophy by Descartes. It can be easily seen that it was by following Twardowski's pattern that Kotarbiński was able to form his own philosophical school within the school of analytical philosophy founded by Twardowski.

Another inheritance was the method of non-historical interpretation of classical philosophical texts. Twardowski interpreted texts without recourse to the established patterns of interpretation, and without complicated philological apparatus. He attempted a logical analysis of meaning in a manner similar to that of Karl Popper. Texts could easily be 'annihilated' by subjecting them to logical scrutiny as it was practised in Poland by Łukasiewicz. This sort of scrutiny was a destructive type of analysis. Twardowski, on the other hand, was concerned with the constructive sort of analysis, a non-historical interpretation of texts. The aptitude for constructive analysis was inherited from Twardowski by many of his pupils, one of whom was Kotarbiński. This is particularly noticeable in Kotarbiński's studies on Bacon.[58]

As to the differences, Twardowski conceived philosophy as 'a whole'; everything was mixed in the same bag. Kotarbiński was for the clear separation of particular departments and took great pains to secure the homogeneity of his own philosophy.

A more important difference, however, was that of philosophical standpoint. Although unwilling to commit himself openly,[59] Twardowski did so indirectly in the paper 'O czynnościach i wytworach' (On Actions and Products) of 1921. Here he admitted the multiplicity of ideal entities—if there are certain terms used as subjects in subject-predicate sentences, there must be entities corresponding to them. Kotarbiński, on the other hand, openly professed his concretism. Therefore, what radically separated them was Kotarbiński's materialism. Twardowski went one way, implicitly admitting a multiplicity of entities, and

[58] 1. 'Myśl przewodnia metodologii Franciszka Bacona' (The Principal Motive of Bacon's Methodology), *Przeg. Filoz.*, Nos. 3 and 4, 1926.

2. 'Program Bacona' (Bacon's Programme), *Przeg. Humanistyczny*, Nos. 4 and 5, 1932.

3. 'Bacon o przyszłości nauki' (Bacon on the Future of Science), *Nauka Polska*, 1933.

4. 'The Development of the Main Problems in the Methodology of Francis Bacon', *Studia Philosophica* (in English), 1935. Here is the final section of the summary of the last paper:

. . . Mill is looking for constant antecedents for the given subsequents in time, or *vice versa*, in the world of phenomena: he persists in the search for efficient causes (he only liberates the notion of the efficient cause of additional elements with respect to the steady and unconditional sequence in time), he chiefly aims at inductive generalizations on the basis of a minimum number of data, he makes eliminations in masses. Despite all this, he is only a continuator of Bacon, as the pattern implied *in nuce* in Bacon's doctrine. With respect to the heuristic role of quantitative changes in finding out coexistence of factors, Mill represents a step backwards as compared with Bacon who considered that kind of speculation not merely a substitute used in case of necessity, but on the contrary the most fruitful method. If Mill can be called the larva of the theory of induction, then Bacon should be called its caterpillar. (Reprint, pp. 116, 117.)

Bacon was the philosopher whom Kotarbiński particularly appreciated and admired. Kotarbiński translated the *Novum Organum* into Polish, but the manuscript was destroyed during the war.

[59] Twardowski thought, as we saw in Chap. II, that an acceptance of the critical attitude implied restraint from propagating any outlook on the world, since no such outlook could be adequately justified by means of methodical research and with the help of valid logical argument.

Kotarbiński another, reducing all categories to the category of concrete things. It was, in a way, a repetition of the split which occurred in Brentano's school. A number of his pupils (e.g. Meinong and Husserl) developed the line of the early Brentano, accepting a multiplicity of entities; some others (e.g. Kraus and Katkov) attempted to follow the late Brentano.

5 PRAXIOLOGY

A. *A few remarks about the history of praxiology*

Until the twentieth century there was no *general* theory of efficient action which would embrace *all* human activities regardless the kind of activity. As a matter of fact, when we examine various classifications of science before the twentieth century, we are struck by the lack of a science concerned with efficient action. It is rather peculiar that no department of learning was reserved for the theoretical reflection upon practical activities from the point of view of their efficiency and efficacy. It is almost obvious that such a science ought to have been created and elaborated by American scholars, but it was not. Such a science was conceived by Kotarbiński and worked out in some detail. The science of efficient action, whatever the field of activity, physical or mental, and whatever the scale of activity, a one-minute performance or a gigantic undertaking, has received the name of *praxiology*.

Kotarbiński contributed more than anybody else to shaping praxiology into a scientific discipline. Before him, various scholars had attempted to formulate a sort of general theory of efficient action. However, none was as aware of the necessity of the theoretical branch of inquiry concerned with practical activities as was Kotarbiński, and none was as successful. From as early as 1910, Kotarbiński felt it his duty and even his mission to elaborate in detail a new branch of theoretical inquiry—the general theory of efficient action.

It might be appropriate to say a few words on the history of the subject. When a new discipline appears, investigations are made to trace its origins and its embryonic phases. This type of investigation has been conducted with regard to praxiology. It has been discovered that there were some attempts to construct a 'praxiological system' before Kotarbiński.[60] The first seems to be

[60] The most extensive research in the history of praxiology has been made by Jan Ostrowski (writing under the pen name of Jan Jordan). His paper

that of Charles B. Dunoyer.[61] Although the term 'praxiology' was not used, the kind of consideration involved was clearly praxiological. In the work of Louis Bourdeau[62] the term 'praxeologie' is introduced and stands for the 'science of functions, that is of actions'.

Close to Kotarbiński's concept of praxiology is that of 'ponoogy', proposed by the Spanish engineer Meliton Martin.[63] However, the most concrete programme was formulated by a French philosopher and sociologist, Alfred Espinas.[64] His is considered by many to be the direct predecessor of Kotarbiński's praxiology.

The English have had their share in anticipating praxiology as well. In 1911 Charles Arthur Mercier wrote in *Conduct and its Disorders Biologically Considered*:

> It would appear *prima facie* that few studies are more important than that of Conduct. . . . Conduct is what we are all engaged in from birth to death; and yet though many departments of conduct are described in many books, there is not in existence, curiously enough, any comprehensive study of conduct as a whole—any general view of the field of human activity.[65]

More specifically in reference to certain types of action which he called praxiology, he said:

> Apart from the general advantage to everyone who has to engage in conduct of any kind, of having a systematic knowledge of that mode of conduct; and therefore to everyone of having a systematic knowledge as a whole; there are special advantages to be derived from a study of praxiology, if I may so term it.[66]

[61] Charles B. Dunoyer, *De la liberté du travail, ou simple exposé des conditions dans lesquelles les forces humaines s'exercent avec le plus de puissance*, Vols. I–III (Paris, 1845).

[62] Louis Bourdeau, *Theorie des sciences. Plan de science integrale*, Vols. I, II (Paris, 1882).

[63] Meliton Martin, *Le Travail humain, son analyse, ses lois, son évolution* (Paris, 1878).

[64] Alfred Victor Espinas, *Les Origines de la technologie* (Paris, 1897).

[65] Charles Arthur Mercier, *Conduct and its Disorders Biologically Considered* (London, 1911), Introduction, p. vii.   [66] Ibid., p. viii.

'Metody badań nad działaniem' (Methods of Inquiry Concerning Action) published in *Ruch Filozoficzny* (No. 1, 1962) seems to be as yet the most extensive research in the field. Other papers on the history of praxiology have begun to appear in the new praxiological journal, *Materiały praxeologiczne*.

However, Mercier devoted most of his treatise to the general examination of action. Only in two sections of the fifth chapter, entitled 'Action as Crude and Elaborate' and 'Action as Skilful and Unskilful', was he concerned with strictly praxiological matters.

The second line of the predecessors of praxiology consists of practical men interested in the science of management and organization, who often call themselves 'efficiency experts'. They, the 'pragmatists', can be contrasted with the first line, the philosophers and sociologists who were interested in praxiology from a theoretical point of view.

At the beginning of the twentieth century, the science of management was initiated by a number of people (Taylor, Fayol, Le Chatelier, Adamiecki) who formulated their praxiological views in books on the principles of management, industrial organization, scientific management, etc. Also, the 'theory of complex objects', elaborated by Bogdanov and Petrovic in the twentieth century, was a close approximation to praxiology.

All the above works which are historically relevant were unearthed only after Kotarbiński shaped his science of efficient action. There was no continuity in the development of praxiology as might appear from the above references. However, it seems clear that the emergence of praxiology as a *systematic* discipline concerned with a particular aspect of human action—namely with the efficiency of action—was, so to say, an historical inevitability. Various writers hit the nail upon the head, but Kotarbiński drove it in.

B. *The scope and nature of praxiology*

It should be made clear from the start that praxiology is a subject difficult to characterize. The more briefly we attempt to state what praxiology is, the more trivial seems to be its subject matter. To do praxiology full justice would require a treatise. Such a treatise has been written by Kotarbiński.[67]

Praxiology as mentioned above, is concerned with purposeful

[67] Kotarbiński, *Traktat o dobrej robooie* (A Treatise on Good Work) (Wrocław: Zakład im. Ossolińskich, 1955); 2nd edn., Warsaw, 1959.) English translation, enlarged by a number of praxiological essays written after 1955, appeared under the title: *Praxiology—An Introduction to the Science of Efficient Action* (Oxford, 1965).

action, that is to say, with deliberate and conscious action. It analyses such action from the point of view of efficiency. Kotarbiński himself at first called his inquiry a general theory of deeds or practice. Next, he adopted the name 'praxiology' following Espinas. Kotarbiński's work on praxiology was initiated in 1910. In 1913 his 'Practical Essays' were published.[68] In 1955 appeared *Traktat o dobrej robocie* (A Treatise on Good Work), which has become the 'praxiological bible'. In this treatise the author summed up the results of his observations, meditations, and readings on praxiological matters gathered during his entire life. Since any sphere of our activity can be measured in terms of efficiency, the conscious and consistent application of the directives provided by praxiology can bring an improvement in practically every field of human activity. Thus the principal task of the praxiologist is to distinguish those methods which are applicable to all fields of work. In every kind of work we strive to use as few physical resources, as little time and effort as are necessary to reach the intended objectives. One way of achieving this purpose is to replace therapeutics (broadly understood as the repairing of damages and defects) by prophylaxis (broadly understood as the prevention of damage). Another way is to perform many actions at one stroke.[69]

Many people have doubted whether praxiology is a branch of philosophy. Kotarbiński wrote:

> The business of praxiology is ... to investigate the essence of the process of action, and to clarify all those concepts which are indispensable for the description, appraisal and planning of action and for the general theory of efficient action.[70]

Apart from the logical clarification of the concepts of paraxiology which is no doubt an extension of analytic philosophy, there are other arguments for regarding praxiology as a branch of philosophy. Praxiology generalizes in a systematic way all particular facts concerning the efficient action of man. There is only one sphere of considerations in which action is treated in a more general way than in praxiology; this is the general theory of action

[68] 'Practical Essays' and other essays concerning praxiological matters were printed under the title *Thoughts About Action* which appeared as the first volume of *Selected Papers* (Warsaw, 1957).

[69] Kotarbiński, 'The Concept of Action', *Journal of Philosophy*, LVII, No. 7 (31 March 1960), p. 215.

[70] Ibid., p. 215.

as represented, for example, by Maurice Blondel's *Action* (Paris, 1893) and Stuart Hampshire's *Thought and Action* (1959). Both the general theory of action and the general theory of efficient action (praxiology) can be correlated with and considered as parts of the general theory of causality, and in this way shown to belong unquestionably to philosophy.

C. *Some basic concepts of praxiology*

We shall now consider some of the basic concepts of praxiology. 'Elementary action' means an act of voluntary *pressure*. The term 'pressure' is understood here in a broader sense than in everyday life, where only 'positive' pressure is considered, e.g. as in kicking a ball to score a goal. In praxiology, the term 'pressure' also includes 'negative' pressure, e.g. when shooting with a bow, we let go the bowstring in order that it will propel the arrow. Both positive and negative pressures have something in common—a change of pressure occurs in both. Therefore, the concept of elementary action is defined in terms of a *change* of purposeful pressure rather than in terms of purposeful pressure without qualification.

The above account of a single action refers not only to actions directed towards external objects. Internal processes taking place in our minds satisfy the above description as well. When, for example, we restrain ourselves from reacting after being provoked, our successful action is performed by no change in the external environment. However, we experience an inner pressure[71]—concentration of will, strain of imagination, etc. In short, the elementary process of action is characterized in praxiology exclusively and sufficiently by a purposeful change in pressure.

Although in the elementary act there is one pressure, it may give rise to many effects. 'It is the property of action, so pregnant with dramatic consequences, that even an elementary act produces a countless number of most varied effects which reach extremely far into time and space.'[72]

When we consider the *complex activities* performed in daily life,

[71] This 'inner pressure' is, of course, not to be considered as a metaphysical entity, but as a state of an experiencing subject who is to be considered according to the thesis of somatism as a body, and nothing else but a body. In other words, an 'inner pressure' within an individual means that the person is experiencing something.

[72] Kotarbiński, 'The Concept of Action', p. 216.

in scientific research, or in any other kind of activity, we see that all such activities are composed of elementary acts. Complex activities can be performed by one agent or by many. In the latter case, three different situations can occur:

1. *Positive* cooperation, or simply cooperation when agents work together harmoniously, i.e. strive towards the same goal and help each other to do so (for example, musicians in a symphony orchestra performing the same piece of music).

2. *Negative* cooperation, which Kotarbiński calls 'struggle', when different agents obstruct each other, i.e. they perform the same action but strive in opposite directions (for example, football players of opposing teams in a football match).

3. *Neutral* cooperation, when various agents, participating in the same action, strive towards different goals but do not obstruct each other (for example, when of two persons reading a philosophical text in English, the first person is an Englishman reading to learn something about philosophy, the second is a foreign philosopher reading to improve his English).

But praxiology is concerned not only with the clarification of those concepts which are relevant to certain kinds of human action. It is equally concerned with establishing *norms* of efficient action, and also with *evaluating* the efficiency of performed actions. Therefore, praxiology is a normative discipline.

Praxiology does use a system of *values* to assess various deeds, but practical values are different from ethical as well as from aesthetic values. The deed, excellently performed from a praxiological point of view, can be aesthetically neutral and at the same time morally repulsive. This will be amply illustrated in the next section.

Practical values are, admittedly, different in nature from moral or aesthetic values. Although it is tempting to compare the nature of practical values with that of other values, to trace similarities and differences, it is beyond the scope of this work. Our purpose is to bring to light, so to speak, the existence of practical values and to justify their indispensability rather than to embark upon the comparative study of various systems of values.

Now how can these practical values be analysed? One value of efficient action is *economization*: of energy, time, terrain, materials, and apparatus. (The term 'economization' and other similar expressions such as 'exteriorization' and 'interiorization' are rather ugly words. However, they have become a part of the praxiological jargon and one cannot avoid them.) We say that action A is more economical than action B in relation to the given resources and the given effects, if and only if action A gives the same effects as action B for a smaller consumption of resources.[73]

In analysing the economization of energy, five categories may be distinguished, each of which can have many variants:

1. The minimization of interference. This can be achieved for example, by creating a *fait accompli* (in preparing for negative cooperation by occupying an advantageous position and thereby compelling an opponent to occupy a disadvantageous position).

2. The utilization of the possibility of action. This can have many aspects. One occurs when we show the possibility of action instead of performing it, as in threatening. (For example, in military operations we can surround the enemy and thereby threaten him with annihilation which is equally effective and incomparably more economical than actually destroying his forces by a frontal attack.)

3. The interiorization of action. This consists in replacing physical efforts by reflection. (For example, instead of resorting to the trial and error method in searching for a way out of a difficult situation, we first mentally review the various possibilities, and then eliminate those which seem to be doomed to failure.)

4. Exteriorization of action. This consists in the reverse process. We replace reflection by external activity, providing, of course, that the latter is more economical than the former, which is sometimes the case. (For example, when we want to recollect the day of the week on which an event occurred many months ago, it is easier to reach for a calendar than to make a calculation.)

5. Organization of action. This can imply particular qualities such as coordination, ordering in space and time, preparation, simplification of procedure.[74]

Some other praxiological categories are: activation, automatization, integration. By *activation* we mean an increase of our

[73] Kotarbiński, *Treatise on Good Work*, 1st edn., pp. 124, 125.
[74] Kotarbiński, 'Postulates for Economic Modes of Action', *Methodos*, XIII, Nos. 51, 52 (1961), pp. 6–10.

activity, the application of as many devices as possible, the concentration of our entire energy and ingenuity in order to achieve the goal.

By applying *automatization* as a method of action, we emphasize opposite tendencies; we want to achieve the goal by intervening as little as possible. Automatization is therefore a minimizing of intervention by the agent. When acting according to this principle, our aim is to have tasks perform themselves. Automatization has many forms: habit, imitation, learning, instrumentalization, etc.

Integration is usually the most complex method of action and necessitates planning, preparation, strategy, tactics, choice of action. Integration very often includes both activation and automatization, because the same complex action can be planned, partly in terms of activation, and partly in terms of automation. And indeed in most complex actions we try to automatize some parts as much as possible in order to be able to concentrate on those parts which require ingenuity and creative thinking.

In the search for methods appropriate for action of a given kind, praxiology is close to methodology. Methodology, particularly the methodology of the sciences, is a highly developed form of praxiological investigation; methodology can be considered as the search for methods of inquiry which yield the most fruitful results for the given sciences. An example of this type of methodology is that of Karl Popper, who suggests that those conjectures which are most daring and conducive to the further development of a given science should be followed up irrespective of whether they are true or false. Most, if not all existing scientific theories will be falsified or found inadequate and then replaced by more adequate ones. Consequently, what is of importance for the growth of knowledge is the fertility of scientific theories, that is their potentiality for inducing the growth of science. Viewing theories in the light of the growth of knowledge is a clearly praxiological approach.

Methodology forces us to consider the meaning of the word 'method'. What is meant by 'method' in praxiology? By 'method' or a system of action is understood a certain way of performing a complex action; a way which is planned, which can be systematically applied, and which consists in the proper selection and composition of the elements of the action.

This leads us to consider the notion of *plan*. The term 'plan' has two principal meanings. First, it designates a tangible object which consists of signs perceptible to the sight (e.g. a map or a chart). Secondly, the term is associated with pre-analysis, with meditation upon intended action. Here, a plan does not necessarily have to be expressed in perceptible signs.

A plan of intended action[75] is usually taken to mean a system of sentences describing the choice and sequence of the component actions leading to an over-all goal. A good plan should have the following 'virtues'[76]:

1. Purposefulness. The plan should indicate the aim or aims which it serves.

2. Feasibility. This characteristic is obvious, but can be tested only after the event.

3. Inner harmony. In other words, consistency, harmony, logical cohesion.

4. Maximum simplicity. The simpler the plan, the more easily we bridge the gap between conception and realization. This, of course, depends on its structure, and generally on everything which makes the programme tangible and comprehensible.

5. Flexibility or elasticity.

6. Particularity. The plan should be reasonably detailed.

7. Long-term view. The plan should be constructed to cover the longest period possible in the light of the existing knowledge of future conditions.

8. Terminal definiteness of the plan. The date of the completion of work must be specified (taking into account point 5).

9. Rationality. The more rational the plan, the more scientifically based are its elements.

Planning is itself an action, therefore it too should conform to the above nine criteria. In short, a good plan must itself be 'good work'.

D. *Some illustrations of praxiological thinking*

To recapitulate: praxiology concerns itself with general principles of efficacious action common to all kinds of work, both intellectual and physical. Here I should like to give a few examples of how different kinds of work—from political science to climbing a

75 A plan becomes a programme when the decision as to its realization has been reached.

76 See Kotarbiński's *Sprawność i błąd* (*Efficiency and Error*) (Warsaw, 1956), pp. 73–82.

mountain, from pedagogy to judo—can be analysed from a praxiological point of view.

The usefulness and even the inevitability of praxiological values become apparent when we analyse the reasons why many disputes in moral philosophy have remained unresolved. For centuries philosophers and moralists argued about the cynicism and moral rottenness of Machiavelli's *The Prince*. Principles and devices recommended there were thought to be manifestations of un-mitigated evil. The praxiologist would say that these moral disputes and moral evaluations of the treatise were simply irrelevant, because Machiavelli considered the techniques of political action from the point of view of their efficiency in the same sort of way as an engineer considers the technique of con-structing a ship, irrespective of whether his project will be realized by the friends or enemies of his country. Machiavelli, in short, did not ask which actions are morally worthy, but only which methods are more *efficient* in the struggle for and maintenance of power. Before praxiology provided evaluations of action different from moral evaluations, it was difficult to see that actions which had some moral implications, could be considered from a non-moral point of view. Such is the case with Machiavelli's *The Prince*, which was truly a praxiological treatise. If we accept this we see immediately that moral discussions about the treatise were really irrelevant.

Some philosophers, by mixing praxiological and moral con-siderations, were equally muddled about the essential issues of moral philosophy. Thus, for example, when Spencer in *First Principles* wished to establish the moral connotation of the term 'good' by examining the question 'What is a good knife?', he was unaware of slipping from the realm of moral considerations to the realm of praxiology. The conclusions of his examination were not very relevant nor interesting for moral philosophy because he chose to consider practical values, not moral ones. In the field of aesthetics many heated controversies remain curiously unresolved because, under the guise of aesthetic values, practical values are at issue. In architecture and in the useful arts particularly this problem can be rather troublesome if it is insisted that given objects can be considered as aesthetically satisfying only insofar as they are useful. In a modern idiom, this is the problem of 'func-tionality'. Clearly, for functionality we require a combination of two different virtues, aesthetic and praxiological.

The general conclusion can be expressed as follows. Only by

recognizing the realm of practical values and its active interaction with the realms of aesthetics and morals can we bring order, clarity, and understanding to many issues which have been muddled because of the lack of this recognition.

The conquest of Mount Everest demonstrated the indispensability of the praxiological 'virtues'. It was an example of a complex action which, although performed with no conscious knowledge of praxiology, was nevertheless a praxiological performance. The ultimate goal, in praxiological terms, was a minimization of energy, which consisted in delivering a team of two (or four) people to a final camp in good condition so that they would be able to make the final short ascent. All actions were *coordinated* around this goal. From shoes, anoraks, tents, and oxygen masks, which were selected and tested months in advance, to the final moves between camps everything was arranged and described as a huge and complex exercise in preparation. Of course, other praxiological categories such as coordination and integration were involved; the overall pattern, however, was one of preparation. Consequently, the story, which for the layman appears as a dramatic and romantic struggle of man against the elements, will be read by the praxiologist as an unromantic account of efficient preparation.

To give another example which demonstrates the usefulness of praxiology in complex actions, consider some dilemmas of the teacher. One is the problem of combining intelligibility with precision and exactness in a lecture. A formula must be found to resolve these conflicting demands. Why is it a praxiological problem? Because its successful resolution implies a hierarchy of purposes, the hierarchy which cannot be established or analysed within the domain of pedagogy proper.

Usually the system of education is a resultant of the factual knowledge and the methods of teaching contained in particular subjects. The formation of the system starts from the bottom. Specialists of various disciplines decide upon the knowledge to be transmitted to students and upon the methods of this transmission. The totality of all the subjects (with their factual knowledge and methods) composes what might be called the system of education. This system moulds a type of specialist, a man educated within this system. He faces the needs and challenges of his society. Usually there is a considerable discrepancy between what he can offer, as a product of his university, and what society demands. And almost always substantial adjustments are required on the part of scientists, engineers, and other specialists.

The praxiological approach to the teaching problem will consist in 'starting from the top'. The praxiologist would say that only after establishing a consequential chain, and after correlating the particular links of this chain, can we resolve the problem. To simplify the matter, let us consider only students of science and engineering. The consequential chain is as follows: *the tasks* set for a scientist by contemporary society will imply the type of scientist capable of fulfilling these tasks; the *type of scientist* will imply the system of education suitable for producing this type; *the system of education* will imply suitable methods of teaching.

The problem of intelligibility and precision in transferring knowledge can be successfully resolved only in relation to the whole pattern explained above. Of course, the basic assumption might be different, namely that the main point is to educate a man in such a way that he would be comfortable in an ever-changing technological world. It is precisely this point that accounts for the basic difference between the American and the British systems of education. In America scientists and technologists are clearly emerging as the high priests of the society; in Britain classicists remain the high priests; from their point of view, scientists and engineers are useful technicians who make life more comfortable. However, even when we start with a different assumption about the needs of society, the rest of the inferential chain will retain its validity; it will imply the system of education, next the scope of disciplines, and finally the methods of teaching.

In either case, a praxiological consideration must enter; in order to make the system of education rational and the method of teaching intelligible, a hierarchy of goals must be established. During the process itself or afterwards, efficiency in fulfilling the established goals should be checked. Particular educational operations should be related to and assessed within the framework of the system of education itself with an eye to the main goals of the system. All this should be analysed and described in praxiological terms. Recent disputes over higher education, about the future of universities and so on, are bogged down and confused mostly because the problems tackled are misleadingly formulated and consequently cannot be resolved within the praxiological frame of reference.

The praxiological ways of thinking are also convenient for

explaining less abstract matters. Iigoro Kano, who is recognized as the creator of Judo, explained the main principle of Judo in this typically praxiological way:

> Let us suppose that the strength of man will be estimated in units from 1 to 10. The strength of my opponent is equal to 10, mine is equal to 7. Therefore I should be defeated. However, if I manoeuvre skilfully at the right moment, then my opponent attacking me may lose his balance and his strength will be diminished to 3 units. I shall preserve my 7. I can now overthrow him using only half of my power and preserving the other half for the future course of the fight, or for the next fight.

An ancient maxim proclaimed: 'Whatever is worth doing is worth doing well.' To this we can add: whatever is to be done well may and should be analysed and assessed in praxiological terms. Therefore, praxiology is called for on countless occasions whenever an action is really worth doing.

E. *Recent developments in Poland*

Kotarbiński conceived of praxiology as the major goal of his life. In Poland and elsewhere, however, he is mainly known as the originator of concretism. His praxiology has been comparatively underestimated. This might be due to two factors. First, praxiological concepts, once presented, seem to be obvious and 'known' immediately. The second factor has to do with timing; usually a new discovery, new creation, or new conception, to be duly appreciated, must wait some years. When the *Treatise* was published in 1955, the term 'praxiology' seemed very odd. After five years it became fairly popular, and today it has become part of the Polish language. Moreover, praxiology is becoming more widely used as an instrument for the analysis and appraisal of action in various fields.

In the late 1950s a group appeared who made praxiology the centre of their theoretical activity. Their official organ since 1965 has been the quarterly *Praxeologia* (established in 1962 under the title *Materiały Praxeologiczne*). The most accomplished among these younger praxiologists are: A. Podgórecki,[77] T. Pszczołow-

[77] Adam Podgórecki, (i) *Zagadnienia polityki prawa* (The Problems of the Politics of Law) (Warsaw, 1957)—an analysis of the construction of legal norms from the praxiological viewpoint.

(ii) *Charakterystyka nauk praktyczynch* (A Characteristic of Practical Sciences) (Warsaw, 1962)—an analysis and classification of practical sciences based on praxiological criteria.

In recent years Podgórecki has moved to the field of sociology of law.

ski[78] and T. Zieleniewski.[79] They work in the praxiological workshop of the Polish Academy of Sciences in Warsaw to develop praxiology theoretically and to find its application in science and everyday life. In 1962 the first praxiological Congress took place in Poland sponsored by the Polish Academy of Sciences. Recently praxiology has acquired its first genuine historian, Jan Ostrowski[80] (Jan Jordan) of London. His collection of materials on the history of praxiology is unofficially called 'The Historical Station of the Non-Existent Institute of Praxiology'. It is thus evident that Kotarbiński's favourite discipline shows every sign of healthy growth.

As a postscript it might be added that praxiology is beginning to make a career for itself in the United States. The term 'praxiology' appears to be finding its way into general circulation. Works on praxiology are beginning to appear.

RÉSUMÉ

Kotarbiński might perhaps be characterized finally by the contrasts in his philosophy.

He was a staunch defender of common sense when developing his concretism, but did not hesitate to assert that 'every soul is a body.' In this he differed drastically from Moore. He joined the ranks of those classical philosophers who did not hesitate to violate common sense in order to achieve consistency in or completion of their systems.

Although he had little affection for mathematical logic, he was recognized as an authority in the field. Moreover, his system of

[78] Tadeusz Pszczołowski, (i) *Praxeologiczna koncepcja pracy* (The Praxiological Concept of Work) in *Fragmenty Filozoficzne* (second series, 1959).

(ii) *Zasady sprawnego działania* (The Principles of Efficient Action) (Warsaw), 1st end, 1960; 2nd edn, 1961; 3rd edn, 1962—a popular version of the Kotarbiński's *Treatise*.

(iii) *Umiejętność przekonywania i dyskusji* (The Art of Discussion and Persuasion) (Warsaw) Ist edn, 1962; 2nd edn. 1963—a praxiological analysis of the art of argument.

(iv) *Praca człowieka* (Human Work) (Warsaw, 1966).

[79] Tadeusz Zieleniewski, *Organizacja zespołów ludzkich* (The Organization of Human Teams) (Warsaw, 1964).

[80] Jan Ostrowski, 'Narzędzie i kultura' (Tool in Man's Culture) in the *Journal of the Institute of Polish Engineers Abroad* (London, 1960). See also footnote 60.

philosophy was partially erected on the scaffolding of concepts worked out in mathematical logic.

At the start of his philosophical career, his sole concern seems to have been to analyse the meaning of concepts in philosophical discourse as a programme of intellectual reform. However, the residue of his analyses became a philosophical system.

He objected to being placed in traditional pigeon-holes, and preferred to be called a concretist or a reist. However, there is no doubt that his is a modern type of materialism; the materialism which grew out of concretistic semantics. Hence it might be called semantic materialism.

Kotarbiński's praxiology, that is the science of efficient action, was undoubtedly an original achievement, and it will be a great achievement if it consolidates into a fully-fledged science; as yet one wonders if it is no more than common sense and proverbial practical wisdom dressed up in polysyllables.

Kotarbiński's 'independent ethics', although only sketched and therefore requiring much theoretical elaboration, has nevertheless been very influential in a practical way, and has gained many adherents in Poland.

Kotarbiński was one of the very few philosophers who understood and creatively acted upon the idea that philosophy has as its subject not only theory, but also *praxis*. However, his praxiology was quite independent of the rest of his philosophy.

V

KAZIMIERZ AJDUKIEWICZ—

EPISTEMOLOGY REFLECTED IN

LANGUAGE

---

1 A GENERAL CHARACTERIZATION

Kazimierz Ajdukiewicz was born on 12 December 1890, at Tarnopol, Galicia, and died in Warsaw in 1963. Between 1908 and 1912 he studied philosophy at the University of Lwów under Twardowski and Łukasiewicz. He received the degree of Doctor of Philosophy for the dissertation: 'Apriorism of Space in Kant's Philosophy'. At the same time he studied mathematics under W. Sierpiński and physics under M. Smoluchowski. In 1921 he obtained a dozent degree for a dissertation entitled: 'Z metodologii nauk dedukcyjnych' (On the Methodology of the Deductive Sciences) and he began to teach at the University of Lwów. In 1925 he became a professor of philosophy at Warsaw University and remained there until 1928. Then he moved to Lwów University until 1939.

During the Second World War, between 1940 and 1941, and between 1944 and 1945, he was assigned to lecture on physics at the Russian Medical Institute at Lwów. After the war, when the city of Lwów was annexed by the U.S.S.R., he chose to be in Poland and in 1945 was appointed to the Chair of the Methodology of Science at the University of Poznań. Between 1948 and 1952 he was Rector of that University. In 1955 he moved from Poznań to Warsaw University, where he held a Chair of Logic. In 1961 he retired from the chair but continued to direct the Division of Logic of the Philosophical Institute of the Polish Academy of Sciences. He took an active part in international congresses of philosophy between the wars, when scientific philosophy was the watchword. These were at Oxford (1930), Prague (1934), and Paris (1935). He also attended many congresses after the war.

He was the founder and the first editor-in-chief of the journal *Studia Logica*. In 1960–1962 he was Vice-President of the Division of Logic, Methodology and Philosophy of the Sciences of *l'Union International de l'Histoire et Philosophie des Sciences*.

A. *Some remarks on Ajdukiewicz's style of philosophizing*

Ajdukiewicz was led to philosophy by reading Berkeley. As a pupil in secondary school, he discovered Berkeley's treatises and was so fascinated by the question of 'how things really are' that he decided to devote himself to philosophy. From that time onwards, he maintained a keen interest in traditional problems, particularly in the controversy between idealism and realism, and that between apriorism and empiricism. His views underwent continual change and evolution throughout his life, like Russell and unlike Kotabiński. The major changes in his outlook occurred after the war, when he shifted from idealism to realism, and from apriorism to empiricism.

The main difficulties in presenting Ajdukiewicz's philosophy are: (1) the variety of topics with which he dealt, (2) his changes of mind on some topics, and (3) his way of philosophizing and of presenting his results; he gives incisive analyses of particular problems in such a highly condensed, consequential, and subtle form that his arguments are almost impossible to summarize. Kotarbiński, describing Ajdukiewicz's style of philosophizing, emphasized this particular trait: the ability to work through a problem to its bare bones.

> I do not know any philosopher more acute in analysing and criticizing the philosophical works of others than you. In this field, you are a champion not to be surpassed in skill. I suppose that if an international competition were to be arranged to judge the highest standard of philosophical work, you could certainly stand as a candidate fully entitled to the prize.[1]

In his philosophical work, Ajdukiewicz was a thinker first and a teacher second. However, on many occasions his teaching gave rise to theoretically important results. From it sprang the idea of

[1] T. Kotarbiński, published in commemoration of Ajdukiewicz's 70th birthday in *Kwartalnik Filozoficzny*, No. 4, 1962.

writing a textbook on logic. Apart from his other enterprises, Ajdukiewicz was occupied throughout his life with writing 'the' textbook on logic. By 1962 he had written about ten in all, and published three of them, trying in each to solve a number of old problems in a novel way. His *magnum opus* on logic, *Logika Pragmatyczna* (Pragmatic Logic), was published posthumously in 1965.

Apart from Kotarbiński, Ajdukiewicz was the major figure in the Polish analytical movement. Kotarbiński enunciated a minimalistic programme of a 'small' philosophy, but later developed a system of philosophy in the traditional sense. Ajdukiewicz, on the other hand, did not announce any programme, but invariably and consistently maintained a minimalistic attitude towards philosophy. Before the war, Ajdukiewicz, more than anyone else in Poland, tied philosophical investigations to inquiries into language. He also applied logic, particularly semantics, to formulating and solving philosophical problems. Although he was originally a zealous advocate of the logical reconstruction of philosophy, he himself admitted the limitations of logic when the expected results did not emerge.[2]

From the early years of the Vienna Circle, Ajdukiewicz was in close contact with that group and published some of his most important papers in *Erkenntnis*.[3] But, as with most Polish philosophers, his philosophical credo had crystallized before the Vienna Circle came into being. Ajdukiewicz sympathized with many of the undertakings of the Circle although with some important reservations. In the paper 'Logistical Anti-Irrationalism in Poland', delivered to the Prague Congress of Philosophy in 1934, he said:

An affinity between Polish philosophers and the Vienna Circle consists mainly in the similarity of methodological standpoint. The characteristic features of this standpoint are: firstly—anti-irrationalism, that is to say, a requirement that only those assertions are recognized which are justified in an intersubjective way; secondly —a requirement of exactitude of thought and language; and thirdly —application on a large scale of the method and language of symbolic logic. As regards the subject-matter, the two movements

---

[2] 'O stosowalności czystej logiki do zagadnień filozoficznych' (On the Application of Pure Logic to Philosophical Problems), *Przeg. Filoz.*, XXXVII, 1934. Also in *Actes du VIII Congrès International de Philosophie*, Prague.

[3] K. Ajdukiewicz, 'Sprache und Sinn', *Erkenntnis*, IV, 1934: 'Das Weltbild und die Begriffsapparatur', *Erkenntnis*, IV, 1934.

share a predilection for problems concerned with scientific cognition, that is to say, with meta-theoretical inquiries according to the assumption that cognition can be investigated only through its linguistic expression.[4]

Thus Ajdukiewicz called the analytical movement in Poland logistic anti-irrationalism. He wished to contrast a rational attitude with an irrational one. However, because the term 'rationalism' is burdened with too many associations, he preferred to use the term 'anti-irrationalism'. The adjective 'logistic' indicates that the method applied was that of logic, mainly symbolic logic. It should be firmly borne in mind at this point that this description refers to Ajdukiewicz's philosophy rather than to the analytical trend in Poland as a whole. Ajdukiewicz's belief in rationalism, as expressed on many occasions, was one of the basic pillars of his philosophy; methodologically speaking, it was a principle which was to guard the intersubjective and cognitive character of his philosophical inquiry.[5]

B. *An analytical attitude towards social issues*

Ajdukiewicz was a scholar of academic type, and, unlike Kotarbiński, participated, but to a small extent, in public affairs. However, he did write some papers on general topics, such as justice, the concept of man, academic freedom. The paper 'On the Freedom of Science'[6] is a good example of his conception of the rôle of a philosopher in society. It was written at the time of social ferment in Poland (1957) when the problem of freedom of research, science, and learning was by no means purely academic. Even in this paper, however, Ajdukiewicz was first and foremost a scholar, an analytical philosopher for whom theoretical analysis is of prime importance. When Kotarbiński, on the other hand, took part in public affairs, he did so primarily as a member of the community

[4] K. Ajdukiewicz, 'Logistyczny antyirracjonalizm w Polsce' (Logistic Anti-Irrationalism in Poland), delivered during the Prague Congress in 1934, published in *Przeg. Filoz.*, XXXVIII, 1934, p. 400.

In 1960, the first volume of Ajdukiewicz's *Selected Papers, Język i poznanie* (Language and Cognition) appeared. Therein the three above-mentioned papers are contained, along with the 19 papers published originally before the war. The second volume, containing essays published in the years 1947–1959, appeared in 1965.

[5] See Section 4B of this chapter, 'The principle of rationalism'.

[6] Delivered first as a public lecture at the University of Warsaw in March 1957, and published in *Nauka Polska*, No. 3, 1957.

protesting against injustice or appealing to the better side of human nature; his analytical attitude at such moments was not obvious at all.

Because Ajdukiewicz's paper 'On the Freedom of Science' is particularly characteristic of his treatment of more general problems, we shall present it in some detail.

The four 'freedoms' which must be achieved in order to secure scientific freedom are:

1. Freedom of choice.
2. Freedom of method of inquiry.
3. Freedom of thought.
4. Freedom of speech.

Each of these requirements are related to restrictions which had been imposed on academic freedom in Poland in the 1950s. Ajdukiewicz talked in an abstract way and did not bring to the picture the most relevant examples of these restrictions. We shall supplement his abstract argument with some concrete examples in order to make quite clear what sort of barriers he wished to remove.

Regarding point (4), Ajdukiewicz observed that freedom of speech requires:

(*a*) that a person can say, write, and publish what he wants to, and

(*b*) is not compelled to say, write, or publish what he does not wish to.

However, scientific freedom does not mean a freedom of speech so unrestricted that it would permit the dissemination of rubbish or unintelligible gibberish. Consequently, freedom of speech should be restricted to opinions which show:

(i) meaningful and significant content (from a scholarly point of view);

(ii) coherence and precision of formulation;

(iii) rationality of approach;

(iv) the competence of the author in the given field.

Regarding point (3)—freedom of thought implies:

(*a*) a right to believe in that and only that which can be rationally justified, and

(*b*) a right to disbelieve everything that is not supported by rational argument and, even more so, everything that rational argument actually speaks against.

Compelling people to believe in unjustifiable assertions is called by the author 'normative dogmatism'. It can be open or disguised. Disguised dogmatism does not openly declare its dogmas and does not produce lists of heresies, but it suppresses any opinion which goes against the grain of the established orthodoxy. Apart from normative dogmatism, Ajdukiewicz distinguishes methodological dogmatism, which occurs when assertions are made without rational justification, or when a rational justification is actually much weaker than is claimed. Many pronouncements of Marxist philosophy and Marxist sociology are cases in question.

Regarding freedom of method of inquiry, 'A recommendation of this or that method which has been successfully applied does not mean an exclusion of all other methods of research. An exclusion does take place whenever one method has a monopoly and is recognized as the only valid or the only scientific one.'[7] This can occur when, for example, the laws of dialectics are considered the supreme method to be used in explaining the structure of the world, and other methods are discarded as antiquated and unscientific.

Finally, freedom of the choice of problem entails (*a*) that a person is free to deal with any problem of his own choice, and (*b*) is not compelled to investigate those problems he does not wish to deal with. Violation of either of these two requirements constitutes a limitation of scientific freedom even if all the other 'freedoms' are guaranteed.

In the conclusion, Ajdukiewicz protested against the crudely pragmatic policy which supports science insofar as it is immediately utilizable. This Ajdukiewicz considered to be 'erroneous and detrimental to science'. Scientists and scholars are responsible members of society, he said, and are able to adjust the scope and direction of their theoretical investigations in accordance with social needs. However, if this 'adjustment' is superimposed from outside, 'it should never lead to the destruction of intellectual potentialities and to the diversion of science from its path for the sake of satisfying the needs of an insignificant and momentary occasion.'[8]

The essay 'On the Freedom of Science' was written in specific circumstances to counteract specific obstacles. However, this analysis applies to all circumstances in which scientific freedom is suppressed or violated. Various orthodoxies violate the four 'freedoms' in different degrees. In periods of severe limitation,

[7] Op. cit., p. 14.   [8] Ibid., pp. 18, 19.

usually more than one of the required conditions is violated. None the less, even in circumstances which are called 'liberal', there are usually some measures of limitation contained in unformulated mores. One is not supposed to tackle certain problems or to use certain methods. For example, in most academic institutions, academic freedom is limited by fashions and predilections prevalent at a given time.

Among Polish philosophers, Ajdukiewicz was closest to the ideal of the analytical philosopher. His philosophy was always minimalistic, concerned with particular problems which were closely scrutinized. Great syntheses, he felt, could be achieved only at the expense of logic or by extravagant indulgences in fantasy. In his inquiry, language played the most instrumental part. However, language never became the ultimate goal of his investigation; important as it was, it was always a means to the solution of some philosophical, non-linguistic problems.

2 THE THEORY OF MEANING

'Preoccupation with the theory of meaning could be described as the occupational disease of twentieth-century Anglo-Saxon and Austrian philosophy.'[9] And the same could be said about Polish philosophy. The most important contributions of the two major Polish analytical philosophers, Kotarbiński and Ajdukiewicz, were very closely related to their works on the theory of meaning with this difference that in Kotarbiński semantic research served his ontology, whereas in Ajdukiewicz it served as a basis for his epistemology.

In *The Diversity of Meaning*,[10] which is the first comprehensive study in the theory of meaning since Ogden's and Richards' *The Meaning of Meaning*, Jonathan Cohen groups modern theories of meaning into two classes which he calls *de facto* theories and *de jure* theories. In *de facto* theories, meanings are treated as:

(*a*) timeless subsistent entities (e.g. Frege);

(*b*) facts causally related to the utterance of a word or sentence (e.g. Russell);

(*c*) facts purposively related to the utterance of a word or sentence (e.g. Popper).

[9] Gilbert Ryle, 'The Theory of Meaning,' in Raymond Klibansky (ed.), *British Philosophy in the Mid-Century* (London, 1957), p. 239.
[10] L. Jonathan Cohen, *The Diversity of Meaning* (London, 1962).

It appears that all these theories have been recently superseded by the *de jure* theory of meaning which claims that statements about meanings are or should be construed as statements about rules of certain kinds. In other words, meanings are to be considered as, or constructed in terms of, normative rules. The main representatives of this theory of meaning are, according to Cohen, Alonzo Church so far as formal languages are concerned, and Ryle and Wittgenstein so far as natural language is concerned.

Thus, 'for *de facto* theories a language is a pattern of events, for *de jure* ones a system of rules'.[11]

It is a pity that Cohen did not find enough space to mention Ajdukiewicz even once while considering the *de jure* theory of meaning. Ajdukiewicz was probably the first to formulate the *de jure* theory: with respect to artificial language in 1921 ('Z metodologii nauk dedukcyinych'); and in relation to natural languages in 1930 and 1934 ('O znaczeniu wrażeń' and 'Sprache und Sinn' respectively). The works of 1921 and 1930 were in Polish and no doubt were not accessible to readers outside Poland. However, 'Sprache und Sinn', where Ajdukiewicz's theory of meaning was worked out in detail and formulated with exactitude, was published in *Erkenntnis*.

Ajdukiewicz's theory grew out of his interests and researches in the deductive sciences and, later on, the methodology of science. In his dozent-degree thesis of 1921, 'Z metodologii nauk dedukcyinych' (On the Methodology of the Deductive Sciences), he analysed deductive theories from a logical point of view and provided, independently of Frege, a definition of mathematical proof in terms of its formal structure. It was the first formulation of a structural theory of proof in Poland, and one of the first in Europe. In his treatise, Ajdukiewicz considered mathematical symbols as figures similar to those in chess, with which we operate according to established rules. In deductive theories the rules are rules of proof. The comparison with chess is a very close one; in chess the whole meaning of the different pieces is entirely comprised in the moves prescribed for them, i.e. in the ways in which we can use them. Likewise, in formalized deductive theories, the sense of symbols is comprised entirely in the ways of operating with them, that is to say in the rules of proof.

In Poland this work first put forward the structural method of defining methodological concepts, such as the concepts of proof

[11] Op. cit., p. 24.

or inference. Together with similar ideas introduced independently by Leśniewski, this method greatly stimulated the development of the methodology of the deductive sciences, metamathematics particularly.

The approach which Ajdukiewicz employed for defining the rules of proof was later elaborated and generalized in his perhaps most significant papers on the theory of meaning: 'O znaczeniu wyrażeń' (On the Meaning of Expressions), and his well-known 'Sprache und Sinn' in which he put forward the thesis that the meaning of an expression, and in particular of a sentence, is determined in a given language by the rules which govern the use of this expression. To recognize language as such implies following the rules of its use. If we do not respect the rules of use (workings of language), we do not operate with the language in question. In a word, meaning is use.

At the time when Ajdukiewicz formulated and developed his theory of meaning in the early 1930s, the way to the correct formulation of semantic concepts (i.e., terms which describe the correlation between expressions of a language and the objects 'these expressions are concerned with') was paved with antinomies. The definition of the notion of denotation was endangered by the antimony of heterological expressions; in the way of a correct and adequate formulation of the theory of truth stood the antimony of the liar. The construction of a valid definition of any semantic concept seemed to be an impossible task; and to talk simultaneously about language and the objects with which this language is concerned did not seem possible either. This pessimism was premature. Correct and adequate definitions of semantic concepts were first provided by Tarski and later by other logicians. However, in the early 1930s, because of apparently insurmountable difficulties, philosophers and logicians, including Ajdukiewicz, avoided defining semantic notions such as a true sentence. Instead they concentrated on syntactical notions and attempted to provide definitions of a meaningful sentence in such a way that the concept of denotation would not be involved. If we cannot use expressions which we know to be true, let us at any rate use expressions which we know to be meaningful in a given language.

The theory of meaning, based on rules which determine the meaning of expressions in this language, was emerging in the late 1920s. The theory, so to speak, hung in the air. However, it was

Ajdukiewicz's good luck to formulate and expound the theory explicitly and in detail. He claimed that for every language there are certain rules which we must obey if we are to talk that language meaningfully. If those rules are violated, we simply are not talking the language in question. If we are to talk English meaningfully, then to the question: 'Is a square a quadrangle?', we must answer affirmatively. However, if someone is unable to answer this question at all, or answers it negatively, this would simply prove that, providing he has no deceitful intentions, he does not understand the meaning of the English words 'square' and 'quadrangle'. These rules, which determine the meaning of expressions and consequently force us to accept certain expressions as meaningful and to reject others, are jointly called the rules of sense (of meaning) of language. In the formative stage of his theory of meaning in 'Sprache und Sinn' (1934), Ajdukiewicz distinguished three kinds of rules:

(*a*) axiomatic,
(*b*) deductive,
(*c*) empirical.

Axiomatic rules of sense (meaning) determine the meaning of those expressions or sentences which must be accepted in all circumstances and can never be rejected if we are to talk the language in question. The sentence 'Every square is a quadrangle' is an example of such a sentence.

Deductive rules determine the meaning of a pair of sentences which are connected in such a way that the acceptance of the first necessarily implies the acceptance of the second if, again, words are being properly used. For example, if we accept the sentence 'Some animals are mammals', we cannot, if we use English properly, reject the sentence 'Some mammals are animals'.

Empirical rules determine the meaning of certain sentences in certain situations in such a way that, in a given situation, we must use certain expressions in a certain way if we are not to violate the language we speak. For example, if a person is pricked with a needle and is asked 'Does it hurt?', the answer 'Yes' must be given.

With empirical rules the case is not so clear-cut as with the first two, because the classification of 'empirical situations' may be difficult. Ajdukiewicz's idea was this. If we find ourselves in a particular situation (being pricked by a needle) in which people using ordinary language would say 'it hurts', and we, in this situation with our nervous system intact, say 'It does not hurt', we would simply violate some empirical rules of the language.

At the time when Ajdukiewicz formulated his theory of meaning (early 1930s), he thought that apart from the three kinds of rules it was conceivable that there are further rules of language. Perhaps, had he tried to discern further rules, he might have come to an elaborate classification of linguistic expressions which might have been in accord with the Oxford philosophy of ordinary language. Later, however, he did not look for new kinds of rules, but rather attempted to reduce the three groups to two, or even to one. At one time he dispensed with one kind of rule, and at another with another kind of rule.

The concept of language, based on the rules of sense, implied a twofold relationship: (*a*) it implied that the meanings of expressions determine the rules of sense of a given language L, and (*b*) conversely, that the rules of sense determine the meanings of expressions. The second relationship allowed Ajdukiewicz to formulate his definition of meaning in terms of synonymy of two expressions in language L. If, as the result of the replacement of two expressions one by another, the rules of sense remain unchanged, then these expressions are synonymous. In other words, two expressions are synonymous if and only if the rules of sense are invariant with respect to replacement of these two expressions or, more briefly, if and only if the rules of sense assert the same thing about each expression.[12]

The characterization of language in terms of the three rules of sense, and the admission that the meaning of expressions in a language determines the rules of sense of this language and *vice versa*, facilitated the definition of synonymy and also provided a

---

[12] In 'Sprache und Sinn' the following definition is given: '*A* has in language *L* the same meaning as *A'* in language *L'*, if and only if *A* is an expression of language *L* and *A'* is an expression of language *L'*, and when there is a relationship R such that *L* is translatable into *L'* according to this relationship, and this relationship R holds between *A* and *A'*.' (In *Selected Papers*, Vol. I, p. 170.)

How is this relationship R to be understood? Languages *L* and *L'* are translatable into each other, according to relationship R, if and only if R is a one—one relationship where for every expression in *L* there is a corresponding expression in *L'* and *vice versa*, in such a way that matrix *L* (or *L'* respectively) turns into matrix *L'* (or *L*), when all expressions in the matrix are replaced by corresponding expressions according to relationship R.

clear distinction between two expressions of the same denotation, but different meaning. For example, two expressions: a 'pentagon', and a 'polygon with the sum of its angles 540°' denote the same object but mean something different. The rules of sense precisely indicate the difference because two different rules are to be applied to these two expressions. We certainly violate language if we reject the statement: 'A figure of five sides is a pentagon'. In virtue of the meaning of its terms, the statement is true; the axiomatic rules of sense secure the truth of the statement. But the axiomatic rules do not secure the truth of the statement: 'The polygon, the sum of whose angles is equal to 540°, is a pentagon.' In this way the rules of sense provide a clear distinction between meaning and naming—the problem with which contemporary philosophers have been absorbed since Frege.

When developing his theory of meaning, Ajdukiewicz's main concern was to escape the treatment of meanings as abstract entities or mental acts subjective for a given person. Instead, he wished to treat meanings as 'something intersubjective which is attributed to a given sound of human speech with respect to a given language, and not with respect to a particular person'.[13] It was precisely in order not to hypostasize, something to which Polish philosophers were acutely allergic mainly because of the influence of Kotarbiński, that Ajdukiewicz defined meaning in terms of the sameness of meaning of two expressions, or synonymy, rather than ventured a definition of meaning as such. It is enough to observe the pains with which Ajdukiewicz tried to define and re-define the concept of sameness of meaning or synonymy to realize what importance he attached to the definition of meaning in terms of synonymy.[14]

It can be clearly seen that Quine's views on the subject, as well

[13] K. Ajdukiewicz, 'Sprache und Sinn', in *Selected Papers*, Vol. I, p. 145.

[14] Because a detailed technical discussion of this problem is beyond the scope of our presentation, we shall only mention that the complete definition of the expression: 'The expression A is in language L synonymous with the expression B' as provided in 'O znaczeniu wyrażeń' (On Meaning of Expressions) goes on for about 150 words. It appears that in *Word and Object* Quine referred to this definition when, in the section 'Synonymous and Analytic Sentences', he said that he was not 'taken aback' when it was pointed out to him that similar ideas to his on synonymy can be found in Bolzano. To this Quine added: 'I was [taken aback] at recently uncovering an anticipation of my specific exposition in Ajdukiewicz.' *Word and Object* (Technology Press of the M.I.T., 1960), p. 65.

as those of his followers, are reminiscent of Ajdukiewicz's. In 'Two Dogmas of Empiricism' Quine wrote:

> Once the theory of meaning is sharply separated from the theory of reference, it is a short step to recognizing as the primary business of the theory of meaning simply the synonymy of linguistic forms and the analyticity of statements; meanings themselves, as obscure intermediary entities, may well be abandoned.[15]

In reference to the definition of meaning, he argued in 'On What There Is':

> The useful ways in which people ordinarily talk or seem to talk about meanings boil down to two; the *having* of meanings, which is significance, and sameness of meaning, or synonymy. What is called *giving* the meaning of an utterance is simply the uttering of a synonym, couched, ordinarily, in clearer language than the original. If we are allergic to meanings as such, we can speak directly of utterances as significant or insignificant, and as synonymous or heteronymous one with another.[16]

Also, in 'The Problem of Meaning in Linguistics':

> What happens in this maneuver is that we fix on one important context of the baffling word 'meaning', namely the context *'alike in meaning'*, and resolve to treat this whole context in the spirit of a single word 'synonymous', thus not being tempted to seek meanings as intermediary entities.[17]

The theory of meaning, as formulated by Ajdukiewicz in the early 1930s, underwent evolution. When retaining the axiomatic rules Ajdukiewicz insisted, as we have pointed out, that it is not only that the way in which expressions are used determines the rules of sense of the language, but also that the rules of sense determine the meaning of expressions of the language. The second part of the thesis led Ajdukiewicz to believe that aprioristic elements are inevitable in science. This attitude was particularly striking with respect to logic.

Łukasiewicz, when constructing his systems of many-valued logic, asserted that only future experience would show which of the systems of logic is the valid one, the two-valued, the three-valued, or a many-valued one. Ajdukiewicz disagreed with this. Experience in his opinion could not have the decisive voice in this

[15] In *From a Logical Point of View* (Cambridge, Mass., 1953), p. 22.
[16] Ibid., pp. 11, 12.
[17] Ibid., p. 48.

matter. If the axiomatic rules of meaning are observed, it follows that the axioms of logic and rules of inference are determined by the language we use. Because the choice of the language or the choice of conceptual apparatus must precede any experience, future experience cannot affect the existing conceptual apparatus. For example, it followed from Ajdukiewicz's theory of meaning that the law of contradiction could not be proved or disproved by experience. In order that the law of contradiction be rejected, experience would have to force us to admit both a statement and its negation. But if we admit two such statements, one of which contradicts the other, then they would not be equal to a pair of contradictory statements in the English language (or any other Indo-European language for that matter) because for that language there is an accepted axiomatic rule which asserts that if we use the negation sign in current usage for the English language, we must not accept two statements one of which differs from the other by the introduction of the negation sign. In virtue of the axiomatic rules of the language, the law of contradiction must be held true. Ajdukiewicz adhered to this aprioristic view of the nature of logic until the early 1950s.

The transition began with the paper 'Logic and Experience' of 1950 in which axiomatic rules were demonstrated to be dispensable. The idea was the following. While testing a scientific hypothesis, we in fact test not only our new conjecture, but also many other scientific theories which are assumed in our hypothesis. The results, which are usually taken to confirm our new conjecture, in fact confirm quite a range of theories implied in our hypothesis, and also confirm the laws of logic which are used as means of inference. Consequently, we may assume that axiomatic rules, which appear as logical theorems, can be regarded as auxiliary hypotheses tested alongside working hypotheses.[18]

Ajdukiewicz's theory of meaning was important for at least three reasons. First, it provided perhaps the first explicit and exact formulation (to use Cohen's terminology) of the *de jure* theory of meaning. Secondly, it was on the basis of his theory of meaning that Ajdukiewicz developed some other, more philosophical enterprises: radical conventionalism, a refutation of subjective idealism and affirmation of epistemological realism, and a resolu-

[18] A more detailed account of the problem of reducing deductive rules along with axiomatic ones will be given in section 5 of this chapter, entitled: 'Methodological Empiricism'.

tion of the apriorism-versus-empiricism controversy. The evolution of his views on meaning brought about the evolution of his views on the above issues. Thirdly, the measure of exactitude achieved in the formulation of Ajdukiewicz's theory of meaning was regarded in Poland as a paradigm of philosophical inquiry. Many Polish philosophers have subsequently attempted to achieve the same degree of precision in their endeavours.

3 RADICAL CONVENTIONALISM

'Ordinary' conventionalism, proclaimed by Le Roy and Poincaré, held that there are scientific problems which cannot be solved by reference to empirical reality alone. In other words, with regard to some problems we must first introduce certain conventions which, together with empirical data, will lead us to a solution. The solutions are therefore obtained partly by reference to empirical reality and partly by introducing some conventions, the choice of which is to a certain extent arbitrary.

In the paper 'Das Weltbild und die Begriffsapparatur' (The Picture of the World and the Conceptual Apparatus),[19] Ajdukiewicz formulated and attempted to justify the thesis of radical conventionalism which consisted in a generalization and radicalization of the thesis of 'ordinary' conventionalism.

What exactly was radicalized? Ordinary conventionalism distinguished those empirical statements which state facts from those which interpret facts. If we compare the length of two iron bars A and B and observe that they coincide, we can say that the bar A is equal in length to the bar B; this is a statement of fact or, in other words, a report-statement. However, if we do not observe the coincidence of two bars C and D, and nevertheless assert a statement 'The bar C is equal in length to the bar D', this is not a report-statement but an interpreting-statement for the confirmation of which we must have some criteria. For the confirmation of a report-statement, it suffices to recognize the empirical rules of meaning, and at the sight of two bars coinciding with each other, to assert accordingly that 'The bar A is equal to the bar B'. If we are not prepared to make such an assertion at the sight of two coinciding bars, we simply violate language (or, to be more pre-

---

[19] Published originally in German in *Erkenntnis*, IV (1934), pp. 259–287; Polish translation incorporated into *Selected Papers*, Vol. I,

cise, one of the ordinary languages in which such a statement can be asserted or denied). Therefore, a statement is a report-statement if empirical rules of meaning of ordinary language (one of the ordinary languages) together with some empirical data are sufficient for the assertion of this statement.[20] On the other hand, for the assertion of an interpreting-statement, some new rules of meaning must be added. These new rules are called conventions. Thus, the main difference between the report-statement and the interpreting-statement is that the assertion of the latter is conditioned by the admission of some conventions of arbitrary choice. This is the position of ordinary conventionalism.

Ajdukiewicz's radical approach consists in asserting that there is no real difference between report- and interpreting-statements. The data of experience alone do not force us to accept either interpreting- or report-statements. We can restrain ourselves from acknowledging either of the two kinds of statements when confronted with given empirical data, if we choose a different conceptual apparatus in which neither report- nor interpreting-statements can be formulated.[21]

In other words, Ajdukiewicz's thesis is that not only some but in fact all the statements which compose our picture of reality depend, at least partially, on a choice of conceptual apparatus. That is to say, empirical data, out of which we construct a picture of the world, can provide different pictures of the world if fitted into different conceptual apparatuses. Certain empirical data do not force us to accept one picture of reality or another. The choice of the conceptual apparatus is a decisive element in obtaining this or that picture of the world. This is the thesis of radical conventionalism.

In actual fact, all the semantic distinctions required for an understanding of the doctrine of radical conventionalism were made in 'Sprache und Sinn', published a year before 'The Picture of the World and Conceptual Apparatus'. By *conceptual apparatus* in the above discussion is meant the totality of meanings of expressions of a given language. By the *world perspective* of that language is meant the totality of propositions which are meanings of sentences of the language considered, together with the given empirical data and accepted rules of meaning.

Two pictures of the world can be formulated in such a way that statements of each are untranslatable into statements of the other.

This is the only case when languages of the respective conceptual apparatuses are *closed* and *connected*. Ajdukiewicz distinguished between open and closed languages, and between connected and unconnected ones. A language is open if there is another language which (*a*) contains all expressions of the first one, (*b*) ascribes the same meanings to these expressions, and (*c*) is richer than the first one. That is to say, includes expressions the first one does not include. Besides, Ajdukiewicz introduced the concept of a *connected* language, a language whose expressions can be divided into two non-empty classes in such a way that none of the expressions of the first class is connected in meaning to any expression of the second class. According to common sense, it would seem to be exceedingly difficult to find such a language among existing languages actually in use. It should be observed that Ajdukiewicz treated language in a rather abstract and semi-formal way.

Ajdukiewicz characterized open and closed languages in this way:

> Let us suppose that there are two languages L and L', and that for every word and for every expression of language L there is a corresponding expression in language L', but not *vice versa*. Furthermore, let the corresponding expressions of the two languages be mutual translations of each other. Let us now suppose that an expression A' of the richer language L', which possesses its translation A in language L, is directly connected in meaning with another expression A'_1, and this A_1' has no translation in language L. In this case we shall call language L open with respect to language L'. If we wish to say that a language is open with respect to another language, we shall simply say that this language is open.

And here is a characterization of a closed language:

> Language which is not open is called closed.[22]

About 'connected' and 'unconnected' languages Ajdukiewicz said:

> A non-empty, partial class of expressions of a language (we shall say instead a 'part of a language'), whose elements have no relation in meaning with any expression of the remaining part of the language, we shall call the isolated part of this language. If a language possesses no isolated part, we shall call it 'connected'. From the above, the

[22] Ajdukiewicz, *Selected Papers*, p. 177.

following conclusion can be drawn: if a closed language L is enriched by a new expression E, which possesses no meaning equal to the meaning of any former expression, and if former expressions preserve in the richer language L_e the same meaning which they had in Language L, then this richer language L_e is unconnected.[23]

When expressed by means of a closed and connected language, two conceptual apparatuses are 'either identical or have no common elements at all'. In his considerations on the structure and properties of closed and connected languages, Ajdukiewicz was not thinking of any specific languages, ordinary, scientific, or artificial, but rather of a sort of schematic laboratory language. Closed and connected languages, as well as other languages with some very specific characteristics attributed to them by Ajdukiewicz, were not his discoveries but rather his inventions. He was aware that his concept of language was much 'idealized'. However, he pointed out that an 'idealizing tendency' is characteristic for many sciences. In physics we formulate laws for ideal gases; in mechanics we deal with movements which are never observed in reality. In the same sort of way an idealized concept of language is of help to us, as Ajdukiewicz contended, in investigating reality and in particular comprehending more thoroughly the process of human cognition.

What consequences follow from the doctrine of radical conventionalism? One seems to be the relativity of truth. However, Ajdukiewicz insisted that this is not the case. Statements may not be translatable from one language to another; none the less, it can never happen that certain statements, true in one conceptual apparatus, can be false in another. If conceptual apparatuses are different, then a statement formulated in one may not be expressible in another. The problem which may appear is that of the untranslatability of statements from one conceptual apparatus to another, but this has nothing to do with change of truth-value; a statement true in one apparatus, if expressible in another, must also be true. This is Ajdukiewicz's position. However, if we accept the conception of untranslatable languages, it is hard to talk about objective truth at all. There are no objectively true statements, but only accepted ones, because in every language truth can mean something different. Ajdukiewicz wished to adhere to the classical concept of truth, but if we stay within the framework of radical conventionalism, we cannot talk of the conformity

[23] Op. cit., p. 177.

or lack of conformity of a statement with reality. A statement is not related to reality but to a picture of the world. Ajdukiewicz would reply that although we cannot say that one picture of the world is more true than another we can say that one is more significant than another. However, the criteria for determining the measure of significance are extralogical; they are not to be found within the framework of radical conventionalism itself.[24] The conclusion is that even if the relativity of truth does not explicitly follow from Ajdukiewicz's doctrine, it is hard both to adhere to the doctrine and to retain the classical concept of truth.

Another problem is whether or not radical conventionalism does imply a sort of subjective idealism. If our picture of reality depends on the conceptual apparatus in which it is expressed, and if our conceptual apparatus depends on some freely admitted conventions, then reality is to a certain extent a subjective creation dependent on one set of conventions or another. This is one of the theses of subjective idealism.[25] Ajdukiewicz opposed this interpretation. For him, the acceptance of radical conventionalism does not commit one to the view that a change in the world results from a change of our conceptual apparatus. What changes is our picture of reality, not reality itself. The world perspective is a class of statements about the world, not the world itself. A change of conceptual apparatus changes our relation towards the world; in other words, it changes the set of problems with which we refer to the world. If we ask different questions, we accordingly obtain different answers, but this does not mean that the world which is being investigated is changed because we investigate it by means of different conceptual apparatuses. By posing different questions, we examine different aspects of the world. But the world itself does not change.

Ajdukiewicz's conception of radical conventionalism was undoubtedly an original and bold one. However, we should realize that the whole construction is based on the distinction between open and closed languages. Only after we admit the existence of closed and connected languages, can we arrive at different conceptual apparatuses, and consequently at entirely

[24] *Selected Papers*, Vol. I, p. 193.
[25] This point was particularly insisted upon by Marxists, notably by L. Kołakowski in 'Filozofia nieinterwencji' (Non-Intervention Philosophy) *Myśl Filoz.*, 2/8, 1953.

different world-pictures. Only then can we claim that cognition is dependent on our conceptual apparatuses and conventions built into them.

The concept of the closed and connected language turned out to be a fiction. It was too extreme an idealization of actually existing languages. Indirectly Ajdukiewicz admitted this in 1936; explicitly (under criticism by Marxists) in 1953. He then abandoned radical conventionalism, which, as he put it, had 'enticed him by its originality and the prospects of far-reaching philosophical consequences'. However, although he overtly gave up the doctrine, Ajdukiewicz never really rejected some of its consequences. It seems plausible that after a reconstruction of its semantic basis, it might be possible to defend a version of 'semantic' conventionalism, which admittedly would not be *radical* conventionalism. Ajdukiewicz did not try to rescue his doctrine by some such reconstruction; instead he moved on to new problems.

The story of radical conventionalism is an illuminating one. That such a doctrine was conceived by Ajdukiewicz, who connected cognition with language perhaps more than anyone else, should not be surprising. Even if the final outcome was negative, and the main thesis of radical conventionalism (that every statement, empirical or not, is a reflection of our conventionally chosen conceptual apparatus) proved invalid, the attempt was daring and, in a sense, historically inevitable. The realization that language is not transparent, not a mere vehicle for transmitting thoughts conceived outside linguistic reality, has come to many a twentieth-century philosopher. No wonder, therefore, that some philosophers, in examining the relation thought–language–reality, have been carried away in assessing the significance of the middle element.

Benjamin Whorf, an American linguist, came in the 1930s to conclusions similar to Ajdukiewicz's about the rôle of language in theoretical inquiry. Whorf investigated primitive languages which he called 'exotic'. The structure and grammar of these languages are quite unlike Indo-European languages with which linguists are familiar and in which philosophers formulated their doctrines. The analysis of one of these languages, namely Hopi, led him to believe that some fundamental philosophical categories, such as time and matter, are quite differently conceived in Hopi as compared with Indo-European languages.[26] Observations of this kind prompted Whorf to formulate the linguistic relativity principle 'which holds that all observers are not led by the same physical evidence to the same picture of the universe, unless their linguistic backgrounds are similar, or can in some way be calibrated.'[27] Languages which can be 'calibrated' in Whorf are those which are 'translatable' in Ajdukiewicz. Languages of 'different' linguistic backgrounds correspond to Ajdukiewicz's languages which are 'closed' and 'connected'. But in the course of time Ajdukiewicz acknowledged that there are no such languages, most probably considering only Indo-European languages. Whorf stated that 'different' languages are to be found outside Indo-European languages, such as Hopi. His hypothesis that 'every language contains its own metaphysics' or differently, that 'each language performs this artificial chopping up of the continuous spread and flow of existence in a different way',[28] or still differently, 'We dissect nature along lines laid down by our native languages'[29] has been tested by many linguists in recent times. It has been neither proved not disproved.

Though it would be hard to defend the view that every language contains its own metaphysics, we can easily agree with more moderate formulations of the thesis that 'each language is not

[26] 'Our own "time" differs markedly from Hopi "duration". It is conceived as like a space of strictly limited dimensions, or sometimes as like a motion upon such a space, and employed as an intellectual tool accordingly. Hopi "duration" seems to be inconceivable in terms of space or motion, being the mode in which life differs from form, and consciousness *in toto* from the spatial elements of consciousness. . . . Our "matter" is the physical subtype of "substance" or "stuff", which is conceived as the formless extensional item that must be joined with form before there can be real existence. In Hopi there seems to be nothing corresponding to it; there are no formless extensional items; existence may or may not have form, but what it also has, with or without form, is intensity and duration, these being nonextensional and at bottom the same.'
These ideas were expressed in the essay 'The Relation of Habitual Thought and Behavior to Language' in the selected writings of Benjamin Lee Whorf, *Language, Thought and Reality*, ed. John B. Carroll (Technology Press of the M.I.T., 1956), p. 158.
The essays were originally published between the years 1933 and 1941. Perhaps the most significant was 'Science and Linguistics' of 1939 in which the linguistic relativity principle was formulated.
[27] B. L. Whorf, 'Science and Linguistics', *Language, Thought and Reality*, p. 214.
[28] Ibid., p. 253.   [29] Ibid., p. 213.

merely a reproducing instrument for voicing ideas, but rather itself the shaper of ideas',[30] and that the 'formulation of ideas is not an independent process, strictly rational in the old sense, but is part of a particular grammar and differs from slightly to greatly between different languages'.[31] For a decision as to the degree of shaping (of the content of our thought by our language), the concept of language itself would have to be more thoroughly elucidated. In Whorf the concept of language is not clearly defined; hence, he can afford such huge and impressive statements as: 'We dissect nature along lines laid down by our native languages.' In Ajdukiewicz language is more precisely characterized, at times perhaps too precisely; and it seems that occasionally language tailored to suit the solution of philosophical problems.

Ajdukiewicz's theory of meaning, developed as a preparatory stage and as a sort of foundation for the development of radical conventionalism, has survived, while the main edifice has fallen. The thesis that language cannot be characterized by syntactic rules alone, but must also be characterized by empirical rules of meaning, became widely accepted in the 1940s and 1950s.

4 IDEALISM VERSUS REALISM

A. *The first encounter*

The problem of idealism versus realism was thrust upon Ajdukiewicz at a very early age through Berkeley's arguments against matter. After that time, this problem occupied him constantly.

Before the Second World War, in spite of all his qualifications and stipulations as to the correct understanding of his conception of 'pictures of the world', his inclination towards some kind of subjective idealism was quite apparent. It seems that subjective idealism followed from his theses as a logical consequence, as he himself admitted years later.

Although somewhat inclined towards idealism himself, Ajdukiewicz launched an attack against transcendental idealism as conceived by Kant and his revivers, neo-Kantian philosophers of the Marburg and Baden Schools. The paper in which he made his attack, 'Problemat transcendentalnego idealizmu w sformułowaniu semantycznym' (The Problem of Transcendental Idealism in

---

[30] Op. cit., p. 212.   [31] Ibid., p. 213.

the Semantic Formulation),[32] is a characteristic sample of Ajdukiewicz's treatment of philosophical doctrines, particularly of his
semantic treatment of doctrines in the theory of knowledge. In
this paper the strengths and weaknesses of the semantic method
are magnified and thus can be clearly seen.

To anticipate the course of the argument. Ajdukiewicz's treatment of the problem consists in a double superimposition: first of
the structure of deductive systems on to the structure of language;
and second, the superimposition of language, as so conceived, on
to the traditional formulation of a philosophical problem, in our
case the problem of transcendental idealism. These two points will
be further developed.

Ajdukiewicz starts with distinguishing two parts of the theory
of knowledge: psychological (dealing with mental processes) and
logical (dealing with the end-products of mental processes, that is
with the meanings of terms and sentences in the logical sense). If
there are meanings independent of mental processes which are
common to many people using the same language, then to each
statement in a language there corresponds an equivalent statement
which makes an assertion about this first statement.[33] This leads us
to a new treatment of the theory of knowledge; instead of talking
about judgements and notions, we may talk about their linguistic
equivalents in a certain language. This relativization to a particular language is essential. In other words, instead of talking about
the inference-relation or the relation of contradiction, we may
talk about contradictory sentences or sentences inferable from
one another. In short, the semantic theory of knowledge, while
dealing with the logical part of the process of cognition, can be
compared with the theory of deductive systems, so at any rate
Ajdukiewicz contended. And here lies the first superimposition,
that of the structure of deductive systems on to the language with
which we operate.

It is shown that a deductive system is characterized by (*a*) rules
determining the set of expressions of the system, (*b*) rules distinguishing certain sentences as axioms, and (*c*) rules determining
immediate inference of some sentences from the others. If the
concept of immediate inference is understood in a broad sense
(i.e., if by axioms are meant sentences which follow immediately
from any class of sentences), then only two classes of rules remain:

[32] *Przeg. Filoz.*, XL, 1937; also in *Selected Papers*, Vol. I.
[33] Ibid., p. 265.

(*a*) rules determining the set of expressions, and (*b*) rules sanctioning immediate inference. And Ajdukiewicz defined the deductive system as 'a specified system of expressions for which the relations of the immediate inference are determined'.[34]

Now, if we accept Ajdukiewicz's concept of language with its rules of sense (meaning), it is not difficult to show that language can be conceived as a deductive system in the above sense. If there are expressions with established meanings, then, in order not to violate the language, we must recognize relationships following from the meanings of those expressions. So, if the rules of meaning (axiomatic and deductive) are observed, the established meanings of the expressions of the language determine the relations of immediate inference between sentences of the language. And hence, as Ajdukiewicz succinctly put it: 'A language conceived as a class of expressions with established meanings is a deductive system.'[35] Ajdukiewicz expressly tells us that it is not true that language is nothing but a deductive system, but other characteristics of language, although the author mentions some, are not taken into consideration at all on this occasion.

Thus, the first superimposition, that of the structure of a deductive system upon the structure of language, has been achieved. Next comes the second superimposition, a reformulation of the problem of transcendental idealism so as to fit the already prepared language, and thus be suitable for treatment as an epistemological problem of the semantic theory of knowledge.

Out of many formulations of the thesis of transcendental idealism, Rickert's is chosen because, as Ajdukiewicz claimed, it is the most tangible and definite: the real world is only a correlate of certain judgements in the logical sense, that is to say, ideal meanings of certain sentences. Some transcendental idealists claimed that the truth of our judgements depends on their conformity with absolute transcendental norms. These transcendental norms are a kind of Platonic essences. The class of all these transcendental norms is called the transcendental *subject*, whose correlate is reality. This transcendental subject is a kind of Platonic universe *in toto*; our universe, being a pale shadow of the real one, is called a correlate of the transcendental subject.

To achieve the second superimposition, Ajdukiewicz paraphrased the standpoint of transcendental idealism, cut it to the

[34] Op. cit., p. 268.   [35] Ibid., p. 269.

appropriate shape, and dressed it up in semantic attire so that it could be treated as a problem within the framework of deductive systems. The attempted reformulation had to be such that the rules of immediate inference would correspond to Rickert's transcendental norms; the norms establishing axioms would correspond with axiomatic rules; and logical norms would correspond with deductive rules. However, there was one catch—the empirical rules of meaning, which are admitted as a part of Ajdukiewicz's theory of meaning. On this occasion they were claimed to be reducible to the axiomatic ones. However, if axiomatic rules can be treated as rules of immediate inference, as Ajdukiewicz claimed, so can empirical ones.[36]

The third step of Ajdukiewicz's argument (before the final refutation of the thesis of transcendental idealism) is presented as follows. If Rickertian norms are paraphrased as specific rules of immediate inference of the language of the natural sciences, then the transcendental subject will correspond to the theorems of the axiomatic system constructed from the expressions of the language of the empirical sciences, and will de determined by the rules of immediate inference specific to this language. In the semantic paraphrase, the main thesis of transcendental idealism, which asserts that only statements following from transcendental norms are true, will be translated into the sentence which asserts that in the language of the natural sciences, the only true sentences are those which follow from the rules of immediate inference specific for that language, that is to say, the sentences which are the theorems of the language.[37]

Now comes the final argument which rejects the thesis of transcendental idealism: if we accept the rule of the excluded middle, and if we agree that the language of the natural sciences is a deductive system, and if we admit that the language of the natural sciences contains as a part the language of arithmetic, and if we agree that the language of arithmetic is undecidable, that is to say, that it includes a pair of contradictory sentences neither of which

[36] This seems to be the only occasion on which Ajdukiewicz suspended the empirical rules of meaning. After the war, on the contrary, he demonstrated that axiomatic and deductive rules can be reduced to empirical ones. It is worth observing that this manipulation with rules of meaning of a language can lead to effective results, but it also makes the semantic theory of knowledge a bit dubious; if solutions to philosophical problems were solely dependent on such manipulation, philosophy would be an easy task.

[37] Ajdukiewicz, *Selected Papers*, Vol. I, pp. 273–4.

is a thesis of the system (language), then the thesis of transcendental idealism fails because it is not true that 'the only true sentences are those which are the theses of the language'.

This is Ajdukiewicz's semantic formulation and refutation of the thesis of transcendental idealism. In the conclusion of his ingenious and persevering paper, Ajdukiewicz wrote: 'Among crucial philosophical problems there are some whose solution could not be provided earlier because of the inadequacy of the previous conceptual apparatuses which did not facilitate a precise formulation of these problems.'[38] Ajdukiewicz thought that his logical reconstruction provided both the formulation and the solution of the problem. However, it seems that neither of the two was achieved. The problem which was *constructed* and subsequently resolved by Ajdukiewicz is remote indeed from that of transcendental idealism. It is so remote that transcendental idealists would probably not recognize their doctrine. The whole operation, which was called the formulation and the solution of the problem of transcendental idealism, although performed with finesse and exactitude, is no more than a highly sophisticated exercise in the theory of deductive systems; it seems that the 'substance' of a philosophical problem has been transformed into a problem from the field of deductive theories.

Besides, Ajdukiewicz in his reformulations, deserted his own position. In 1937 when the essay was written, he still 'believed' in the conceptual apparatus. That is, he would still have theoretically asserted that a substantially different reformulation of the same problem leads to a different problem. After so many reformulations, hypothetical assumptions, and paraphrases, the so-called problem of transcendental idealism must have inevitably changed its content.

The solution of the problem of transcendental idealism by the semantic method is not at all satisfactory. It has been examined here to convey something of the virtues and the weaknesses of the semantic method.

B. *The second encounter*

Ajdukiewicz's second encounter with idealism after the war was much more successful and significant. This time he fought against all forms of idealism, subjective idealism in particular. In the paper

---

[38] Op. cit., p. 277.

'Epistemology and Semiotic'[39] he declared himself to be a realist. According to his own opinion, the argument contained in his paper provided a weapon for the ultimate defeat of subjective idealism for the first time.

Ajdukiewicz's analysis and criticism of idealism is based on the assumption that in epistemology it is possible to use statements about thoughts to arrive at conclusions about the things with which these thoughts are concerned. However, this is only possible when the language used by the epistemologist contains from the start not only the names of thoughts, but also expressions denoting the things which are the objects with which these thoughts are concerned—or, in Ajdukiewicz's words, when the metalanguage of our discourse used contains the object language.

In semantics (but not in syntax) it is possible to pass from sentences about words to sentences about the objects these words refer to. It was only after Tarski's work on the semantic concept of truth that Ajdukiewicz turned to semantic problems. Before that time, he deliberately confined the scope of his inquiry to problems of a basically syntactical nature, such as the theory of meaning.

In 'Epistemology and Semiotic', Ajdukiewicz claimed that a philosopher concerned with epistemological problems, if he recognizes the distinction between syntax and semantics, is confronted with two alternatives:

1. He may confine the language of his epistemological inquiry to the language of syntax, that is the language which contains names of the expressions of the object language, or names of the thoughts which constitute the meanings of those expressions. Then the philosopher in question, operating with such limited language, would not be able to tackle, let alone resolve, any problem of the object language; he would have no expressions for doing this; moreover, he would be in no position to say anything whatsoever about trees, tables, and other material objects because this would require terms involving semantic relationships which by definition are excluded from any purely syntactical language.

2. He may, from the start of his epistemological inquiry, use

[39] Ajdukiewicz, 'Epistemology and Semiotic', Library of the Tenth International Congress of Philosophy, *Proceedings of the Congress,* Vol. I, pp. 386–8.

a language containing the object language. But then he would have to follow the rules of this language. That is, he would have to resolve all questions formulated in the object language in exactly the same way as they are resolved in ordinary language. Ordinary language does include semantic relationships, that is it possesses expressions referring to non-linguistic objects. In other words, it contains in itself the standpoint of epistemological realism. Briefly, the philosopher in this case would have to accept the realistic standpoint. It means that he would share with scientists and ordinary people the belief that houses, trees, mountains, etc., exist in the literal sense—in the sense in which these words function in the object language.

The philospher who chooses the first alternative and confines himself to the language of syntax is, or at any rate ought to be, prevented from saying anything in the object language, and consequently can, or at any rate should, take no part in ontological discourse. He can neither deny nor assert existential statements if they belong to the object language, provided that they are taken in their literal sense.

If we examine some approaches of idealistic philosophers, we realize at once that they do not use the object language. However, they do not hesitate at all to deny existential statements formulated in the object language and understood in the literal sense. Moreover, and interestingly enough, they are prepared to make statements about the objects with which ordinary people are concerned, on condition that an unusual meaning is attached to these statements. Berkeley, for instance, was eager to make existential statements concerning houses, trees, mountains, etc., on condition that houses, trees, mountains, etc., exist only in virtue of someone's perceptions of them.

In actual fact, idealists, of Berkeley's type at any rate, do not make assertions in their language about the world, but only about cognition. Their language is not concerned with the objects of the external world, although they try to make it appear so; it is concerned with what might be called 'linguistic' objects constituted by their language. In other words, idealists start with the language of syntax (in the broader sense), which contains no expressions of the object language, but they make this language masquerade as an object language. In this way, by using this quasi-object language, idealists can 'prove' certain statements, Berkeley's *esse est percipi* for example, which is erroneously supposed to belong to the object language. However, in the object language, when the semantic rules of this language are followed, Berkeley's maxim *esse est percipi* is manifestly false. Consequently, it is only by twisting and abusing language that idealists can arrive at their erroneous conclusions. And this explains the paradoxical state of affairs, because on the one hand their 'proofs' seem to be infallible, and on the other their arguments offend our common sense.

Ajdukiewicz's argument against idealism is certainly of considerable weight. Thus, the semantic theory of knowledge can be effective in dealing with important problems of philosophy.[40]

5 METHODOLOGICAL EMPIRICISM

A. *Radical empiricism and the analytic*

In Poland the problem of empiricism was not very extensively discussed before the Second World War. The problem of physicalism, which stemmed from the resuscitation of Hume's empiricism, did not attract Polish philosophers as it did those of the Vienna Circle. True, there was some interest in Hume and the British empiricists. The *Treatise* was a standard text in Twardowski's seminars, and the writings of the British empiricists were considered excellent for the sharpening and developing of the students' philosophical acumen and sensitivity. No neo-Humanisms, however, emerged from this.

The focus of interest was centred on deductive systems and the methodology of deductive sciences. It was not physics, as in the Vienna Circle, but logic and mathematics that captured the attention and inspired the work of Polish philosophers. Investigations into the nature of logic and mathematics led some philosophers to more general reflection on the nature of knowledge, and this in turn led to an examination of the issue of empiricism *versus* apriorism. Only after the war, when the hope no longer prevailed that a new philosophy could be constructed with the aid and in the likeness of deductive systems, did the focus of interest

---

[40] It appears that Max Black and E. Beth followed Ajdukiewicz's pattern, or at any rate were inspired by Ajdukiewicz's argument, while dealing with the problem of idealism in their respective publications: Black in 'Linguistic Method in Philosophy', *Phenomenological and Philosophical Research*, Vol. 8, 1948; and Beth in *The Foundations of Mathematics* (Amsterdam 1959).

gravitate towards the methodology of the natural sciences. Consequently, the problem of empiricism was tackled more frequently, but even then only in an attenuated form—in the 1950s the Marxists had battered all philosophical discussion out of shape.

In recent times the main dispute has been centred around the controversy between radical and moderate empiricisms. Both versions of empiricism accept empirical statements, but radical empiricism asserts that *only* empirical statements can be admitted as scientific.[41] Analytic statements, statements true (or false) in virtue of their meaning, cannot, according to the doctrine of radical empiricism, be recognized as scientific statements. Empiricism in its moderate version finds a place in science for analytic as well as observation statements.

However, the controversy is not only between the two forms of empiricism. Some philosophers also wish to include in the realm of scientific knowledge statements which are non-analytic, that is synthetic, and which at the same time are not empirical, that is to say, *a priori*.

The complete classification may be set out as follows:

Standpoint	Characteristics in terms of admission of the statements		
	Empirical	Analytic	Synthetic *a priori*
Empiricism: (*a*) radical (*b*) moderate	Yes Yes	No Yes	No No
Apriorism (*a*) moderate (*b*) radical	Yes No	Yes Yes	Yes Yes

Both empiricisms reject the synthetic *a priori*. Radical apriorism, which is included here for the sake of completeness, is not a

[41] It is now less violently argued whether or not only observation statements should be regarded as empirical and in what way other statements, if they are to be recognized as empirical, should be related to the observation statements. Apart from observation statements it is now usual to accept as empirical also those statements which function as hypotheses verifiable or falsifiable by empirical tests, or non-observation statements deductively inferred either from observation statements or from verified hypotheses.

position nowadays defensible. In antiquity, however, some philosophers denied that empirical cognition had any value and considered *nous* as the only means of penetrating reality.

Ajdukiewicz's position in relation to the problem of empiricism shifted from that of a *moderate* to that of a *radical* empiricist. His views on this matter were clearly expressed only after the war when he became involved in the philosophy of science, which increasingly absorbed him during the last years of his life. He said: 'I have wasted too much time in semantics when such a wealth of problems has been clamouring for solutions in the philosophy of science.'[42] Needless to say, Ajdukiewicz's radical empiricism, like nearly all his philosophical constructions, had its roots in his theory of meaning.

In the book, *Trends and Problems in Philosophy*, and in the paper, 'Logic and Experience',[43] Ajdukiewicz defended the standpoint of moderate empiricism. If meanings are determined by the rules of sense of a given language, and if axiomatic and deductive rules are accepted (as is almost always the case with natural and even artificial languages), then we can justifiably utter statements which are not empirical but which nevertheless must be recognized as valid. Therefore, the radical version of empiricism collapses. Ajdukiewicz argued that 'Radical empiricism seems to overlook the fact that every statement and therefore every observation statement is formulated in a certain language' and that 'Every language is bound by certain rules governing the acceptance of statements'.[44] If we reject in English such sentences as 'Every square is a quadrangle', or 'No mountain is higher than the highest', it clearly indicates that we do not understand the language or else that we are deliberately attaching idiosyncratic rather than ordinary meanings to words contained in the sentences in question. In virtue of the meanings of the terms 'every', 'square', 'is', and 'quadrangle', the above sentence containing them is true irrespective of experience. Thus, axiomatic rules compel us to accept some statements as true regardless of external circumstances. These statements cannot be rejected unless we are

[42] From conversation in Warsaw, October 1962.

[43] Ajdukiewicz, (i) *Zagadnienia i kierunki filozofii* (*Trends and Problems in Philosophy*) (Warsaw, 1949); (ii) 'Logic and Experience', *Synthese*, VIII, Nos. 6, 7 (1950–1951).

[44] Ajdukiewicz, 'Logic and Experience', p. 291.

prepared to violate the language in which they are formulated. The same is true for statements which are based on the deductive rules of language, e.g. if 'John is younger than Harry', and 'Peter is older than Harry', then without any reference to experience we can assert 'John is younger than Peter'.

Thus, axiomatic statements, which can be called the axioms of a given language, and also the statements which can be derived from them according to the deductive rules, are *analytic* statements. Ajdukiewicz claimed that:

> Such a definition of these sentences seems to express better the intention which induced Kant to introduce the notion of analytic sentences than his own well-known formulation which can be applied only to affirmative subject–predicate sentences and which therefore is not general enough.[45]

Ajdukiewicz's paper 'Logic and Experience', in which he declared himself a moderate empiricist, examined most of the difficulties which logic poses for empiricism. According to him all the languages in which logical theory has been formulated are languages governed by axiomatic and deductive rules. It therefore follows that in these languages analytic statements can be accepted without recourse to experience. Everyday language, as well as the various known artificial languages (whose syntax is exactly specified and the rules of inference given) seem to belong to one and the same group of languages in which axiomatic and deductive rules are observed. With regard to such languages, the thesis of radical empiricism—that in order to be accepted, every statement must pass the test of experience—will not do.

> ... if logical theorems are analytic sentences, then the rejection of one of these sentences must be, or at least must lead to, a violation of some axiomatic or deductible rules; such a violation will in turn produce a change of meaning of the words and therefore a change of the language.[46]

Thus, the radical empiricist, by rejecting the laws of logic, quite unknowingly substitutes a different language which does not possess axiomatic rules. In dispensing with axiomatic rules we dispense with analytic statements and *vice versa*. If by analytic statements are understood axioms and those statements which can

---

[45] Op. cit., p. 292.   [46] Ibid., p. 298.

be inferred from them by means of deductive rules, then if there are no axiomatic rules, deductive rules alone cannot originate analytic statements. In short, no axiomatic rules, no analytic statements.

If the radical empiricist insists on subjecting all statements to experience as 'the only criterion of truth', then, by reinterpreting the concept of the analytic, he changes the language; otherwise he must, quite arbitrarily, declare that he will recognize as statements only those which are empirical. The advantage to be derived from this arbitrary linguistic decision is rather dubious.

However, the standpoint of radical empiricism can be adopted as a programme for scientific work, and as such it need not be proved to be true. Such programmes are to be appraised from the point of view of their pragmatic fruitfulness; their truth or falsehood is irrelevant. In order to be workable, they must serve a purpose and be practicable. As a programme, Ajdukiewicz believed, radical empiricism could be put into effect.

From the above considerations an important question arises. Are languages possible which possess no axiomatic rules and, consequently, within which laws of logic can be regarded as empirical statements? A tentative answer to this question was provided by Ajdukiewicz in the paper 'Logic and Experience' already discussed. In what way could logical laws be verified? They could not be verified separately, but only jointly with other scientific hypotheses. The process of verifying or falsifying logical laws, assumed as auxiliary hypotheses, would run as follows. First, it should be observed that, apart from auxiliary hypotheses, we would have to deal with ordinary, working scientific hypotheses. From these working hypotheses, in conjunction with auxiliary (logical) hypotheses, some conclusions would be drawn by the application not only of primary deductive rules, but also of secondary ones, derived from the former. If appropriate empirical tests confirmed the conjunction composed of working and auxiliary hypotheses, then each of the sets of hypotheses would be confirmed. If, as the result of testing, the conjunction was refuted, then at least one of the components would be invalid and need to be replaced. Usually it is by replacing working scientific hypotheses and by retaining the logical laws that new hypotheses are formed. In the language without axiomatic rules, logical laws could be questioned and regarded as subject to replacement as well. In such a case working hypotheses would be retained as correct and all steps in which secondary rules[47] were applied would be rendered subject to questioning and possible rejection.

This is closely similar to the position held by Quine. In Quine's opinion we retain a wide latitude of choice as to which statements of the system of our knowledge we preserve and which we revise. That is to say, 'any one of many revisions will be sufficient to unmake the particular implication which brought the system to grief. . . . Mathematical and logical laws themselves are not immune to revision if it is found that essential simplifications of our whole conceptual scheme will ensue.'[48]

B. *The principle of rationalism*

It seems clear that radical empiricists have tended to operate with the narrower concept of science, as knowledge empirically testable—as confirmable or as is sometimes held refutable. Apart from that knowledge which is called science, it appears that radical empiricists have also recognized mathematical and logic as justifiable knowledge, and have definitely rejected as unjustifiable 'knowledge' based on revelation and other extra-rational means. When we adhere to the narrower concept of science, it is possible to reconcile the positions (1) that only empirical statements are to be regarded as scientific, and (2) that analytic statements can be recognized as cognitive or as 'accepted'. The extensions of the two terms 'scientific' and 'accepted' are then different; every scientific statement is within the range of cognitive or 'accepted', but not conversely.

Ajdukiewicz's concept of science was the broader one. Science was identified with rational knowledge and consequently analytic

---

[47] In this new language without axiomatic rules of meaning, deductive rules would be nevertheless valid such as *modus ponendo ponens, modus tolendo tollens*, or de Morgan's law. The logical system taken as a set of auxiliary hypotheses would justify some *secondary* rules derived from the logical laws contained in the system. These secondary rules could not, however, figure as rules of language—this would violate the language in question—but would remain valid only as long as we accept our hypothetical logical theorems. Ajdukiewicz characterized secondary rules in this way: 'To say that the rule R is secondary with regard to rule D and the assertion T means that every sentence which may be inferred from arbitrary sentences Z according to rule R can be inferred from the sentences Z and the assertions T according to rule D.' (Ibid., p. 298.)

[48] W. V. Quine, *Methods of Logic* (London, 1952), pp. xii, xiv. See also 'Two Dogmas of Empiricism'.

statements were recognized as scientific. Hence a discrepancy appears between the radical empiricists and Ajdukiewicz in relation to the meaning of the expression 'The analytic is to be recognized'. Radical empiricists meant to say that analytic statements are to be recognized as justifiable knowledge but they are *non-scientific*. Ajdukiewicz, particularly in the paper 'Logic and Experience', claimed that because analytic statements are to be recognized as justifiable knowledge, they are *scientific*.

The principle of rationalism, which Ajdukiewicz often called anti-irrationalism (to stress that it is diametrically opposed to irrationalism and to prevent association with philosophical doctrines appearing under the name of rationalism) contained two theses: (*a*) rational knowledge must be intersubjectively communicable; (*b*) rational knowledge must be intersubjectively checkable.

> Scientific cognition is only such content of thought which firstly can be communicated in words understood literally, that is to say, without using metaphors, parables and other poetic means of expression; and secondly, an assertion can be regarded as scientific only if its validity can in principle be checked by anyone who happens to be in the appropriate circumstances. . . . Rationalism would thus be interpreted as a thesis claiming that a value can be ascribed only to such cognition as is intersubjectively communicable and checkable.[49]

It was the identification of science with rational cognition that caused Ajdukiewicz's difficulties in dealing with the problem of empiricism. However, if rational cognition is split into two: science and other justifiable although non-scientific knowledge (in the narrower sense of the word), the difficulties raised by Ajdukiewicz disappear. Empirical statements represent science; analytic statements the rest of justifiable knowledge. (For apriorists, justifiable knowledge will be also represented by the synthetic *a priori*.) It is then possible to claim that only empirical statements are scientific and that analytic statements ought to be accepted.

The principle of rationalism[50] has often been used in philo-

---

[49] Ajdukiewicz, *Trends and Problems in Philosophy*, p. 73.

[50] This concept of rational cognition substantially affected Ajdukiewicz's manner of writing; in attempting to express himself without any metaphors or other poetic means, he developed a rather pedantic style, perhaps unnecessarily scrupulous and even a little pompous.

sophy, but hardly ever made clear. Ajdukiewicz gave this principle an explicit justification which was *social*, and therefore extra-cognitive. It is 'to protect society from the domination of the cliché which is meaningless but which, in spite of this, often evokes a strong emotional response and consequently influences the behaviour of the individual and of large social groups';[51] it is also to protect society from uncritical acceptance of views, often pronounced with unbending conviction, which are untestable and which consequently can be meaningless and even false although they often appear to be unquestionable. In short, the purpose of the principle of rationalism in critical scholarship is 'to protect society against nonsense and against falsehood'. Ajdukiewicz was aware that rational cognition pays a high price for its inter-subjective character. Nevertheless, he argued:

> The voice of rationalism is a healthy social reaction, an act of self-defence against the domination by uncontrollable forces among which there might be a saint announcing a revelation, as well as a madman prophesying the figments of his sick mind, or finally an impostor desiring to find supporters for the views which he advocates with an eye to his egoistic and ignoble purposes.[52]

Ajdukiewicz's justification of cognitive knowledge in the final resort is non-cognitive. By emphasizing the social significance of rational cognition, Ajdukiewicz approached the pragmatist standpoint in the theory of knowledge. He even admitted at one time that it was in pragmatism that he tended to seek a shelter for his epistemology.[53]

C. *Towards the semantic concept of radical empiricism*

Ajdukiewicz had the temperament of a classical philosopher and liked to construct philosophical edifices with sharp outlines, radical in approach. To achieve clear-cut constructions, his theories abstracted from many 'irrelevancies', and this usually resulted in extreme positions. He had his 'visions' first, and constructed arguments to support them afterwards. This was the case with his radical conventionalism and in intention with his

---

[51] Op. cit., p. 73.   [52] Ibid., p. 77.
[53] In a private conversation in Warsaw, October 1962, he said: 'When I was at Harvard, Quine and I agreed that we are inclined to consider pragmatism as the final justification for our epistemological pursuits.'

radical empiricism. He attempted to provide an empiricist foundation for all rational knowledge and to demonstrate that the thesis
of radical empiricism can be maintained even given the broader
understanding of science—when by 'science' is meant not only
empirical or testable knowledge but in fact all rational knowledge.
The first step was taken by eliminating axiomatic rules and treating
logical theorems as auxiliary hypotheses. Further developments
led to the elimination of deductive rules as well. But his 'construction' of radical empiricism was not completed.[54]

The problem of empiricism was not conceived by Ajdukiewicz
as a separate technical problem to be considered out of the context of fundamental philosophical issues. Before the war, his
radical conventionalism was complemented by apriorism (the
chosen language determines at least partly the content of empirical
statements), and by idealism (the conceptual apparatus chosen
determines a picture of the world which in fact amounts to a
construction of an ideal world). This followed consistently from
his concept of language at that time. In 'Sprache und Sinn' as well
as in 'O znaczeniu wyrażeń' (On the Meaning of Expressions),
it was contended (*a*) that the meanings of expressions determine
the rules of sense of language, and hence it follows that we cannot
change the rules of sense without changing the meaning of expressions, and (*b*) that, *vice versa*, the rules of sense determine the
meanings of expressions, and hence it follows that, since every
science uses a language with its axiomatic and deductive rules,
aprioristic elements in science are inevitable. In particular, if
axioms and logical rules of inference are determined by the language in which they are formulated, and if the choice of a conceptual apparatus corresponding to this language precedes all
experience, then there is no point in referring to experience as a
possible arbiter which is to decide whether bivalent logic or one of
the many-valued logics is the most adequate medium for the
description of reality.

If we wish to avoid these aprioristic elements in our conception

[54] The gist of Ajdukiewicz's radical empiricism was presented in two
addresses: the first was delivered to the Warsaw Philosophical Society in
1958, and the second in February 1962, at a special conference convened to
celebrate his 70th birthday. Only the second address was published (posthumously) but in an incomplete form. The following remarks aiming at
the reconstruction of Ajdukiewicz's radical empiricism are based on these
two lectures, on private conversations which took place in Warsaw in
October 1962, and on some of Ajdukiewicz's unpublished notes.

the structure of any science, we must revise the concept of language and particularly reject (*b*), that the rules of sense determine the meanings of expressions. Hence it will *not* follow that because every science uses a language, it must contain some aprioristic elements. This was precisely Ajdukiewicz's position. A revision of his philosophical views was almost always accompanied by a revision of his concept of language and, obviously, of the rules of sense (of meaning). On the surface it appears that Ajdukiewicz's new philosophical pronouncements were preceded by some changes in his theory of meaning. Thus, from internal reconstructions of the theory of meaning, philosophical assertions seem to follow as consequences. But in fact, the actual procedure seems to have been the other way round; new philosophical convictions brought about consequential changes in the concept of language, in the theory of meaning.

After the war, the change of outlook from idealism to realism, and from apriorism to empiricism, as well as the change of interests from semantics to the philosophy of science led Ajdukiewicz to some radical changes in his concept of language. The centre of attention became for him the structure of science and the procedures that occur in science. As to the procedures, the point is whether science, understood as the totality of rational cognitive endeavours, both in the course of its history and at the present time, has been derived entirely from experience, or whether some *a priori* assertions have also been assumed. Ajdukiewicz considered the tracing of the actual procedures which occur in science as a 'hopelessly difficult task', and instead concentrated on another aspect of the problem, whether science can be reconstructed in such a way that all aprioristic assertions are eliminated. The latter approach in the methodology of science can be called *structural* because it is concerned with the structure of science, whereas the former can be called *procedural* in that it is concerned with scientific procedures.

It is in relation to the structure of science that Ajdukiewicz attempted to develop his version of radical empiricism, which he called methodological empiricism. The point was to demonstrate that it is possible to conceive science as grounded entirely in experience; consequently, all its elements must be shown to be either directly experiential, or derived from experience. Then the thesis of radical empiricism, that all scientific statements are empirical, could be held valid.

The solution to this problem is once again provided by reference to the rules of sense. The elimination of axiomatic rules by means of treating logical laws as auxiliary hypotheses was a half-way measure. As long as deductive rules are retained, the task is not completed. The admission of this or that set of deductive rules may have an important significance for the rest of our empirical knowledge. So empirical knowledge will be dependent to a certain degree on non-empirical (aprioristic) elements accepted as deductive rules. In order to avoid this consequence, deductive rules must be eliminated as rules of meaning of language, along with axiomatic ones.

The concept of language which would be compatible with the thesis of radical empiricism requires that deductive rules be treated and tested as auxiliary hypotheses in the same sort of way as axiomatic rules. Consequently, the rules of inference would be liable to change. If a discrepancy appears between immediate data of experience and assertions of a theory and if we do not wish to change our language, that is, the meaning of its expressions, then we might replace the set of rules of inference employed for drawing conclusions from the data of experience with another set which would allow an inference of consequences compatible with the theory in question.

The concept of language presented above without the axiomatic and deductive rules, although it offers some advantages, also has drawbacks. True, as the consequence of the elimination of deductive rules, logic will be freed from its aprioristic legacy and therefore the structure of science can be founded on entirely empiricistic grounds. The treatment of deductive rules as auxiliary hypotheses might help to overcome many deadlocks in science. Scientists, when faced with some discrepancies between observation and a hypothesis, instead of checking their reasoning and rules of inference, generally give up the hypothesis entirely. According to Ajdukiewicz, scientists might attempt to revise the rules of inference as well. However, this might lead—one is inclined to think—to the construction of *ad hoc* logics in order to bolster up 'shaky' hypotheses. It is a disturbing possibility that logic should be treated on the same level as ordinary hypotheses and changed or reshaped at will. The soundness of the scientific enterprise has always included as one of its constants the soundness of logic, which has been regarded as a touchstone of scientific theories. This disregarded, confusion between what *is* and what *is not* scientific, is almost inevitable. The danger inherent in the resultant pattern is manifest. If reality does not agree with our theories, let us whittle away our logic so that its revised rules will make reality consistent with our theories. Obviously, some restrictions would have to be superimposed on what is to be called logic and what is not. But then would this not be the admission of some aprioristic elements?

Ajdukiewicz's concept of radical empiricism (called by him methodological empiricism), which was provided to secure the empiricist structure of all science, raises some questions and many doubts. Since it was not elaborated in detail, questions and doubts will remain.

Another difficulty in relation to Ajdukiewicz's concept of radical empiricism, and some of his other constructions as well, arises from an excessively abstract level of consideration. No concrete examples or illustrations are provided. Hence it is often difficult to see the relevance and validity of his argument in relation to more specific philosophical issues.

RÉSUMÉ

It would be perhaps premature to aim at a complete assessment of Ajdukiewicz's semantic epistemology. Although some attempts were too radical and therefore misfired, the approach seems to promise much. No one can afford to pass over indifferently the philosophical implications of the recognition that a language functions through its rules of meaning. Unless one is an objective idealist and holds that language is a mere vehicle for the expression of Platonic essences, one must realize that cognition cannot be separated from its linguistic expression. Ajdukiewicz followed this consequence certainly more persistently and more consistently than most philosophers.

With the aid of his theory of meaning, he attempted to dismantle the arguments of subjective idealism. This doctrine appears in the guise of object-language discourse, but in fact Ajdukiewicz showed that it operates entirely with a sort of syntactical language which does not have empirical rules.

Through the same theory of meaning he attempted to formulate his doctrine of radical empiricism upon which the structure of science without aprioristic elements was to be founded.

The thesis of radical conventionalism, claiming that different philosophical doctrines are manifestations of different accepted languages, also grew out of the theory of meaning.

From Ajdukiewicz's philosophical endeavours we might distil the following maxim: there is no solution to philosophical perplexities without an understanding of the rôle of language and its rules.

VI

PHILOSOPHERS OF LINGUISTIC

ORIENTATION

I THE FOUR TYPES OF ANALYTICAL PHILOSOPHERS

In order to avoid misunderstanding, I shall say at once that there was no philosophical movement in Poland which, in the strict sense, corresponded to the Oxford philosophy of ordinary language. There were, however, some philosophers who believed in following language rather than in forcing it, in recording actual uses of terms rather than in proposing new ones. Their attention, however, was focused on philosophical problems quite different from those with which Oxford philosophers have been preoccupied.

Before the differences between the Polish and Oxford linguistic trends are singled out, let us examine the types of analytical philosophy in terms of its relation to language. There is at the present moment a tendency to classify all analytical philosophers into two main groups. Anthony Quinton appears to be the first to have suggested the distinction between *formalists* and *non-formalists*. The former, 'considering language to be the servant of thought, have treated it with a disdainful lack of respect by infringing its rules and putting it to unsuitable tasks'; the latter 'have uncritically accepted the logical and metaphysical hints and have drawn inferences about thinking and the world from the grammatical properties of the sentences used to describe them'.[1]

José Ferrater Mora attempted to improve upon this division

[1] Anthony Quinton, 'Linguistic Analysis', in Raymond Klibansky (ed.), *Philosophy in the Mid-Century* (Florence, 1959), II, p. 151.

and suggested the distinction between *formalists* and *linguists*. The formalists

(*a*) emphasize the importance of logic and tend to use an idiom close to the one employed by scientists;

(*b*) are, or have been, greatly concerned with problems of meaning, and

(*c*) are interested in problems.

The linguists

(*a*) separate themselves increasingly from strictly logical analysis and tend to employ an idiom closely resembling the one used by any sophisticated common talker,

(*b*) are spending most of their time and energy in tackling problems raised by use, and

(*c*) are interested in puzzles.[2]

All analytical philosophers are to be put into one of these two pigeon-holes, formalistic or linguistic.

Useful as these distinctions may be, they are not quite adequate for the location of *all* types of analytical philosophers. In Poland and certainly elsewhere, at least two further types can be distinguished. A new division is therefore required in order to make the classification more adequate. The first and main line of division appears between those who trust language and those who mistrust it; or, in other words, between the *followers* of ordinary language and the *rebels* against it. Both followers and rebels could be subdivided into *extremists* and *moderates*. So we have come to four types.

The extreme rebels condemn ordinary language unconditionally, 'treat it with a disdainful lack of respect', and consider artificial languages as the only vehicle suitable for the unambiguous formulation of their ideas. Because they form new artificial languages, they could be called *formists*; because their languages are formalized, the name 'formalists' would not be unsuitable either.

The moderate rebels do not condemn ordinary language entirely but only reshape it according to their needs. They claim that ordinary language is an amorphous mass out of which many different languages can be shaped, each of which could be equally compatible with (what is called) ordinary language. They do not

[2] José Ferrater Mora, *Philosophy Today* (New York, 1960), p. 53.

form new, artificial languages, but only *reform* ordinary language. Therefore they could be called the *reformists*.

The extreme followers of ordinary language accept it uncritically and attempt to 'draw inferences about thinking and the world from the grammatical properties of the sentences used to describe them'. They consider ordinary language to be the only medium of expression which does not lead to the over-simplification and distortion of thought. Because they are principally concerned with codifying usage, they could be called *codifiers*; because the homage they pay to ordinary language is unprecedented, the name 'linguists' would not be unsuitable either.

The moderate followers accept and follow ordinary language, but not without reservations. They codify the usage, but also do not hesitate from time to time to rectify language. The difference between extreme and moderate followers is similar to that between unwritten law, which has the sanction of tradition, and written law, which is an improvement upon customary law. Although customary law 'works', it works still better with rectifications. Because moderate followers have some tendency towards tidying up or, so to speak, rectifying ordinary language, they might be called *rectifiers*.

In more concrete terms the difference between rectifiers who *follow* ordinary language and codifiers who *obey* it is the difference between the majority of linguistic philosophers at Oxford and the ultra-linguistic philosopher, J. L. Austin, who carried the linguistic approach and indeed the programme of linguistic philosophy to a sublime extreme.

In a linear representation the classification into four types may be presented in this way:

1 Formists (formalists)	2 Reformists	3 Rectifiers	4 Codifiers (linguists)

The formists by definition are anti-codifiers or anti-linguists; conversely, the codifiers are anti-formists. There is no reconciliation between these two groups. They are at opposite poles. They gravitate towards quite different disciplines—the formists towards mathematics, the codifiers towards linguistics.

The linear distance between these groups indicates the degree of animosity or approval. The formists do not disapprove of the reformists, but insist that the latter would be much better off if they would try to be more exact, that is to say, more formal. But the formists are rather at odds with the rectifiers for whom they have a low regard. The codifiers are in sympathy with the rectifiers but wish that the latter were more faithful to language. But they rather disapprove of the reformists, though without the animosity they feel towards the formists. The reformists and the rectifiers live in perfect co-existence and mutual understanding, particularly because they are often under fire from both extreme wings.

In Poland the first three types were fully represented; those of the fourth type were only negligible.

Leśniewski, Łukasiewicz, and Tarski were the prominent formists. Because of their unmitigated drive towards formalization, they were called anti-philosophers. Their technical language and the requirements they established for their theories brought them nearer to mathematics than to any other discipline.

The prominent representatives of the second type (reformists) were Kotarbiński and Ajdukiewicz. It is enough to examine the growth and the nature of their doctrines to conclude at once that to pigeonhole them, either among the formalists or the linguists, would be quite misleading. Kotarbiński was far from attempting to formalize the assertions of concretism; on the other hand, he moved far away from everyday usage in his attempt to translate all statements into statements in which only references to bodies occur. The fact is that he constructed his own semantics, *ergo* his own language. He would, however, insist that this was not an artificial language, but a slight reform, a sharpening of ordinary language for the sake of clarity.

Ajdukiewicz might make the hair of many a codifier stand on end by his doctrine of radical conventionalism according to which we are to a large extent free to choose our own philosophical language. He was idiosyncratic towards ordinary language which he considered to be too 'swampy'. However, his theory of meaning is based on the rules of sense which, roughly speaking, are rules of usage. Far from being a codifier, he was also quite apart from the formalists. Like Kotarbiński, he accused the formalists of spending too much effort and attaching too much significance to playing with empty formulae.

It is clear that quite a number of other philosophers can be classified as reformists. One might even risk a thesis that most of *the* philosophers of the past were reformists; under the guise of ordinary language, they were in fact shaping their own languages to fit their philosophies.

2 THE OXFORD IDIOM AND THE OXFORD TRADITION

A conspicuous feature of Oxford philosophy of ordinary language has been its preoccupation with the problems of the philosophy of mind and moral philosophy. Other domains of philosophy have hardly been considered. The specific character of the Oxford linguistic movement, its novelty, its distinctiveness from all other philosophies, and even its idiom was worked out and manifests itself most strikingly in the field of the philosophy of mind and in moral philosophy. This is where the codifier's approach is most valuable. The leading exponents of the philosophy of ordinary language: Austin, Ryle, Wittgenstein (if the last is to be included) are all philosophers principally concerned with the analysis of terms concerning mental phenomena.

Austin's penetrating analyses are analyses of the concepts of moral discourse and above all of the philosophy of mind. Even in such a celebrated essay as 'Ifs and Cans', the title of which might suggest the analysis of logical concepts, his primary concern is the 'ifs' and 'cans' in the ethical writings of G. E. Moore and P. H. Nowell-Smith.

The subject-matter explains the peculiarity of the Oxford idiom only in part; another part of the explanation is to be found in the singularity of Oxford itself. The sheer power of tradition must not be underestimated when considering the peculiar position of Oxford in English society and in English philosophy. Owing to its ancient tradition of classical studies, Oxford acquired first an outstanding level of scholarship and secondly a confident certainty in its judgement in all spheres of the humanities. An awareness of its tradition became after a time linked to a conviction of the infallibility of its judgement. Whatever changes have taken place in the world, whether geo-political or social, economic or ideological, Oxford has always remained essentially unchanged. This resulted in a tacit presumption that ideas originating there tend to have a special value, as permanent and lasting as the place itself.

Oxford has always been a place of sophisticated argument and subtlety of thought. For better or worse, verbalism seems to be the touchstone of Oxford learning: verbalism as a basic ingredient of the undergraduate's education, as a basic ingredient of the tutor's life, as an essential part of all Oxford writing. The word 'verbalism' is not used here in an evaluative sense, and in particular it is not used pejoratively, but according to the definition given by the *Concise Oxford Dictionary*: 'Verbalism—minute attention to words.' Oxford linguistic philosophy may then be regarded as a continuation of the Oxford verbal tradition and the twentieth-century expression of the Oxford idiom, rather than as a perpetuation of Moore's or Wittgenstein's philosophy.

The spoken word has become so important at Oxford that some philosophers thought it almost a virtue to read little and to write still less. This opinion has been pointedly expressed by one of the exponents of the Oxford movement.

On the whole we do not write long or difficult books; *if ideas are understood by our colleagues in the course of verbal discussion, that is enough for us*...we do not think it a duty to write books; still less do we think it a duty to read more than a few of the books which others write.[3]

The tradition of fostering sophisticated philosophical dialogue and cultivating subtlety in linguistic nuance goes back to the fourteenth century when Oxford philosophy produced scholastic distinctions of remarkable finesse and reasoning schemata of exemplary force, thereby securing for itself a place in the history of human thought. Since that time it appears to be in the Oxford spirit to paint delicate, sophisticated ornaments rather than huge frescoes in the temples of human knowledge. The extraordinary subtlety of argument of fourteenth-century Oxford philosophers lapsed in succeeding centuries and was subsequently underrated as mere scholastic hair-splitting. Although not as prominent as it had been in the fourteenth century, Oxford remained a centre of classical learning during the following centuries, and the tradition of verbalism (in the sense specified above) was continued. Cook Wilson and Prichard in the first decades of the twentieth century were the heirs of this verbal tradition with its finesse of philosophical argument. Austin, rightly regarded as 'the emperor in the kingdom' of Oxford linguistic philosophy, perhaps inherited more from Cook Wilson and the Oxford verbalist tradition than

[3] R. M. Hare, 'A School for Philosophers', *Ratio*, II, No. 2 (February 1960), p. 113 [Italics mine].

he himself might have been willing to admit.[4] Characteristically enough, as an undergraduate he read classics in Greats and won a university prize for composing Greek prose. Indeed, almost all philosophers, who are included in the school of Oxford philosophy of ordinary language, were first Greek and Latin scholars and only afterwards turned to philosophy. Therefore, it should not really be surprising that language *qua* language has become their passion.

Thus, when we trace the ancestry of Austinian linguistic analysis, and seek an explanation of Oxford linguistic philosophy, we are struck by the same sharpness of argument in Cook Wilson, and by a similar subtlety of linguistic nuance as in fourteenth-century Oxford philosophy. Austinian analysis, of course, is on a qualitatively new level.

It has been pointed out, as a means of explanation, that the linguistic movement was foreshadowed in Ryle's paper 'Systematically Misleading Expressions' of 1931. It seems that the relevance of this paper was discovered only when the movement had taken shape and was trying to discover its origins. At the time this paper did not make a great impact on British philosophers. Moreover, as it stands, it can be taken as a programme for reductive analysis; the main tenor of the work remarkably resembles Kotarbiński's reduction of categories, as in his *Elements*.[5]

Only when we accept that the Oxford idiom is one of virtuosity of philosophical argument and manifold patterns of verbal discourse can we understand better what has happened in philosophy at Oxford. To accept a foreign idiom, whether that of Russell's philosophy or that of the Vienna Circle, would be to go against the grain and against the tradition. On the other hand, to continue Cook Wilson's type of argument would mean to fall behind the times. Quite naturally, Oxford did not wish either to

---

[4] Not only is it the case that Austin's actual practice stems from Cook Wilson, but Wilson himself provided the *raison d'être* for Oxford linguistic philosophy. In a letter to Bosanquet, Wilson wrote: 'Distinctions current in language can never be safely neglected', and 'It is the business of the student of logic to determine the *normal* use of an idiom or a linguistic expression. Everything depends upon that.' (In J. Passmore, *A Hundred Years of Philosophy*, p. 244.)

[5] I shall argue in the last chapter that the content of 'Systematically Misleading Expressions' can hardly be reconcilable with the idiom of Oxford philosophy of ordinary language in its mature phase. (See Chap. IX, section 2D, entitled 'Ryle and Kotarbiński'.)

cultivate foreign plants or to fall behind. It had to find a realm of its own in which the Oxford idiom would be in place.

After the great discoveries in mathematical logic had been made, and after logical analysis was introduced into philosophy, it was no longer possible to philosophize in the old manner without being considered an outsider. New standards of sophistication had to be observed. In order not to fall behind, Oxford philosophy had first to exhibit the weaknesses of mathematical logic as the main tool in logical analysis, and secondly to work out a method of its own. Formal logic had to be reduced in influence and significance, and so informal logic was introduced. Moreover, all strictly technical analyses, conducted within the framework of the language of mathematical logic and therefore inappropriate to the Oxford idiom, had to be replaced by something more compatible with the existing tradition, and the method of ordinary language analysis was given this rôle. Of course, the above described process has been a slow and gradual one, and not as self-conscious or straightforward as presented here. An historical process is never the same as its logical reconstruction. The point is that this process brought about a form suitable for the expression of the Oxford tradition. Oxford's fortes—the refinements of verbal discourse, the subtleties of verbal distinctions —were made an integral part of a new philosophy. In the form of the philosophy of ordinary language, the Oxford verbalist tradition flourished as illustriously as in its great period in the fourteenth century. Whatever differences we may observe among Oxford philosophers of ordinary language, we notice common elements: finesse of philosophical argumentation, sophistication, and subtlety.

At this point it is perhaps worth while to add a word about the Cambridge type of philosophy. The appearance at Cambridge of Russell and Whitehead and then of Ludwig Wittgenstein, all with their rather technical styles of philosophizing, should not be surprising. The tradition of science at Cambridge provided a fertile ground for this more professional and more specialized type of philosophy, elaborated in conjunction with the newest achievements in science. It seems that Russell and the early Wittgenstein were rejected by Oxford, not so much because they were Cambridge men, though it would not be true to say that this did not matter at all, but because they represented a different and alien philosophical idiom. The acceptance of Russell's type of philosophy would have violated the Oxford tradition because this would have meant: (1) a thorough study of mathematical logic, (2) the acquisition of specialized knowledge of the exact sciences, and (3) the replacement of rich, subtle, and sophisticated argument by the dry formulae of mathematical logic. Logically speaking, all these changes might have occurred. But tradition is not governed by logic. The encounter between the Oxford tradition of eloquent, non-technical, and non-erudite argument and the philosophy of Russell, manifestly technical, professional, and erudite, led inevitably to the rejection of the latter.

To recapitulate, Oxford philosophy of ordinary language is the twentieth-century embodiment of the Oxford verbalist tradition. The concentration of this philosophy on the problems of the philosophy of mind and some problems of moral philosophy is explained by the fact that the method of linguistic analysis is particularly suitable and rewarding in these fields. It is much less rewarding, however, in other domains of philosophical inquiry.

In order to illustrate the last point concretely, I shall briefly turn to Stephen Toulmin's *The Architecture of Matter*. The author is considered to be an adherent of the Oxford linguistic movement; the work belongs to the field of the history and philosophy of science. The result is that the method employed diverges considerably from that of a codifier; instead of recording the actual usage in ordinary language, the author traces and reconstructs the meaning of concepts as they were used in scientific discourse over the centuries.

> Any theory of matter must draw a distinction between those things which are genuine *bodies*, and those which are not—between 'material substances' and 'immaterial agents', 'corporeals' and' incorporeals'. Far from agreeing on definite lists of corporeals and incorporeals, men in 1700 did not even agree on the *meaning* of this distinction; and the intellectual contortions which resulted from the ambiguity were responsible for many of the birth-pangs of chemistry.[6]

That our ordinary language and our common sense were not always 'ordinary' and not always 'common', Toulmin argues in this way:

> The crucial importance of mass, though clear enough in dynamics and astronomy, was not established in chemistry for nearly a century;

[6] Stephen Toulmin and J. Goodfield, *The Architecture of Matter* (London, 1962), p. 202.

and the very word 'imponderable' is recorded by the *Oxford Diction-ary* only from 1794. It was in fact the middle of the nineteenth century before men were in a position to draw our 'common sense' distinctions between (1) genuine chemical substances, which are both ponderable and capable of acting physically—and so 'material' in both senses; (2) spiritual things, which are neither ponderable nor physical in their direct affects—and so doubly 'immaterial' and (3) the intermediate class, consisting of physical agencies such as heat and magnetism—which appear to be devoid of mass, even though their physical effects are unquestionable.[7]

These two passages are too eloquent in themselves to need comment. The crucial point with linguistically oriented philosophers is this. When the method of linguistic analysis is applied in fields other than the philosophy of mind and moral philosophy, then it acquires a modified form; no longer are philosophers codifiers, but rather rectifiers. Such is the case with Toulmin in his works concerning the history and philosophy of science. And such is the case with Polish analytical philosophers. Owing to a different educational orientation, more of a Cambridge than an Oxford type, and to a preoccupation with the problems of the philosophy of science, epistemology, and the history of philosophy rather than with the philosophy of mind, the Polish linguistically oriented philosophers were rectifiers rather than codifiers.

It is by no means my purpose here to establish *per fas et nefas* a 'linguistic movement' in Poland in the Oxford sense; there was nothing of the sort. If, however, we agree that analytical philosophers exhibit various degrees of fidelity towards ordinary language; and if we agree furthermore that the division into formists, reformists, rectifiers, and codifiers characterizes these various degrees of fidelity, then we cannot fail to notice that there were in Poland philosophers who quite consciously followed ordinary language rather than attempted to force it. Perhaps the most accomplished in this category was W. Tatarkiewicz.

3 WŁADYSŁAW TATARKIEWICZ AND THE HISTORY OF IDEAS

Kotarbiński and Ajdukiewicz were the most outstanding of Polish reformists; Tatarkiewicz[8] was the most prominent of

---

[7] Op. cit., p. 203.

[8] Tatarkiewicz (born 1886) studied at Marburg at the time when it was the stronghold of neo-Kantism. After receiving his doctorate, he moved

Polish rectifiers. Kotarbiński and Ajdukiewicz made their names through their contributions to systematic philosophy; Tatarkiewicz established his reputation through his contributions to the history of ideas.

Tatarkiewicz did not build new philosophical edifices in the manner of Ajdukiewicz or Kotarbiński. His originality lay in his extraordinary ability for systematizing other philosophers' ideas. He declared himself a pluralist in his 1912 work, 'Über die Naturalische Weltansicht'. And he remained a pluralist until the present day. He had a multiplicity of interests, and no desire to weld his views into one whole. The fields of his accomplishments were the history of philosophy, the history of aesthetics, and the history of morals. Here he had no rivals in Poland. It would be hard indeed to find elsewhere a philosopher equally accomplished in all these three areas. He was immensely erudite, but free from German pedantry; a painstaking analyst in tracing the usage of concepts, but without tediousness. In fact his philosophical writing is a paradigm of Polish prose; the clarity, lucidity, and flexibility of his language can be compared with the best French prose. His influence in history of philosophy and aesthetics can be compared with the influence of Kotarbiński in epistemology and logic. The names of the two were equally well known to the layman in Poland.

If we wish to extend the method of linguistic analysis to the field of the history of ideas, it is hard to see how it could acquire a form different from that of Tatarkiewicz—a careful and thorough

---

to Lwów to study under Twardowski. The influence of the Marburg School was rather insignificant and can be seen only in the intensification of his interest in the ancient masters, Plato and Aristotle. Twardowski's influence, on the other hand, is easily seen in his method, in which he showed an appreciation of caution and common sense in philosophizing, and above all in his acceptance of analysis as the main instrument of philosophical inquiry.

In 1923 he was appointed to the Chair of the History of Philosophy at Warsaw University, which he held for 25 years except, of course, during the war. In 1923, he became the editor-in-chief of *Przegląd Filozoficzny*, the most important philosophical periodical in Poland in the first half of the twentieth century. This position he also held for 25 years, until *Przegląd Filozoficzny* was closed down by the Marxists. In the 1950s he was not allowed to teach philosophy at all, and his Chair was taken from him. In 1956, when the period of Marxist domination was over, Tatarkiewicz returned to Warsaw and obtained the Chair of Aesthetics at Warsaw University. He retired from this chair in 1960.

examination and recording of all meanings used and implied by the philosophers of the past. In the historian's work analysis, though necessary, is not sufficient; after the analysis must come organization, the synthesis in which a pattern is presented. At this stage, Tatarkiewicz advocated the principle of *historical interventionism*,[9] which calls for an active rôle on the part of the historian. It is not enough for the historian of philosophy to know philosophy; he must be a philosopher himself. It is on this basis that his monumental *History of Philosophy* was written.

Tatarkiewicz's peculiar interests and aptitudes were, so to say, *synoptic*; he first attempted to juxtapose historical facts and trends, and next to weigh them in order to find their place and proportion in relation to other trends and facts. The method which he worked out for achieving his sharp and clear synoptics may be called the method of *non-continuous* representation of facts. In his *History of Philosophy*,[10] this method consisted in dividing the subject into the same rubrics repeated regularly in every chapter. Each philosopher is presented in a series of separate sequences: his life, work, predecessors, opponents, successors, development, chronology, terminology, disputable issues, etc. This was a formal procedure without precedent in the history of philosophy. By the application of this method, Tatarkiewicz's history is concise, clear, and comprehensive. There are some who claim that no other history of philosophy succeeded in presenting so much material on relatively few pages, which was so lucid and intelligible to the layman without being oversimplified for the sake of popularity, and which did so much justice to philosophers and philosophical trends without favouring any particular one. The method of non-continuous representation introduced by Tatarkiewicz in 1931 was later followed by other historians of philosophy, as for example Gilson and Boehner.

Tatarkiewicz's presentation of the history of philosophy and Windelband's *Lehrbuch der Geschichte der Philosophie* are, one might

[9] Tatarkiewicz, 'The History of Philosophy and the Art of Writing It', *Diogenes* (Winter, 1957).

[10] Tatarkiewicz, *Historia filozofii* (*History of Philosophy*), (Lwów, 1931), Vols. I, II; 2nd edn., 1933; 3rd edn., Warsaw, 1946; 4th edn., 1948; Vol. III, 1950; 5th edn., 1958. This history was unrivalled in Poland and eclipsed all others, foreign translations included. It also served as a university textbook from the time it first appeared. Even in the period 1950–1956, when it was 'on the index', so to speak, students used it secretly to prepare themselves for examinations in the history of philosophy from the Marxist point of view.

say, at opposite poles. Windelband applied the principle of continuity. For him the history of philosophy is one uninterrupted stream. To describe the two approaches figuratively, Tatarkiewicz constructed his history in the way a film is made, one shot after another, each separate. Windelband constructed his history as a film is shown to the public, as a continuous flow of pictures. To use another simile, Tatarkiewicz resembles a pre-Renaissance painter who paints the history of an event in a series of separate pictures (first St. John is in the Wilderness, next his head is cut off, etc.) whereas Windelband resembles a Baroque painter who represents the whole series of events on one canvas.

Tatarkiewicz's contribution to the history of philosophy was not only in terms of the structure within which he presented the growth of ideas. He also made a number of detailed contributions relating to particular philosophers. To mention a few, his doctoral thesis, 'Die Disposition der Aristotelischen Prinzipien',[11] showed that Aristotle's conceptual apparatus had many layers. About this work W. D. Ross wrote:

> The cumulative value of these [Tatarkiewicz's] arguments is very great. Nor is the general character of the treatise unworthy of Aristotle. The method followed is truely Aristotelian—a careful classification of the possible views, followed by a discussion of each, coupled with names of their supporters.[12]

In 1931 Tatarkiewicz in 'Les Trois Morales d'Aristote'[13] set as his aim to show that Aristotle had not one, but three ethical systems.

The *History of Philosophy* contains much else that is new. When discussing the philosophy of the Enlightenment, Tatarkiewicz sharply distinguished and separately analysed its various components, as for example, sensualism, naturalism, materialism, positivism. This had not been done before. He also discussed French moralists—La Bruyère, Chamfort, La Rochefoucauld—along with philosophers in the strict sense, in order to emphasize that the history of philosophy should not be limited to the examination of 'professional' philosophers only. He also felt it

[11] Tatarkiewicz, 'Die Disposition der Aristotelischen Prinzipien', *Philosophische Arbeiten* (Giessen, 1910), IV, Bd.2.

[12] W. D. Ross, review of 'Die Disposition der Aristotelischen Prinzipien', *Classical Review*, 24, p. 252.

[13] Tatarkiewicz, 'Les Trois Morales d'Aristote,' *Séances et travaux de l'Académie des Sciences Morales et Politiques* (Paris, 1931).

should present facts of the social, economic, and cultural back-ground against which various philosophies developed.

However, most innovations are to be found in the third volume of his *History* (1830–1945). Both the division into periods and the arrangement of the material are quite original. Tatarkiewicz was probably the first to examine simultaneously all philosophical trends of the twentieth century; when analysing one trend, he attempted to trace its influence on other trends. His originality also consisted in attempting to characterize every philosophy in terms of, so to speak, its 'essences'. The first positivism (of d'Alembert) was presented in this way:

1. Delimitation of science to asserting facts.
2. Following from it the elimination of metaphysics, and not only that which affirms, but also that which denies.
3. The consideration of science against the background of biological and social circumstances.
4. The limitation of philosophy to the inquiry concerning the principles of exact sciences.[14]

Nietzsche's philosophy was characterized in this way:

The fundamental conviction of Nietzsche was that bodily life, the biological fact, is the basis of human existence, whereas spiritual life is only its offshoot. From this followed Nietzsche's naturalism and relativism, both epistemological and ethical, as well as a new morality, the revaluation of all values, the rising above the good and the bad, opposition between the master and the slave, between Apollonian and Dionysian, the concept of superman and the necessity to oppose decadence.[15]

In moral philosophy Tatarkiewicz also combined systematic and historical interests. In 1931, in his address to the Seventh Philosophical Congress held at Oxford, he distinguished four types of ethical judgements:[16]

1. *Judgements of value*, which are made when a given quality or action is regarded as valuable in itself. We may assert, for example, that to speak the truth is a good thing in itself, inde-pendent of results. It is better that the truth should be spoken rather than concealed because the truth is a value in itself.

2. *Judgements of rightness*, which are made when a given action

---

[14] In Volume II, 1st edn. (1931).
[15] In Volume III (1958 edn.), p. 225.
[16] Tatarkiewicz, 'On the Four Types of Ethical Judgements', *Proceedings of the Seventh International Congress of Philosophy*, 1931.

is assessed in terms of its consequences. If we assert that to speak the truth is the best course to follow in a given case, since together with its consequences it will produce the maximum of good, or at any rate the minimum of evil, we are making a judgement of rightness.

3. *Judgements of morality*, which are made when the intentions of the agent performing the act are judged. If, in the case of speaking or not speaking the truth, we judge the intention of the agent, we are within the realm of judgements of morality.

4. *Judgements of merit* have to do with the effort made in performing a moral action. If we are concerned with the amount of effort necessary for overcoming the reluctance of a person to expose himself to painful consequences of telling the truth, then we have a judgement of merit.

The above types of judgements, although related to one another, have to do with different questions; therefore they ought not to be confused. But, as Tatarkiewicz argued:

> It has become customary to link up the ethical doctrines which have appeared in the course of time in a single historical series under the title 'history of ethics'. This series is very irregular, and it is not surprising that, if ethical doctrines have to do with various problems, judgements are also of various kinds. Thus, the ethics of ordinary life operate exclusively by means of judgements of value which we have placed under the first type. The same is true of the ethics of Socrates and of Plato in the latter's early phase. In the ethics of Aristotle, on the other hand, we already have judgements of rightness. A considerable portion of the religious ethics, which prevailed especially in the Middle Ages, is concerned primarily with the enunciation of judgements of merit. The ethics of Kant has as its object morality in the sense of the intention of the action.[17]

Tatarkiewicz was fortunate in completing his major philosophical undertakings. The first was *History of Philosophy* (the first two volumes in 1931, the third in 1949). Next, his fundamental work on moral philosophy, *On Happiness*,[18] was completed in 1946. His third important undertaking, *History of Aesthetics*, appeared in 1960.[19] The qualities which enabled Tatarkiewicz to

[17] Op. cit., p. 400.

[18] Tatarkiewicz, *O szczęściu* (*On Happiness*) (Warsaw, 1947); 2nd edn., 1949, 3rd edn., 1962.

[19] The first two volumes have already been published; the last two are to come.

complete all three enterprises were his extraordinary gift for words and his synoptic aptitude. By following his synoptic approach, he concentrated on the question of *how* and not *why* ideas and systems emerged and developed. In answering the 'how' question, the centre of focus was on *types* of philosophy, art, etc. Hence typology occupied an important place in Tatarkiewicz's philosophy.

The treatise *On Happiness* is as 'typological' as the *History of Philosophy*. It is analytical and descriptive rather than didactic and moralistic, critical rather than normative. It is a survey of the opinions and thoughts of philosophers and moralists, of poets and novelists, of dramatists and biographers on happiness— covering centuries and even millennia. It is in a sense an empirical study. In the Introduction Tatarkiewicz wrote:

> There are many treatises on happiness. . . . But in the extensive literature on this subject of the last few thousand years, there is really no book which embraces all the problems and which offers all the solutions. The complete treatise on happiness has never been published. This is almost unbelievable, particularly when we reflect that there are so many books about matters less important for human beings.
>
> I should like this book to be such a treatise; that it should, at any rate, give an outline of all that can be objectively said about happiness; that it should not be confined to one problem, even the most important; neither to one conception, even the most valid; nor to one road to happiness, even the most successful. I should like this book to be 'Summa de Beatitudine' as it would have been called in the Middle Ages, but which was not written even then.[20]

Whether or not Tatarkiewicz's treatise can be considered *the* 'Summa de Beatitudine' is for the expert to determine. It is a work characteristic of those several Polish philosophers who have had a thorough classical education and adopt a thoroughly modern approach. Łukasiewicz's *O zasadzie sprzeczności u Arystotelesa* and *Aristotle's Syllogistic from the Standpoint of Modern Formal Logic* are two further examples. In the first half of the twentieth century there were many philosophical scholars with a profound understanding of the ancient masters; on the other hand, there were many who took up the modern approach. Few, like Tatarkiewicz, Łukasiewicz, and Kotarbiński combined the two approaches.

[20] Tatarkiewicz, *On Happiness*, 3rd edn., p. 8.

Aesthetics was the third field of Tatarkiewicz's interests, although it would be more true to say that it was his first—he considered himself primarily an aesthetician. In his systematic studies in aesthetics, he practised what J. L. Austin recommended: *field work*. For example, his students and assistants were given the task of examining literary and non-literary writings and of recording what various authors said explicitly and implicitly about different aspects of modern art, e.g. how the term 'modern' in the phrase 'modern painting' was used. This was the method which was practised in Warsaw before a plea for field work appeared in Austin's essay 'A Plea for Excuses'. Tatarkiewicz's 'linguistic-empirical' approach to aesthetics made aesthetics to a large extent a tangible subject, accessible to unambiguous and concrete formulation.

Among various elucidations, Tatarkiewicz introduced a distinction between aspective and prospective art.[21]

Aspective art (from the Latin *aspectus*—appearance) can be identified with realism, and aspires only to representing the outward appearance of things.

Prospective art (from the Latin *prospectus*—a distant view) often appears under the name of expressionism and aims at reaching the essence of things. This term was suggested by Poussin, who discriminated two ways of seeing: the ordinary way and that one where we observe objects with our minds as well as with our eyes. Philosophically speaking, aspective art is akin to realism and empiricism, whereas prospective art is linked to idealism, Platonism in particular. This distinction is desirable, Tatarkiewicz argued, because of the existing terminological confusion and abuse of such terms as 'naturalism', which have become almost meaningless.

Tatarkiewicz's work on aesthetics was crowned by the publication of the *History of Aesthetics*[22] in which he attempted to give 'an *overall* picture of the development of European aesthetics . . . a systematic *exposition of aesthetic opinions prevailing in different times*, their essence, their development, and their relation to each other'.[23] In the nineteenth century there were some histories

---

[21] Tatarkiewicz, 'Abstract Art and Philosophy', *British J. of Aesthetics*, II (1962). Also in an augumented version in *Jahrbuch für Aesthetik*, VI (1961).

[22] Tatarkiewicz, *Historia estetyki*: Vol. I—*Estetyka starożytna*, Vol. II—*Estetyka średniowieczna* (Wrocław-Cracow, 1960).

[23] Ibid., Vol. I, Introduction, p. 5.

which covered the whole development of aesthetics, but the sources known at that time were not so numerous. In the twentieth century, when knowledge of the sources immensely increased, only one comprehensive history of aesthetics has been written, that by K. Gilbert and H. Kuhn. Since that time, Tatarkiewicz's is the only attempt to embrace the whole history of aesthetics. The project is very ambitious indeed. This is the author's account of how he conceived his undertaking:

> This work . . . is not confined to the general aesthetics of philo-
> sophers, but includes in its scope also the more detailed aesthetics
> of theoreticians of the arts—the theory of poetry, music, painting
> and sculpture; and also the aesthetics of artists, not only as they
> themselves expressed it, but as it can be deciphered from their deeds,
> at least in more important moments of history.[24]

All the methods and procedures which Tatarkiewicz employed in his *History of Philosophy* are applied in his *History of Aesthetics*, possibly in a more condensed and purified form. It is a rare occasion when a learned treatise of this kind becomes a best seller, as was the case with the *History of Aesthetics*. The leading Marxist in the field of aesthetics in Poland, S. Morawski, Tatarkiewicz's adversary in the early 1950s, called this history 'Tatarkiewicz's "Opus Magnum"', and with characteristic reservation said: 'In spite of all shortcomings previously analysed, Tatarkiewicz's book is, I must repeat again, the best of its kind in world literature.'[25]

It is difficult to summarize the philosophical accomplishments of a historian of philosophy. Tatarkiewicz, a historian of philosophy, was also a systematic philosopher who participated in the philosophy of analysis; most of his contributions were incorporated in his histories of philosophy and of aesthetics, and the treatise on happiness. These contributions are so fitted into the presentation of philosophical ideas, that it is often difficult to discern their source. His success as a historian is only partly to be explained by his analytical bent of mind. Partly a historian, partly a philosopher, and partly an artist, he consciously decided on certain omissions; what is omitted, however, is omitted deliberately according to the principle that the art of synthesis is the art of omission.

[24] Op. cit., pp. 5, 6.
[25] S. Morawski, 'Tatarkiewicza "Opus Magnum"', *Studia Filoz.*, Vol. 24 (3), 1961, p. 199.

4 JANINA KOTARBIŃSKA—THE LINGUISTIC APPROACH
IN THE PHILOSOPHY OF SCIENCE

Mme Janina Kotarbińska's[26] approach much resembles the style which Toulmin has adopted in the history and philosophy of science. Partly under the influence of Tatarkiewicz, she inherited a synoptic attitude. Kotarbińska's forte lies not so much in arguing for or against this or that standpoint, but rather in systematizing various views concerning the subject under discussion. She never openly declared her philosophical standpoint because, as she said, she 'did not wish to talk about things if this could not be done precisely and accurately'. Consequently, the realm of problems she examined was suitably narrowed to those which could be discussed without becoming involved in any kind of philosophical doctrine.

The source of her inquiry—and this gives the clue to all her pre-war writing—lies in the idea of compiling a philosophical dictionary.[27] This was to be done by giving the usage of philosophical concepts as thoroughly and exhaustively as possible, not by giving short and more or less arbitrary definitions. Kotarbińska thought that, as the result of these thorough analyses, some philosophical problems would be rejected as spurious and meaningless, and some others might be solved as a consequence of proper formulation. This, as can easily be seen, was very much in accordance with the attitude of the logical empiricists.

The problem of determinism was one of Kotarbińska's considerations. In the essay, 'The Problem of Indeterminism in Modern Physics, Biology, and the Humanites',[28] she wrote that at

[26] Janina Kotarbińska, *née* Dina Sztejnberg, was Kotarbiński's pupil, and then his assistant. She collaborated with him in the preparation of the *Elements*, and afterwards became his wife. Since 1957 she has held one of the Chairs of Logic at Warsaw University.

[27] She began this undertaking in the early 1930s. In 1931 she published a paper 'Analiza pojęcia przypadku' (An analysis of the Concept of Chance) with the subtitle 'A Contribution to a Philosophical Dictionary'. When the project of this dictionary was far advanced, the war broke out and her manuscript, over a thousand pages, containing a great deal of the dictionary, was burnt and buried in the ruins of Warsaw in 1939. At this point it should be mentioned that *The International Encyclopaedia of Unified Science*, which appeared quite independently twenty-five years later, was a realization of a similar idea.

[28] J. Kotarbińska, 'Problem indeterminizmu we współczesnej fizyce, biologii i naukach humanistyczych' (The Problem of Indeterminism in Modern Physics and in the Humanities), *Przeg. Filoz.*, XXXV–XXXVIII (1932–1935).

the present time the dispute between determinism and indeterminism is not mature enough to be resolved decisively by means of the empirical method. What was most important for the controversy was an unequivocal formulation of the meanings of the terms involved in the dispute. 'Only an unequivocal formulation of the problem will definitely show whether the dispute between determinism and indeterminism has indeed been a genuine one, and whether it deserves to be the object of such heated discussions.'[29]

The analysis of the concept of determinism in Kotarbińska's above-mentioned essay was carried on in a scrupulous, systematic, drily professional, typically Austinian manner. The analysis of the problem of determinism *versus* indeterminism begins with an examination of the concept of the law of nature. Because there is no agreement about the meaning of the term, the author takes great pains to analyse all possible meanings involved. It has often been held that simplicity is an essential condition of a law of nature, and accordingly Kotarbińska examines what various authors meant by the *simplicity of laws*.

We shall briefly present here Kotarbińska's findings regarding the notion of *simplicity of laws* because (1) this investigation is highly typical of her approach to the philosophy of science, because (2) recent discussions about scientific laws still refer to simplicity as a defining component of scientific laws, and because (3) in the 1960s analytically-minded Marxists in Poland followed her approach.[30]

Kotarbińska's analysis led her to distinguish a number of uses of the term 'simplicity'. These involved:

   1. Uncomplicated structure. This in turn can mean:
      (*a*) the simplicity of the construction of the law, e.g. Boyle's Law: $pv = $ constant;
      (*b*) the simplicity of the construction in terms of a mathematical function—the simpler the mathematical curve depicting the law, the simpler the law;
      (*c*) the simplicity of the construction in terms of the minimization of the mathematical operations necessary for its application;
      (*d*) the simplicity of the construction in terms of the

[29] Op. cit., pp. 36, 37.
[30] See Chapter VIII—Krajewski's discussion of the problem of sensory cognition and reality.

minimization of the number of variables occurring in the formulae expressing the law.

2. The admission of the smallest possible number of hypotheses. This can mean:

(*a*) the law P_1 is simpler than the law P_2 if the assertion of P_1 involves fewer hypotheses, e.g. Copernicus' theory as opposed to Ptolemy's;

(*b*) the law P_1 is simpler than the law P_2 if P_1 requires fewer 'metaphysical' hypotheses. This postulate consequently necessitates eliminating 'metaphysical' theses wherever possible from laws of nature;

(*c*) the law P_1 is simpler than P_2 if the assertion of P_1 involves simpler hypotheses than P_2 (simpler in terms of 1*a*, 1*b*, 1*c*, or 1*d*).

3. Defining the simplicity of laws in terms of the logical consequences following from them. The law P_1 is simpler than the law P_2 if it leads to simpler consequences in terms of easy comprehension (even if its formulation is more complicated).

4. Defining simplicity in terms of 'intuitive obviousness':

(*a*) Laws which are intuitively obvious are simple.

(*b*) Laws immediately derived from intuitively obvious ones are simple.

5. Defining simplicity as referring to 'simple states of affairs', or as concerned with indivisible elemental particles (such as protons, electrons, etc.).

6. Defining simplicity in terms of indivisibility. Laws which are indivisible, 'atomic' in a sense, are simple.

7. Defining simplicity in terms of generalizations of observational statements, as opposed to laws which follow only from non-observational statements.

8. Defining simple laws as those which do not contain vague or ambiguous terms.

With equal scrupulousness the author examined what we mean by the *generality* of the laws of nature. Next, she considered all the possible connotations of the term *verifiability* in connection with laws of nature. Similar analyses were carried on in relation to every important concept involved in the controversy over determinism and indeterminism. In every case the author attempted to trace all the meanings actually in use in philosophical and scientific discourse.

In another of her papers, 'An Analysis of the Concept of Chance',[31] Kotarbińska distinguished no less than twenty-six current meanings, all of them found in use in various controversies. In conclusion she stated: 'Because of a lack of mutual understanding as to the actual use of one or several of these meanings, many a controversy arose from only terminological confusion.'

Before the war, Kotarbińska's interests were centred around the problem of explanation and the problem of law in science. After the war her domain became semantics. Her post-war papers were mainly published in *Studia Logica* ('Definicja' [Definition], 1955; 'Pojęcie znaku' [The Concept of Sign], 1957).

In one of her later papers, 'On Ostensive Definitions',[32] Kotarbińska analysed 'the specific distinct characteristics of ostensive definition, the mechanism of its functioning and the properties of the terms introduced by ostensive method'. Indirectly, however, it was a study of the significance of the linguistic apparatus in the investigation of empirical reality.

> But it must be borne in mind that, as already mentioned, all non-ostensive empirical terms (we mean here predicative terms) are finally reduced, through equivalent definition or conditional definition to some ostensive terms, usually borrowed from colloquial language, and that it is to this fact that they owe their empirical character. We may say safely that a language which would include no terms introduced by ostensive method would be useless for the implementation of those tasks which face the disciplines that have to investigate reality, because it would include no terms by means of which that reality could be described.[33]

Ostensive definition is a certain kind of procedure which consists in pointing out with a suitable gesture a single designatum of the term being defined, and in simultaneously pronouncing a statement of the type 'This is N', where 'N' stands for the term being defined. In giving an ostensive definition we perform two actions, only one of which belongs to the sphere of verbal language.

---

[31] 'Analiza pojęcia przypadku' (An Analysis of the Concept of Chance) in *Fragmenty filozoficzne*, 1st series (Warsaw, 1934).

[32] J. Kotarbińska, 'Tak zwana definicja dejktyczna' (On Ostensive Definitions) in *Fragmenty filozoficzne*, 2nd series (Warsaw, 1959); also in English under the title 'On Ostensive Definitions' in *Philosophy of Science*, Vol. 27, No. 1 (January 1960).

[33] Ibid., p. 22.

When defining terms by means of ostensive definitions we attempt to arrive at a statement of the kind '*A* is *N*', which in fact is an abbreviated form of the sentence '*N* is such an object as *A*', or even more precisely:

$$\pi x(x \text{ is } N = x \text{ is such as } A)$$

The final formulation of ostensive definition is the following:

$\pi x(x$ is $N \equiv x$ is such as A in the respect R and in the degree D), or in an abridged and symbolic notation:

$$\pi x[N(x) = x \ \text{sim}_{R,D} A]$$

Ostensive definition informs us about the criteria of applicability of the defined term only partially. The rest—the respect R, and the degree (of similarity) D—must be determined by the person who uses the given definition.

In all her papers, Kotarbińska kept close to everyday language. She attempted to analyse what is really talked about, what the procedures of science really are, and not what they should be according to the requirements dictated by mathematical logic. Because she wished to embrace all meanings and all usages occurring in controversies, she usually formulated her final theses so cautiously that her conclusions are 'weak' and, in a sense, ineffectual.

5 MARIA OSSOWSKA—THE SCIENCE OF MORALITY

Mme Maria Ossowska[34] belongs to the same group of linguistically oriented philosophers. Her field is moral philosophy or, according to her own terminology, the science of morality. She attempts an examination and description of moral phenomena by establishing what people have considered as bad and as good. She presents a dispassionate analysis of various ethical systems, both by exposing their logical backbones, and by illuminating their crucial points, but not in order to evaluate. No further attempt is made to improve upon existing systems or to provide another one. The main purpose of this sort of study is to reveal what *does take place* rather than what should take place in the field of morality.

[34] She was educated at Warsaw University and studied under Kotarbiński and Tatarkiewicz. She now holds the Chair of the History and Theory of Morality in the Department of Philosophy in Warsaw University.

Ossowska's approach much resembles that of such Oxford moralists as Hare, Nowel-Smith, Austin, Hart, Hampshire, and Toulmin. In the late 1940s she put forward her science of morality according to which emotive and imperative theories of morals misrepresent the character of moral statements. The business of the moral theorist is to study the 'moral fields', to elucidate and determine the meaning of such key terms of moral discourse as 'good', 'right', 'ought', 'virtuous'. This became the dominant tenet of Oxford moral philosophy in the early 1950s, and was then regarded as a completely new approach.

Ossowska was educated during the period when the Polish analytical movement was already under way. It was a time when specialization prevailed in philosophy, a time when the idea of transforming philosophy into a science was advocated more strongly than ever. No wonder that, following the logicians (who had transformed a philosophical discipline, logic, into a genuine science), representatives of other branches of philosophy made attempts to transform their own disciplines into sciences. Ossowska attempted to reshape moral philosophy into 'the' science of morality, understood as a complex body of at least three disciplines: (1) an examination of the (logical) foundations of morals, (2) the psychology of morals, (3) the sociology of morals. Neither the history of ethics nor an empirical ethics, she felt, could be substituted for a genuine science of morality.

At the time when she started her philosophical inquiry, in the late 1920s, Polish philosophy was dominated by logical analysis. It is thus not surprising that Ossowska tried to present morality in a more systematic way than the code of Oxford philosophy of ordinary language would allow.

Her three main treatises were concerned with the three departments of the science of morality distinguished above. These treatises were: (1) *The Foundations of the Science of Morality*,[35] (2) *Human Motivation*—An Inquiry into the Psychology of Moral Life,[36] and (3) *Middle Class Morality*,[37] which was concerned with the sociology of morals. In each Ossowska adhered to her main

[35] M. Ossowska, *Podstawy nauki o moralności* (*The Foundations of the Science of Morality*) (Warsaw, 1947), 2nd edn. 1957.

[36] M. Ossowska, *Motywy postępowania—Z zagadnień psychologii moralności* (*Human Motivation—An Inquiry into the Psychology of Moral Life*) (Warsaw, 1949), 2nd edn. 1958.

[37] M. Ossowska, *Moralność mieszczańska* (*Middle Class Morality*) (Łódź: ŁTN, Wydz. 1, No. 22, 1956).

principle, which was 'to bring discussions about ethics down from the Platonic sphere to earth'. This attitude and the sobriety of her approach have counterparts in Oxford philosophy.

The Foundations of the Science of Morality is the Polish equivalent of *Principia Ethica*. Since it was written four decades later (after the prolific growth of syntactics and semantics), it is more penetrating, more incisive, and more exhaustive, although *Principia* is more readable, lucid in style, and perhaps better composed. Ossowska, *nota bene*, was Moore's follower; she came to Cambridge specially to study with him in 1927.

The *Foundations* is a logical examination of morals, particularly moral norms and moral evaluations. This examination reveals that ethical systems are illogical and chaotic, and shows that from a logical point of view the problem of evaluation is hopelessly entangled.

Moral evaluations are expressed in statements. Statements to be considered morally evaluative must possess some specific characteristics. Thus Ossowska examines various classes of attributes which supposedly make statements morally evaluative. The peculiarity of moral evaluations has often been characterized in terms of psychological statements expressing moral indignation or approval. However, in order to be a statement of a moral type, a psychological statement expressing blame or praise must be impartial. But then the psychological characterization of moral judgements ceases to be adequate. Ossowska goes on to examine theories in which the peculiarity of moral evaluations is characterized in terms of *objects* (situations) giving rise to those moral evaluations. Various theories advance different objects (situations) as those evoking moral evaluations: deeds, motives, intentions, decisions, feelings, personalities, and finally the people performing deeds, experiencing intentions, etc. The general conclusion about objects (situations) which evoke moral evaluations is this. As a rule, the conditions required for objects to be praiseworthy stand in an asymmetrical relation to the conditions required for objects to be morally condemned, but there appears to be no clear pattern in this asymmetry.

We can readily agree with Ossowska that the difficulty in defining moral norms and moral evaluations, as contrasted with other norms and evaluations, is a consequence of the blurred edges of the domain of morality. We may further agree with Ossowska that some definitions of the concept of moral evaluations appropriate for a section of moral life become inadequate when generalized to cover the whole sphere of morality.

Our inability to define adequately moral evaluations prevents us from defining the realm of morals. Ethical treatises in fact are concerned with very diverse topics. No comprehensive and cohesive system of ethics can be constructed out of this diversity. Consequently, Ossowska claimed that the construction of ethics must be preceded by a science of morality. This study, however, indicates that the topics traditionally appearing under the label of ethics should be separated into at least four departments: (1) general axiology or the theory of values, (2) felicitology, a science of happiness, (3) perfectionistics, a discipline concerned with ideal patterns of behaviour which people consider worth following, and (4) ethics in a narrower sense, a discipline providing principles for a harmonious life in society.

This is very roughly the substance of Ossowska's *The Foundations of the Science of Morality*.

The second treatise, *Human Motivation*, which is concerned with the psychology of morality, is as incisive in its analytical aspect as *The Foundations*. To present her approach in the psychology of morality, we have chosen her analysis of psychological hedonism. In investigating those theories which claim that man's behaviour is actuated by pleasure or pain Ossowska drew distinctions between:

1. A theory which claims that we should never have arrived at a distinction between good and evil had we not been able to experience pleasure and pain.

2. A theory which holds that a value judgement about an object is determined by the object's capacity to produce pleasure or pain.

3. A theory which considers value-judgements as expressions of pleasure or pain.

She concludes that neither partisans of psychological hedonism nor their opponents state explicitly what they are maintaining, and that different forms of psychological hedonism are far from being equivalent.

Existing theories of hedonism claim (*a*) that pleasure is the only determinant, or (*b*) the main factor, or (*c*) a necessary component in the total motivation. The validity of arguments put forward by

o

either hedonists or anti-hedonists entirely depends on which theory they are supposed to support. Also, some moral philosophers who are antagonistic to some forms of hedonism indirectly subscribe to other forms. For example, G. E. Moore discarded the opinion that a thought of a future pleasure determines our actions, but admitted that the presence of a pleasant thought of the desired object was a necessary part of the total motivation.

The third treatise, *Middle Class Morality*, is an inquiry into the sociology of morality. Attacks on bourgeois morality have been launched by various camps: by leftists (Marxists), by writers of aristocratic origin, and by Bohemians. These attacks, however, have mostly been rather vague and overgeneralized. Ossowska clearly discerned three different types of bourgeois (middle class) morality.

(1) The morality of the petty and middle bourgeoisie, as exemplified by Benjamin Franklin. His model man was characterized by financial reliability and was given to hard work, thrift, orderliness, foresight, prudence, and thinking in terms of money. He believed that personal independence should be achieved by everyday monetary gains and that 'every idle moment should be expressed in money terms'. Franklin was not concerned with class aspirations. On the other hand, Defoe, who had ideas similar in many respects to those of Franklin, felt that anyone who made money could aspire to be a gentleman, that is to say, a person of integrity, education, and good manners.

Against the opinion of Weber and Tawney, who had held that there is a causal relationship between religion and morality (e.g. puritanism and bourgeois morality), Ossowska claims that no such causal relationship can be firmly established. Franklin, for example, with his advocacy of and adherence to bourgeois morality, was a product of the Enlightenment rather than of puritanism. In other words Calvinism led to different consequences, depending on social circumstances and the characteristics of peoples and individuals.

(2) The morality which resulted from a fusion of feudal and bourgeois elements, as exemplified by L. B. Alberti. Bourgeois thought in Florentine capitalism was concerned with the efficient organization of estates rather than with getting rich. This was the climate of the ancients (Seneca and the Stoics) rather than of the Old Testament, moderation rather than mediocrity.

(3) The morality of the French bourgeoisie which as a result of their fight against religion, was hedonistic and exhuberant rather than ascetic and Cromwellian. It was produced by the struggle of the middle class for power, and is exemplified by Volney, an ideologist of the French Revolution and a moralist of the Enlightenment.

Whether the moral philosophy of the future will be the study of general axiology or felicitology or perfectionistics or ethics in the narrower sense is, at present, an open question. In adopting this approach, Ossowska in each of her main treatises succeeds in saying something new, interesting, and significant.

The tenor of Ossowska's moral writings, particularly the *Foundations*, is by and large pessimistic; at any rate it has been so regarded by many. The science of morality advocated by Ossowska reveals the inherently subjective, emotional, and even mythical character of moral norms and moral evaluations. In the light of the scrutiny of morality, it appears that no sound foundations can be provided which would justify objectively moral norms and moral evaluations.

If we compare the moral philosopher as traditionally conceived with the moral scientist as conceived by Ossowska, what is the main difference? A moral philosopher is expected to give some justification of moral norms and evaluations, which are taken for granted as indispensable, as basic units of the moral discourse. An attempt to uproot the concept of the moral norm as a meaningful concept, aimed at by the moral scientist, has been regarded by many as disturbing, if not perilous.

The moral philosopher in order to provide a justification for morals must speculate, and sometimes he speculates extravagantly. To emphasize a departure from speculation, Ossowska called her inquiry a theory of morality or the science of morals. In this inquiry the speculative element, indispensable in traditional moral philosophy for justifying the uniqueness and universal validity of morals, has been replaced by a dispassionate logical analysis.

To summarize, What did the British and the Polish linguistically oriented philosophers have in common? Respect for ordinary language. But the degree of this respect was different in the two countries. Among Polish philosophers, the linguistic approach took various forms according to the subject of inquiry. For each particular discipline, the linguistic idiom was suitably adapted. A particular version of ordinary language was chosen depending on the nature of problems to be investigated. In Britain, the extreme followers of ordinary language, the codifiers, represented the linguistic idiom in the purest possible form.

VII

ON THE MARGINS OF ANALYTICAL

PHILOSOPHY

To present Polish inter-war philosophy as solidly analytical would be incorrect. Some philosophers were only slightly influenced by the analytical movement. Others were hostile to it. Although they were not analytical philosophers, their criticism often helped to improve and indirectly to advance the analytical movement. Two other important movements in Polish philosophy—neo-Thomism and phenomenology—although rather indifferent to analytical philosophy, were none the less influenced by its logical rigour.

1 LEON CHWISTEK—THE MULTIPLICITY OF REALITIES

When describing the Polish analytical movement, one cannot ignore Chwistek (1884–1944).[1] He was too prominent a figure, too

---

[1] Chwistek began his university studies at the Jagiellonian University (Cracow) in 1902. He studied mathematics with Straszewski and Zaremba and philosophy with an eminent historian of philosophy, Father Pawlicki. For his doctorate in philosophy he produced a thesis 'On Axioms'. At Cracow he became interested in painting and joined the Academy of Fine Arts.

In the years 1913–1914 he lived in Paris where he became fascinated by new styles of painting. While in Paris, he fought a famous sabre duel with Count Borowski over his future wife, Olga Steinhaus.

In 1928, after many difficulties which stemmed from his rather eccentric style of life, he at last received his dozent degree at his old university in Cracow, and in 1934 the Chair of Mathematical Logic at the University of Lwów. There he remained until the war. In 1940–1942 he was a professor of Mathematical Logic at the University of Tiflis, Georgia. He died in Moscow in 1944.

original and controversial to be neglected. Since he is mainly known in the West as a logician, the 'constructor' of 'The Theory of Constructive Types' and the author of *The Limits of Science*, his other accomplishments will be presented here to make clear his relation to the analytical school.

Chwistek's most original idea in philosophy was that of the multiplicity of realities. He claimed that there is no single reality, but in fact many realities differing one from another. The theory of the multiplicity of realities was first systematically developed with regard to the arts. In his treatise of 1921, *The Multiplicity of Realities in Art*, Chwistek formulated a theory in which he said that: 'Differences among various types of painting correspond to different types of reality.' First he distinguished four basic types of reality and then matched them with four basic types of painting. These four types of reality are as follows:

1. Popular reality, which serves as the basis for the activities of our everyday life.
2. Physical reality, which is constructed by physics.
3. Sensory reality, the world of our immediate sense experience.
4. Visionary reality, which appears in our dreams, in hallucinations, in sub- or super-conscious states.

The types of painting which correspond to the above are:

1. Primitivism. Perspective, anatomy and other technical 'tricks' are out of question. However, it is permissible to imitate existing patterns or proceed by observation. Examples of this type of painting are to be found in Ancient Egypt, in the Middle Ages, and in the twentieth century.
2. Realism. This type of painting parallels the growth of

Hardly any Polish philosopher can be compared with Leon Chwistek as far as the wide and unusual scope of his interests is concerned. He was an avant-garde painter, a theoretician of modern art, a literary critic, and also a novelist. Above all he was an outstanding logician and an original philosopher.

He wrote in a very clear and straightforward manner. He was often pugnacious and even malicious in criticizing other people's opinions. He never bothered to present an opponent's point of view conscientiously. He was too original to repeat literally another person's ideas even while arguing with him.

classical physics. It reached its peak along with classical physics at the end of the nineteenth century.

3. Impressionism. The impressionist does not investigate the essence of things or their relationships to observation. He paints what he finds in his phenomenal field.

4. Futurism. Its approach is diametrically opposed to impressionism and is primarily theoretical. The basic problem of futurism is how to choose, among the totality of reproduced and sensory impressions, those which constitute elements of reality.

The theory of the multiplicity of realities is based on the assumption that a reality can be assumed to exist only if its elements are non-contradictory.

Apart from the distinction made between many types of reality, Chwistek conceived that each reality could be stratified according to a hierarchy of orders. In elaborating his own theory, Chwistek followed Russell's theory of logical types. Because he found Russell's solution to the antinomy of the classes unsatisfactory, he provided his own. Russell's solution was based on the theory of types (later called the simple theory of types). Chwistek's was based on the theory of constructive types, in which a hierarchy of languages replaced the hierarchy of types.

Chwistek's theory of constructive types[2] was an outgrowth of his work on the foundations of mathematics, which, if completed, would have had a value beyond the purely technical; the result would have been a proof of the coherence and non-contradictoriness of mathematics. A decisive argument would have been provided in favour of a rationalistic view of the world and against irrational metaphysics. A mathematician by training and a philosopher by temperament, Chwistek was aware of the difficulties involved in providing solid and consistent foundations for mathematics. In this endeavour, he was a leader of his times. Chwistek began his undertaking in 1928 with the aid of two pupils, J. Herzberg and W. Hetper, but never completed it. His investigations were interrupted by the war, and he died before he could resume them.

Chwistek was an excellent mathematical logician, and a metaphysically oriented philosopher. His penetrating ideas in mathe-

[2] L. Chwistek, 'The Theory of Constructive Types', *Roczniki Polskiego Towarzystwa Matematycznego* (Cracow, 1923–1924), in English.

matical logic were sometimes used to support and develop his dubious philosophical constructions, of which his multiplicity of realities was one.

The hierarchy of multiple realities (along with the careful distinction between their different orders) is a transposition of the theory of constructive types to general ontology. If we assert something about reality in the form of a statement, then this statement is an analysis of reality, or a means of analysing reality. But at the same time, the statement can be an object of analysis. This can lead to an antimony when the same judgement is used in the same argument, once as a means and secondly as an object of investigation. It is therefore necessary to make the content of our inquiry independent of the act of inquiry. The reality of phenomena to be investigated will be called 'reality of the first order'. The reality in which phenomena of the first order are being investigated and described will be the reality of the second order. If we wish to talk about the reality of the second order, to examine or describe it, we need to go a step further, to the third order, and so on *ad infinitum*. A reality of any order can be either popular or physical, sensory or visionary. People in different periods of their lives can live in different types of reality.

In advocating his views, Chwistek did not recognize the classical definition of truth (truth consists in the conformity of thought with reality). Instead, he was an advocate of a sort of coherence theory of truth (truth consists in an inner consistency and coherence within the framework of a particular type of reality of a particular order). His attitude towards the concept of truth was not all that separated Chwistek from the main analytical trend in Poland. His entire concept of philosophy was distinctive. Although Chwistek participated creatively in the development of mathematical logic, he did not believe that a system of scientific philosophy, modelled on systems of formal logic, as suggested by Łukasiewicz, could ever be provided.

... it is an undeniable fact that the construction of a homogeneous system describing reality, which would satisfy all postulates of life and would be based on the principles of formal logic, is inconceivable. Even if such a system were to reach a high point of perfection, we could always imagine forms of life which would transcend the limitations of the system and relegate the reality embraced in the system to an inferior position. ... Reality cannot be grasped and described in one homogeneous system because of this simple reason, that there is not just one reality, but many. Therefore, the theory of reality must contain a multiplicity of possible systems.[3]

A modern painter and a theorist of modern art, Chwistek wished to integrate into his philosophy all aspects of life and art, and therefore was inevitably at odds with analytical philosophers who concentrated only on those problems which have cognitive content and can be tackled rationally and formulated unequivocally. The fulness of life and the richness of art cannot be grasped, in Chwistek's view, by rational means alone; therefore, a sort of irrationality is inevitable. On the other hand, as we have previously seen, Chwistek was a zealous defender of rationality in the philosophy of mathematics. This inconsistency among others made him unpopular and unacceptable to the philosophers of the analytical movement.

To sum up, Chwistek did not create a complete system, either in philosophy or in the arts; his logical concepts connected with his attempt to reconstruct the foundations of mathematics remained unfinished. His interests were too many for him to be able to follow through any one of them thoroughly. However, some of his logical concepts (e.g. the constructive theory of types) were incorporated into the body of logic. His theory of the multiplicity of realities, although a strange creation, was an original one—a proof of boldness and independence of his mind. His ideas about the arts were stimulating and retained their vitality and relevance today.

2 BENEDICT BERNSTEIN—THE CONSTRUCTION OF THE ABSOLUTE BY MEANS OF LOGIC AND MATHEMATICS

Benedict Bernstein (1880–1948) was very different. He was rather a Polish McTaggart, although by training a mathematician. He had studied philosophy simultaneously with mathematics, and thus had a suitable background for participating in the analytical movement. Moreover, he attempted to construct philosophy in a scientific way by the abundant use of mathematics and mathematical logic. However, he had very little in common with the analytical trend in Poland. His was a very ambitious and highly

---

[3] L. Chwistek, *Wielość rzeczywistości w sztuce i inne szkice literackie* (*The Multiplicity of Realities in Art and other Literary Essays*) (Warsaw, 1960), p. 118.

speculative sort of philosophy; he has been rightly described as the posthumous child of Polish romantic philosophy. He was a 'pure' metaphysician, an ontologist concerned with the construction of proofs of Being. The whole complicated mathematical and logical apparatus was used only to support preconceived ontological ideas, to decorate his system. It is not surprising, therefore, that in the period when minimalism, caution, and analysis were dominant in Poland, he had no influence at all. He was recognized in other countries and was invited to lecture in Helsinki and at the Sorbonne; in Poland he was academically recognized only in that a chair of Philosophy, in Cracow, was given to him. Although the titles of some of his works, for example *Elements of Philosophy as an Exact Science* (Warsaw, 1916), might lead us to expect elaborations of analytical philosophy in the strict sense, this is very deceptive.[4] In short, he was not an analytical philosopher.

As one can see from Bernstein's case, a 'scientific programme' and a liberal use of mathematical logic do not automatically classify a philosophy as analytical. The minimalistic standpoint, caution, common sense, and a sharpened sensitivity towards language are indispensable characteristics as well.

3 LESSER FIGURES OF THE TWARDOWSKI SCHOOL

Among Twardowski's pupils there were those who did not make their names known outside Poland but who nevertheless played an important rôle in that country, participating in discussions, writing papers, and teaching in Twardowski's way. Two who particularly deserve notice were Tadeusz Czeżowski and Zygmunt Zawirski.

Czeżowski (born 1890) was a man of broad philosophical knowledge, solid logical training, and a penchant for logical strictness. In the early 1920s he actively participated in the development of mathematical logic in Poland; one might say that he then belonged to the 'avant-garde' of Polish analytical philosophers. He was particularly interested in modernizing Aristo-

---

[4] His main works were: *Architektonika świata* (*The Architectonics of the World*) 3 vols. (Warsaw, 1934); *Struktural-logischer und ontologischer Aspekt des freudschen Begriffes* (Vienna, 1937). His works amount in all to 48 items, all strictly 'philosophical', concerned mainly with ontology and carried out at a very high level of abstraction.

telian logic.[5] Later, however, he did not establish himself in any particular domain. For a few years he left academic life to be Under-Secretary in the Ministry of Education. When he returned to the world of scholarship he did not keep pace with new developments in logic. His paper on singular propositions, published in 1955 in *Mind*,[6] indicates a similar line to that of the 1920s.

Czeżowski was more moderate in his views than his colleagues, and conceived of philosophy in a more traditional way. Because of this he was criticized for eclecticism. He had a fertile mind and moved easily among various branches of philosophy—logic, epistemology, the history of philosophy, and the history of logic. His best known book in Poland is perhaps his *Logic* (1949) where he systematically applied, before Prior did so, Łukasiewicz's notation to the problems of the propositional calculus.

His versatility is evident in his *Philosophical Addresses*, a book of essays published in 1958.[7] The first part, entitled 'Theory and Reality', is devoted to a discussion of more academic problems ranging over all branches of philosophy with the exception of aesthetics. In the second part, significantly entitled 'The Meaning of Life', 'human' problems are discussed such as courage, fear, anxiety, happiness, etc. Czeżowski's philosophical attitude, and in particular his philosophical neutralism, is perhaps best expressed in the essay. 'Two Views on the World', in which he analyses two conflicting tendencies in the history of philosophy. The first, empirical, down-to-earth, and factual ultimately crystallized as materialism; ths second, speculative, metaphysical, and non-commonsensical, ultimately led to anti-materialism. According to Czeżowski, the sharp edges of this dichotomy have been

[5] *Teoria klas* (*Theory of the Classes*) (Lwów, 1918); 'Imiona i zdania' (Names and Propositions), *Przeg. Filoz.*, XXI (1918); 'Zmienne i funkcje' (Variables and Functions), *Przeg. Filoz.* (1919); *O pewnych stosunkach logicznych* (*On Some Logical Relations*) (Lwów, 1921); *Klasyczna nauka o sądzie i wniosku w świetle logiki współczesnej* (*The Classical Theory of Judgement and Inference in the Light of Modern Logic*) (Wilno, 1927); *O pewnym uogólnieniu logiki klasycznej* (*On a Certain Generalization of Classical Logic*) (Lwów, 1931).

[6] A discussion on singular propositions was initiated by Czeżowski with the paper: 'On Certain Peculiarities of Singular Propositions', *Mind*, LXIV, No. 255 (July 1955), followed by J. L. Mackie: ' "This" as a Singular Quantifier', *Mind*, LXVII, No. 268 (October 1958), and Leon Gumański: 'Singular Propositions and "This" as a Quantifier', *Mind*, LXIX, No. 276 (October 1960).

[7] T. Czeżowski, *Odczyty filozoficzne* (*Philosophical Addresses*) (Toruń: Tow. Naukowe w Toruniu, 1958).

blurred by modern science, which has bridged the empirical and spiritual worlds. No particular clash with contemporary physics would occur if we choose to call physical phenomena the manifestation of spirit, or mental phenomena the manifestation of matter, although in either case there would be considerable difficulties in ascribing exact meaning to these phrases. 'The conflict between materialist and anti-materialist attitudes', Czeżowski wrote, 'has been dissolved in contemporary thought because we have ceased to employ contexts in which these two expressions have a tangible meaning.'[8] Although from a scientific point of view, Czeżowski continues, this juxtaposition has sense no longer, the terms in question (materialism, anti-materialism) are still vigorously used—as slogans, as a means of influencing attitudes, and as banners in the fight for realization of non-academic (practical, ideological, and social) goals.

Czeżowski's position of philosophical neutralism was, as a matter of fact, very close to that of Twardowski, and in contrast to those of Kotarbiński and Ajdukiewicz, who were committed to traditional philosophical problems. Czeżowski's lack of strong conviction resulted in a lack of persuasiveness in his argument and in a certain indefiniteness in his views.

Z. Zawirski (1882–1948) was also in Twardowski's tradition; he was an excellent teacher, lucid in lectures and clear in his writing. He was mainly concerned with the philosophical aspects of modern physics and also with the philosophical implications of different views about the nature of mathematics. He was, in short, a philosopher of science. Physics moulded his philosophical outlook. Once acquainted with Einstein's theory, he became its enthusiastic adherent. In *Philosophical Relativism and the Physical Theory of Relativity*, he held that Einstein's theory brings about the defeat of epistemological realism. If Newton's views on absolute space and absolute time are discarded, then it is clear that Mach is right, and therefore that science investigates only 'phenomenological reality'. Later, however, his faith in 'phenomenological reality' was gradually to diminish, and his adherence to epistemological realism was markedly to increase. In 'The Axiomatic Method and the Natural Sciences'[9] he found it inexplicable from

[8] Op. cit., p. 24.
[9] Z. Zawirski, 'Metoda aksjomatyczna a przyrodoznawstwo' (The Axiomatic Method and the Natural Sciences), *Kwart. Filoz.* (1924).

the phenomenological standpoint that the data of experience correspond so closely to each other in various frameworks of reference; this seemed to prove the existence of invariant laws of nature.

In a still later work, *L'Evolution de la notion du temps* (1938),[10] he defended the position which he called 'moderate realism': time exists objectively, but only in conjunction with matter, to put the view very crudely. In this work he argued against conventionalism and against philosophical relativism, which he had previously advocated from the standpoint of the classical theory of truth.

Like most Polish analytical philosophers, Zawirski's attitude towards the Vienna Circle was ambivalent. As one whose philosophical views stemmed from science, he could not fail to appreciate some undertakings of the Circle; of some others he disapproved, particularly of Carnap's formal mode of expression, which he called an 'escape from reality'. In a number of articles on the philosophy of mathematics,[11] Zawirski mainly attempted to inform the Polish philosophical world about new achievements abroad and to relate these achievements to what was being done in Poland. He did not produce new and highly original ideas, but his competence in discussing the problems of modern science was unquestionable and his talent for popularizing the philosophy of science unrivalled in Poland.

The group of analytical philosophers, some of greater and some of smaller importance, was in Poland quite large. However, a proliferation of names is not our intention, and an adequate treatment of *all* contributions to analytical philosophy is far beyond our scope.

In passing I should like to mention some members of the second generation of Twardowski's pupils. The emergence of quite a number of accomplished women philosophers is conspicuous. Perhaps the most distinguished are Maria Ossowska, Janina Kotarbińska, Maria Kokoszyńska, Seweryna Łuszczewska-Romahnowa, Janina Hosiasson-Lindenbaum, and Izydora Dąbska. The contributions of Ossowska and Kotarbińska have already been discussed in Chapter VI. Kokoszyńska was briefly

[10] For which he was awarded the Rignano Prize by *Scientia*.

[11] Z. Zawirski, *Stosunek logiki do matematyki w świetle badań współczesnych* (*The Relation of Logic to Mathematics in the Light of Modern Research*) (Cracow, 1927); *Stosunek logiki wielowartościowej i rachunku prawdopodobieństwa* (*The Relation of Many-Valued Logic to the Calculus of Probability*) (Poznań, 1934); 'Geneza i rozwój logiki intuicjonistycznej' (The Origin and Development of the Intuitionistic Logic), *Kwart. Filoz.*, XVI (1946).

mentioned in Chapter II in connection with the semantic concept of truth; after the Second World War she continued to work within the realm of semantics, following Ajdukiewicz's semantic epistemology. Her main post-war contributions were published in *Studia Logica* and are thus available to the English reader. Mme Łuszczewska-Romahnowa has been concerned with problems similar in nature to those of Kokoszyńska. Mme Hosisson-Lindenbaum (1899–1942) was interested mainly in the methodology of science and wrote at length on the theory of induction. I. Dąbska seems always to have been more traditionally than analytically minded. Her interests ranged over a wide spectrum. Her studies in the history of philosophy (*A History of Ancient Philosophy*, 1931, and *French Scepticism*, 1958) are particularly notable.

Some philosophers educated in the 1920s and 1930s, although they began with inquiries into logical matters, moved away from logic after a time to quite different disciplines. Perhaps the most notable example is that of St. Ossowski. He made some contributions to semantics, moved to aesthetics, and finally chose sociology as his main field. He was not alone in making the transition from logic to sociology.

Some analytical philosophers, although educated in Poland, produced their major works abroad, where they settled permanently. One can hardly say that their contributions belong to the Polish analytical movement.

4 WITKACY—ENFANT TERRIBLE OF POLISH PHILOSOPHY

To conclude this discussion of inter-war Polish analytical philosophy, we shall consider one of the outstanding eccentrics of the period—Stanisław Ignacy Witkiewicz, popularly called Witkacy.[12]

[12] Witkiewicz was born in Warsaw in 1885. He had no proper systematic education and was at the university for a short time only; he never held any academic or official post. He earned his living by painting 'psychological' portraits. In behaviour, he always seemed to hover on the verge of genius and madness. His life was a series of creative eruptions interspersed by periods of acute frustration and intellectual impotence. He committed suicide on 18 September 1939, when the Germans were at the gates of Warsaw.

Before the war, Witkiewicz was not understood at all. He was the subject of derision and was attacked by the establishment. With the passing of time, it has been discovered that immature though some of his ideas may have been, they are highly original. The influence of his work has grown considerably. A sign of final academic recognition is the fact that a book in memory of

To mention him, although he did not belong to the analytical movement, is to contrast even more sharply the development of Polish analytical philosophy with the intellectual and philosophical background of Poland in inter-war times. Witkacy started as an artist and as a prophet of a new art. Later, however, he determined that philosophy was his destiny. In his system of biological materialism, he attempted to grasp all aspects of 'real existence as such', and not to fall into a crippling one-sidedness, so characteristic of all former monistic systems. His doctrine was a kind of monadism. There exist only monads and qualities, but monads exist in one way and qualities in another. The existence of the first is independent, while that of the second is dependent. All particular living beings are monads. Because the system referred only to material objects, it was a materialism; because living beings were given a priority, it was a biological materialism. The main intention was to overcome all the defects characteristic of existing monistic systems which,

. . . [while] operating with the so-called 'sexless' concepts, simultaneously smuggle in by the back door concepts which imply the duality of existence: (*a*) 'I' as a corporeal, existing, lasting and feeling body, and the surrounding world, and (*b*) the division of everything into dependent elements, that of time and that of space.

Witkacy's main philosophical work did not belong to the analytical movement; in fact, he had a singular contempt for analytical philosophy. In his uncompromising attack on the movement, he accused it of narrowness and futility. In a number of articles, [13] he attempted to 'unmask' the real nature of analytical

[13] St. I. Witkiewicz, 'O ontologicznej beznadziejności logiki, fizykalizmu i pseudonaukowego monizmu i o perspektywach koncepcji monadystycznej' (On the Ontological Hopelessness of Logic, Physicalism, and Pseudo-scientific Monism and on the Perspectives of the Monadistic Conception), *Przeg. Filoz.*, XXXIX (1936); 'Błędne koło w kole wiedeńskim' (A Vicious Circle in the Vienna Circle), *Ruch Filoz.* (1939).

Witkiewicz was published in 1957 sponsored by Tadeusz Kotarbiński: *Stanisław Ignacy Witkiewicz, człowiek i twórca* (*Stanisław Ignacy Witkiewicz, Man and Creator*). In this book Kotarbiński wrote: 'All his work bears the signature of a genius; but the seal of one who is very immature indeed . . . Witkiewicz, the philosopher, pored for many solitary hours over works of philosophers . . . and at the end of his life was quite well read in philosophy, but he was never able to overcome the lack of basic, elementary logical training. . . . I do not know any work of his which could be considered as fully mature and free from strangenesses, weaknesses and blots.'

philosophy. He wrote: 'Logistics is more hypocritical than the worst kind of idealistic or materialistic metaphysics. This contempt and carelessness of logisticians, as regards their utter incapability to cope with the most rudimentary and important things, is simply outrageous.'

In spite of his eccentricity, Witkacy, through his exceptional and almost religious devotion to philosophy, and the controversy he aroused, has undoubtedly contributed to the intensity and vivacity of philosophical life in Poland.

Before the war, Polish philosophy presented a lively and diversified picture. Analytical philosophy was supreme but did not inhibit other trends of thought; it attracted the most powerful and original minds, but capable attacks were made upon it. Although its contributions appear to be of permanent value, they are not overwhelming in number. It gained admiration for its lasting achievements, but also aroused doubts because of its narrow scope. It reached a general public and the phrase 'exact philosophy' came into use to designate a new philosophy, different from misty and vague traditional philosophies.

VIII

ANALYTICAL PHILOSOPHY AND MARXISM

Before the Second World War, philosophy blossomed in Poland. The older generation (Twardowski's pupils) were at the peak of their creative productivity and they were joined by their own pupils in the 1920s and 1930s. The hope that a new philosophy could be constructed on the model of the deductive sciences still prevailed.

After the war, the picture was entirely different. The whole country was in ruins. Intellectual and cultural life was paralysed. Universities and libraries were devastated and had to be organized anew. In the face of more urgent needs, what importance had the subtlety of argument so characteristic of the Polish analytical movement? Furthermore, the ranks of philosophers had been seriously thinned. Given these circumstances one can hardly talk of the continuity of analytical philosophy. In any case, there was still another obstacle to analysis. After the initial period of recovery from the devastation of the war, when intellectual and philosophical life began to revive in 1949 and 1950, Marxism was superimposed.

At the end of the 1940s Marxism became the official ideology, with the sanction of law, in all the countries of Eastern Europe. In the arts and humanities all phenomena were to be interpreted in terms of historical materialism. All schools of philosophy were either to be converted to Marxism or liquidated. This subjugation was carried out in most socialist countries fairly severely. In Poland, however, the picture was rather different.

The main campaign in Poland was fabricated against analytical

P   213

philosophy on account of its special significance and influence.[1] Catholic philosophy was less attacked. This may seem rather strange, because analytical philosophy was closer to Marxism, through its secular character, through its realism (and in many instances materialism), and through its determination to eliminate such pseudo-problems as those of the Absolute, the Transcendent and Being. There were no bridges between Catholic philosophy and Marxism. But just because of this, there was no fear of any influence of Catholic philosophy on Marxism. With analytical philosophy there were many points of convergence, and in order to prevent an 'infection' of Marxism, differences were emphasized and over-emphasized. To make these differences effective, a detailed 'Marxist criticism' of analytical philosophy took place which consisted in comparing all the tenets of analytical philosophers with the dogmas of Marxism. Polish philosophers did not remain silent when they were misrepresented. A lively discussion took place. The results of this collision between Marxism and analytical philosophy were far from those anticipated by the Marxists; strangely enough, however, they seem to follow from the principles of Marxist sociology. The Marxists expected to uproot all 'bourgeois' philosophy by silencing some philosophers and converting others to their orthodoxy. However, it is Marxist doctrine that if we act in a certain environment we are bound to be affected by it; the stronger the features of the environment, the more influence it exerts. In any society the environmental forces are the traditions of that society. In a philosophical school, they are the tradition of that school. Because of the tradition of critical thinking and because of the 'logical environment' of the analytical school in Poland, Marxists were influenced more than they anticipated—although no more than they should have predicted.

In short, as the result of the counter-pressure of analytical philosophy on Marxism, something emerged which seems to be a specifically Polish product, and which I would like to call analytical-linguistic Marxism. Three stages can be distinguished in the development of this new Marxism which is, in fact, still in the process of formation.

[1] A detailed technical description of the struggle between Marxism and philosophies in Poland is to be found in Z. Jordan's huge volume, *Philosophy and Ideology*. This book, though meticulous and virtuously thorough, differs in approach from that here adopted.

The Impact of Marxism on Analytical Philosophy

1. The actual collision and the controversy between analytical philosophers and Marxists (1951–1955). At the end of this period the Marxist attack abated; Marxists then reformulated their attitude towards their adversaries and in turn began to evolve along new lines.

2. The period of convulsive, unsystematic revisions in Marxism, interlinked with intense social ferment (1955–1958).

3. The period of systematic growth which incorporated, under the label of 'creative Marxism', many previous heresies and which, by expanding the scope of orthodoxy, changed its previous character (1958–present).

Why did the Marxist offensive lose its impetus in Poland? Why did it not succeed in subjugating all philosophies to Marxism, as in other Socialist countries? At least three further answers can be given: (*a*) the attitude of Polish 'bourgeois' philosophers towards their critics, (*b*) the subject under discussion—abstract and highly specialized and therefore not easily amenable to discussion in terms of the stereotyped dichotomy of idealism-materialism, (*c*) the broad-mindedness and relative tolerance of Polish Marxists.

(*a*) Outstanding representatives of the analytical school in Poland enjoyed a considerable reputation in Europe before the war. They were quite aware of the value of their accomplishments. It was not possible to silence them or to order them to profess a new doctrine and so a controversy occurred. It is to the credit of the Marxists that such a controversy did occur and that analytical philosophers were allowed to defend their views openly and freely. Kotarbiński replied to a critic.

> As I was really much interested in my philosophical and social–political opinions, and wished to be enlightened upon this matter, I acquired a recently published book by Bronisław Baczko concerning this very subject.
>
> While reading it, I learned that my opinions on the above-mentioned matters are, in actual fact, entirely different from what I thought they were. Since, as the author rightly asserts, my opinions have not changed very much for at least twenty years, and are still as they were, a serious discrepancy appears to exist between our opinions about my philosophical views.[2]

Kotarbiński was in a particularly favourable position to argue with Marxists because his concretism was a materialistic system

[2] Kotarbiński, 'Odpowiedź' (A Reply) *Myśl Filoz.*, 2 (4), 1952, p. 315.

par excellence. Therefore, he did not hesitate to assert that the semantic idiom is harmless if we explicitly state that whatever exists is a body, but the admission of such entities as 'the general' and 'the particular' (categories peculiar to Marxist epistemology) is not harmless because they imply concessions to idealism. That Western philosophers were involved in semantics Kotarbiński considered as having little relevance for his doctrine. He insisted that if something was mistaken in his doctrine, the 'what' and 'why' of it should be shown. He was ready to accept criticism insofar as it was logically acceptable; ideological arguments, according to which some philosophical topics are socially poisonous, he discarded as irrelevant.

Ajdukiewicz too replied to criticism. In a lengthy reply to Schaff[3] he asserted that the presentation of his ideas gave such a preposterous picture of them that any philosopher actually holding such opinions would not be considered sane. He argued that the criticism of his works did not include valid arguments, and that his alleged idealism was in fact being criticized from an idealistic standpoint. He pointed out that a valid criticism of any doctrine requires an ability and a desire to understand it; for his part, he thought that his doctrine was not understood by his Marxist critics. In the final part of his reply he wrote:

> The problems I dealt with were different from those Marxist philosophers are concerned with. Different problems require different methods. But that which is different is not necessarily contradictory, and may even be allied. What I advocated was often different from the materialistic doctrine, but it was not contradictory to it because quite different problems were considered.[4]

(*b*) Highly specialized semantic problems dominated the interests of analytical philosophers. Even when tackling traditional problems, they used a rather highly technical language. Marxists thus had difficulty in applying their stereotyped pattern of criticism. The problems at issue were subtle, and the lack of philosophical sophistication of many Marxists stood in the way of competent participation in the controversy.

(*c*) Polish Marxists were relatively tolerant. This was partly due

---

[3] Adam Schaff, O *poglądach filozoficznych Kazimierza Ajdukiewicza (On the Philosophical Opinions of Kazimierz Ajdukiewicz)* (Warsaw, 1951).

[4] Ajdukiewicz, 'W sprawie artykułu Profesora Schaffa o moich poglądach filozoficznych' (With regard to Professor Schaff's Article on my Philosophical Opinions), *Myśl Filoz.*, 2 (8), 1953, p. 334.

to the factors (*a*) and (*b*) and partly to the fact that Polish Marxists, some of whom were educated before the war, had a better comprehension of philosophical problems than, for example, Russian Marxists. Analytical philosophers were not really persecuted. No one was put into prison for advocating non-Marxist philosophy. No one was deprived of the essentials of life for being identified as an 'idealist'. Tatarkiewicz, since he was not a logician and therefore could not teach philosophy under the guise of logic, went to Cracow to teach the history of art. He returned to Warsaw in 1956 to take the Chair of Aesthetics. Ingarden was more dangerous with his idealism, as expressed in his treatise *Spór o istnienie świata* (*Controversy over the Existence of the World*). He was compelled to give up teaching but was given the job of translating Kant. His translation of the *Critique of Pure Reason* is a masterpiece and a valuable contribution to the Polish *Library of Philosophical Classics*.[5] Other scholars did translations of philosophical classics which were published by the State, and by 1966 these exceeded a hundred in number. The publication of these works was one of the enterprises which brought credit to the Marxists. In the *Library of Philosophical Classics*, scholars who were ideological 'risks' could find an occupation either as translators or editors. This 'liberalism' of Polish Marxists is particularly worth mentioning when we consider the situation in other countries of the Socialist bloc. In Hungary, for example, Lukács and Fogarasi, both Marxists before the war, were persecuted in the 1950s for displaying theoretical interests instead of employing their intellects to provide philosophical justification for ever-changing party policies and directives.

It is true that Marxists in Poland exercised a great deal of pressure on non-Marxist philosophers: they tried to discourage everyone from following any philosophy other than Marxism; they attempted to drive all analytically minded philosophers into mathematical logic, conceived as a branch of mathematics.

2 THE FORMATIVE STAGE OF ANALYTICAL–LINGUISTIC MARXISM

1956 is considered to have been the year of Great Change in Polish philosophy and in all of Polish intellectual life. Yet Polish Marxism had been undergoing an evolution long before that.

[5] *Biblioteka klasyków filozofii.*

Adam Schaff's work on the Marxist concept of truth[6] showed that by 1956 he had already assimilated many of the ideas of analytical philosophy. His criticism of the correspondence theory of truth should not overshadow the fact that the Marxist theory of truth was for the first time extensively and seriously discussed. This monograph became a classical work on the theory of truth in the Marxist world.

The years before 1956 were the so-called years of 'militancy' in which Marxism seemed to be dominant. Marxists and analytical philosophers were at odds, particularly since Marxists held that formal logic was an empty game, that only dialectical logic mattered and therefore that the law of contradiction could be ignored. Analytical philosophers considered that disregarding the law of contradiction meant the end of critical, rational, and intelligible scholarship. In about 1955 a kind of reconciliation occurred between the two camps. Marxism no longer claimed to have a monopoly of truth.

Schaff's paper, 'Marxist Dialectics and the Principle of Contradiction',[7] was a decisive breakthrough. In this paper the realm of dialectical logic was clearly separated from the realm of formal logic. Dialectical logic, stemming from the laws of dialectics which govern the development of nature and society, was not to be mistaken for formal logic, whose laws are concerned *not* with developmental processes, but with verbal expressions describing particular aspects of phenomena in particular ways and at particular times. Abandoning the claim that contradictions should be recognized because they 'reflect the intrinsic nature of developmental processes' was of crucial importance. Various contradictions which according to Marxists reflect the nature of reality were shown to be reconcilable with formal logic.

In promoting this new view on the reconcilability of dialectical logic with formal logic, Schaff in many instances followed Ajdukiewicz's argument put forth in 'Change and Contradiction' (1948).[8] This paper was devoted to a critical examination of the arguments which support the thesis that any change, movement

---

[6] *Z zagadnień marksistowskiej teorii prawdy* (*Some Problems of the Marxist Theory of Truth*) (Warsaw, 1951); 2nd edn., 1959.

[7] A. Schaff, 'Dialektyka marksistowska a zasada sprzeczności' (Marxist Dialectics and the Law of Contradiction), *Myśl Filoz.*, 4, 1955.

[8] K. Ajdukiewicz, 'Zmiana i sprzeczność' (Change and Contradiction), *Myśl Współczesna*, Nos. 8 and 9, 1948.

among others, implies contradiction or, to put it differently, that 'if a statement asserting the occurrence of a change is true, then two contradictory statements must be true'.[9] In particular, Ajdukiewicz gave a new interpretation to Zeno's paradox. If an arrow moves from one place to another, then if we consider a point P on its route at a particular moment M, we must conclude that the arrow is at point P and, because it is moving, is not at the point P. Thus the law of contradiction is violated. Ajdukiewicz quite ingeniously argued that this conclusion is based on the confusion between the meanings of the expression 'at a particular moment M'. In the first instance, when we say that the arrow lies in a certain spot P at a particular moment M, the expression 'at a particular moment M' means a point in time, an accent of time. In the second instance, when it is asserted that because the arrow is moving at a particular moment M, it leaves the place P and therefore is not in the place P, by the expression 'at a particular moment' is meant a tiny stretch of time. Hence the contradiction. The contradiction disappears if we replace the confusing expression: 'the arrow is and is not at a point P' by the following one: 'the arrow *passes* point P'. Schaff accepted this interpretation and added that, although reality can be seen as contradictory in itself, the logical law of contradiction must be unconditionally observed. In this Schaff was opposing Engels and Lenin who had questioned the universal validity of the law of contradiction. Schaff considered this a mistake badly in need of rectification. Since Schaff's paper, an overwhelming majority of Polish Marxists and a substantial number of Russian Marxists have agreed that formal logic has a different realm and does not have to be rejected because it disagrees with dialectical logic.[10]

The development of Marxist philosophy was perhaps most accelerated by the young Polish Marxist, Leszek Kołakowski. He is often considered to be *the* revisionist, but the label does not really do him justice. It is not appropriate to consider philosophers

9 Op. cit., p. 35.

10 However, even nowadays in the Soviet Union there are logicians, such as, for example, V. I. Cherkiasov (*Materialistic Dialectics as Logic and the Theory of Knowledge*—originally in Russian, Moscow, 1962) who claim that the apparatus of formal logic is irreconcilable with the directives issued by the Communist Party. Consequently, according to Cherkiasov, Schaff's ideas about dialectical and formal logic are 'incompatible with materialism and hostile to it', as well as 'incompatible with the achievements of contemporary science'.

as 'revisionists'. Revisionism is a term suitable in connection with ideologies, understood as systems of uncritical beliefs, but not suitable in connection with philosophies, understood as sets of statements which are rationally justified. The philosopher, if he is worthy of the name, must question and revise. Therefore he is always a revisionist.

Kołakowski as a philosopher attempted to develop the moral issues of Marxist philosophy. He called himself a Marxist. However, Marxists in Poland, and particularly in other countries of the Socialist bloc, often question his adherence to Marxist philosophy. His work is admittedly individual and unorthodox. It shows, in part, an analytical character. Kotarbiński and Mme Kotarbińska were his teachers during his formative period which accounts in part for the coherence and stringency of his arguments. Kotarbiński's personal influence and his 'independent ethics' most probably inspired Kołakowski's passionate defence of the autonomy of morals. Perhaps no other Polish philosopher in the twentieth century has defended the autonomy of morals as persuasively; certainly no other Marxist philosopher has been more incisive and more penetrating on questions of morals. Kołakowski has summarized his position in this way:

> Practical choice is continually being made in a world in which the category of 'duty' governs, not that of 'being'. These two categories *Sollen* and *Sein* [ought and is] characterize two different attitudes and two different visions of reality between which one attempts to reconstruct a constantly collapsing bridge.[11]

These two attitudes are not reducible to each other. The recognition of historical inevitability does not release us from having to take decisions in particular instances, because it is impossible to separate the elements of inevitability from those of free will. Inevitability is an attribute of past events; with respect to future events, inevitability appears less certain and the room for free choice and independent decisions much larger. Hence it follows that no faith in inevitability can release us from moral choice and moral responsibility.

> It is not true that historiosophy determines the basic choices of our life—they are determined by our moral conscience. . . . The most

[11] L. Kołakowski, 'Odpowiedzialność i historia' (Responsibility and History), Part IV: 'Nadzieja i materia historyczna,' (The Substance and Hope of History), *Nowa Kultura*, 38 (391), 1957, p. 4.

persuasive theory is in itself unable to cause us to lift a finger. Practical choice is a choice of a value, that is to say, a moral act which is something for which everybody individually takes personal responsibility.[12]

This was not a declaration of voluntarism. Moral responsibility, it was argued, is compatible with determinism; moreover, the two do not exclude but supplement each other.[13] Individual destiny cannot be determined by general historical laws of class struggle, just as the behaviour of a particular gas particle in any given instance cannot be predicted from the general laws governing the mechanics of gases. The conditioning of our life through social and economic circumstances and through our own past does not make us the slaves of external reality; 'Individual action remains in the absolute sovereignty of the individual. The main tracks of our life we tread at our own expense.' (Here Kołakowski quotes Walt Whitman):

> Not I, not any one else can travel that road for you;
> You must travel it for yourself.

The culmination of the argument, which is not only an expression of a philosophical standpoint, but also the protest of a humanist, reads as follows:

No one is released from the moral responsibility of condemning a crime because of his theoretical conviction about the inevitability of the crime. No one is released from the moral duty of struggling against a system, doctrine, or social condition which he considers as wretched and inhuman because he regards them as historically inevitable. We protest against any form of moral relativism which assumes that criteria for moral evaluation of human behaviour can be deduced from the knowledge of the secrets of the *Weltgeist*.[14]

Kołakowski's interpretation of historical inevitability and moral responsibility, although topics derived from the classical repertoire of the Hegelian Marxists (as opposed to Marxists of positivistic orientation), is based upon logical tenets. The main arguments against traditional Marxist moral philosophy are of a

[12] Op. cit., p. 4.
[13] L. Kołakowski, 'Odpowiedzialność i historia,' Part III: 'Sumienie i postęp społeczny' (Social Conscience and Progress), *Nowa Kultura*, 37 (390), 1957, p. 5.
[14] L. Kołakowski, 'Odpowiedzialność i historia', Part II: 'Narkotyk wielkiego demiurga' (The Narcotic of the Great Demiurge), *Nowa Kultura*, 36 (389), 1957, p. 4.

logical nature, namely: (*a*) no value judgement can be deduced from statements about facts, and (*b*) no moral evaluation of an individual human action can be extracted logically from the general laws governing the development of society.

The essays discussed above enlivened the intellectual and moral atmosphere in Poland in 1956; they influenced many non-Marxists and gained recognition for Kołakowski in the West. They had little direct influence, however, on the course of Marxist philosophy. His 'leap' was too great to follow. What Kołakowski considered as an attempt to improve Marxism was in official circles called an attempt to liquidate it. Consequently his ideas exerted influence only in so far as Schaff incorporated some of them into his own writings and so in a diluted form, distributed them in the Marxist world at large. Kołakowski had a significant indirect influence on the attitudes of other Marxists; his work brought about an increase of flexibility, greater penetration and insight among Polish Marxists. The peculiarity of his position lies in the fact that while his favourite problems are those with which Hegelian Marxists are principally concerned (e.g. the individual and infinity,[15] historical inevitability and moral responsibility, etc.) his methodological criteria are those of positivist-Marxists.

The division of Marxism into schools has been acknowledged by Marxists themselves, or at any rate by Polish Marxists. Schaff observed in his essays entitled *Marxism and Existentialism* that philosophers are not only divided into materialists and idealists, but also separate into two other lines, one of Ionian descent concerned with external reality and its exploration, the other, a Socratic line, devoted to man and the search for 'self'. The attitude of the first line is best represented in contemporary philosophy by neo-positivists, that of the second by existentialists.

Another Polish Marxist philosopher, W. Krajewski, elaborated in detail the idea of different schools.[16] He distinguished between the *scienticist* and the *humanist* schools of Marxist philosophy, or between positivist Marxists and Hegelian Marxists. Their domains do not exclude one another, but each has specific character-

[15] L. Kołakowski, *Jednostka i nieskończoność* (*The Individual and Infinity*) (Warsaw, 1959). This was an account of the philosophy of Spinoza, Kołakowski's favourite philosopher, but the work contains as much Kołakowski's as Spinoza's ideas.

[16] W. Krajewski, 'Spory i szkoły w filozofii marksistowskiej' (Schools and Disputes Within Marxism) in *Szkice filozoficzne* (*Philosophical Essays*), (Warsaw, 1963).

istics. The former is chiefly concerned with the theory and methodology of science, has a high regard for and tries to apply, in Krajewski's words, 'the characteristically neo-positivistic logical methods, semantic analysis, the structural analysis of science, etc.' The second school is mainly occupied with the problems of man and the history of human society; it is concerned also with such Hegelian problems as the dialectical nature of reality. Philosophers of the second school 'are engaged in developing dialectical logic and tend to underestimate formal logic'. The chief difference between the two schools is that of the method used by the representatives of each in considering the problems of the other. The scienticists (positivists) may be interested in the philosophy of man, but will approach the subject in a scientific manner employing logical analysis: '. . . irrespective of the issues involved, they want to treat philosophy as "une science"—a science as exact as is possible—while the "humanists" regard it rather as "letters".'[17]

The prevailing opinion in the West is that most Marxists are Hegelian Marxists. It is usually not realized that the first school of Marxist philosophy, the positivist or (as it would prefer to call itself, the scienticist school), is growing in size and importance. In Poland particularly this movement is giving rise to new ideas and developing Marxism into a school of philosophy, while Hegelian Marxism is more concerned with worshipping sanctified dogmas. It is among these positivist-Marxists that a new phenomenon, analytical–linguistic Marxism, is emerging.

3 THE MAIN TENETS OF ANALYTICAL–LINGUISTIC MARXISM

Adam Schaff[18] is a prominent member of both schools. He is a leading Marxist philosopher not only in Poland but in the world.

---

[17] Op. cit., pp. 18 and 19.

[18] He was born in 1913 in Lwów. He studied and graduated in economics at the Jan Kazimierz University in Lwów, where Twardowski educated a host of Polish analytical philosophers between 1895 an 1936; and continued his education in Paris at L'École des Sciences Economiques et Politiques. From his early years he belonged to the Communist Party. After the Russians took Lwów in 1939, he went to study philosophy at the Institute of Philosophy in Moscow. His philosophical interests originated from his practical activities. A theoretical reflection upon these activities led him

Apart from being an ideologist, Schaff has *developed* aspects of
Marxist philosophy and thus is a revisionist. Since he attempted
to make his improvements under the umbrella of orthodox
Marxism, he is sometimes paradoxically called an 'orthodox
revisionist'. Marxists may be considered philosophers only in so
far as they develop and not merely conserve the corpus of their
philosophy; otherwise they are ideologists. In this sense Schaff
is a philosopher. He has a special gift for integrating new ideas,
previously regarded as foreign, into Marxist language in such a
way that they became acceptable to the orthodox. In this way he
has done more to inject new ideas into Marxist philosophy than
anyone else in Poland and perhaps elsewhere.

After 1955 Schaff no longer practised Marxist 'nihilistic'
criticism of non-Marxist philosophers, i.e. stretching the meaning
of the concepts of the philosopher, extrapolating his views and
then rejecting them by comparing them with quotations from a
Marxist classic. Schaff seems to have acquired his analytical
orientation as the result of his struggle with analytical philosophers; this was his apprenticeship in the philosophy of analysis.
Not only do his recent writings abound in minute examinations
of the meaning of words, sometimes in the manner of 'ordinary
language' philosophy, but these examinations became an integral
part of his methodological programme.

In case of ambiguous questions, one has first of all to determine—
through the analysis of the statement—what the question is about,
how many different meanings it has. Certainly this does not exhaust
the problem; it is only the beginning. But one must admit that the

to the works of the classics of Marxist philosophy, and from there to more
general philosophical problems. In Moscow Schaff received two degrees—
a 'Candidate' of Philosophy in 1941 (which corresponds to a Western
doctorate) and a 'Doctorate' in 1944 (which is a considerably higher degree).

In 1946 he was appointed to the Chair of Marxism–Leninism at the
University of Warsaw (the first chair of its kind in Poland). From 1951 to
1957 he was the Editor-in-Chief of the quarterly *Myśl Filozoficzna* (*Philosophical Thought*), the only philosophical periodical at that time. He now holds
the Chair of Philosophy at Warsaw University and is the Director of the
Institute of Philosophy and Sociology of the Polish Academy of Sciences.

Between 1945 and 1965 Schaff published nine books, a number of popular
booklets, and a few dozen articles. His vitality is enormous and his gift
for words extraordinary. He has participated in almost all discussions in
Polish intellectual life—from literature, through sociology and ethics, to
epistemology and logic.

analysis alone, if it brings some clarity to the problem, is in itself an accomplishment.[19]

Instead of the previous nihilistic criticism of non-Marxist views, Schaff recommended new principles of controversy. They call for (*a*) a solid knowledge of the doctrine criticized, (*b*) a grasp of the real and significant problems which gained favour for the doctrine, and (*c*) constructive solutions, from the Marxist point of view, of these significant problems. 'Nihilistic' criticism, according to Schaff, never convinces opponents. On the contrary, 'it will make us ridiculous in their eyes, discredit us as ignoramuses who do not know what they are criticizing and who are incapable of understanding the views they criticize . . .'.[20]

Among his other methodological stipulations, Schaff formulated a rather startling definition of 'revisionist'. Because the Marxist system is by definition open, that is, it postulates the necessity for revision in accord with the progress of science, it follows that its theses can and should be modified. Therefore it is the desperate determination to keep Marxism intact that ought to be regarded as revisionism in the strict sense. It implies an unjustifiable revision of the basic principle concerning the creative character of Marxism and is therefore a dogmatic distortion of Marxism. In short, a dogmatist is a revisionist of the worst kind.

There are at least five enterprises which do credit to Schaff as a philosopher: (1) an attempt to elaborate the Marxist theory of truth (in *Some Problems of the Marxist Theory of Truth*, 1951); (2) a clear separation of dialectical logic from formal logic without relegating the latter to an inferior position (in 'Marxist Dialectics and the Principle of Contradiction', 1955); (3) an initiation of the new field of Marxist inquiry, 'philosophy of man' (in *Marxism and Existentialism*, 1961); (4) a rehabilitation of semantics and the first attempt to develop semantics within Marxism (in *Introduction to Semantics*, 1960); (5) an incorporation of the philosophy of language into Marxist philosophy (in *Language and Cognition*, 1964).

Schaff's essays, *Marxism and Existentialism*, were prompted by (*a*) the 'explosion' of existentialism in Poland as a mode of life after 1956, (*b*) Sartre's essay on the same subject, 'Marxism and Existentialism', published in the Polish monthly *Twórczość* in 1957, and (*c*) a conviction that 'he who is absent always loses',

[19] Adam Schaff, *Marksizm a egzystencjalizm* (*Marxism and Existentialism*) (Warsaw, 1961), p. 81.
[20] Ibid., p. 43.

that in the fields where Marxism offers no solutions it is bound to lose.

Sartre, whose evolution from existentialism to Marxism is rather extraordinary, claimed in his essay of 1957 that Marxism is the only contemporary philosophy which is alive and offers prospects for the future. However, he pointed out that there are acute gaps in the corpus of Marxist philosophy, and that existentialism purports to fill in these gaps. Existentialism of the future will be dissolved within Marxism by supplementing it with some elements which had hitherto been lacking. In his *Critique de la raison dialectique* of 1960 Sartre described Marxism as 'an unsurpassed philosophy of our times', and existentialism as 'an enclave within Marxism which Marxism originates and rejects at the same time'. Sartre without hesitation asserted: 'When Marxist inquiries accept the human dimension (that is the existential plan) as the basis for anthropological knowledge, existentialism will lose its *raison d'être*.'[21]

This was a challenge to Marxism which Schaff recognized as valid. He attempted to fill in the gaps within Marxism concerning philosophical anthropology which he called, to avoid unnecessary associations, the philosophy of man. But Schaff definitely did not wish to supplement Marxism with existentialism. The fact that there are two processes—from existentialism towards Marxism, and from Marxism towards problems of existentialist philosophy —does not mean that there must be a point of intersection. The fusion of Marxism and existentialism, according to Schaff, will never occur. The crux of the matter is the concept of the individual. Schaff's analytical bent of mind showed itself in clearly discerning a single element from which follow further consequences that make existentialism irreconcilable with Marxism. For existentialism, the individual is autonomous and is the starting-point; for Marxism, the individual is a product of society, the end-product of social determinants. The extentialist concept of the individual implies indeterminism and the negation of historical materialism. It is clear that it cannot be compatible with Marxism.

While arguing with Sartre, Schaff attempted to sketch some positive answers to questions raised by existentialism. The question: 'What is the sense of life?' is transformed to: 'What is the aim of life?' In order to answer this question, in Schaff's

[21] Op. cit., p. 53.

opinion, the philosopher should not only be erudite but also a sage, because he must justify preferences for values differently from the way in which he justifies philosophical views. A Marxist reply to the question concerning the aim of life is, simply, social eudaemonism. This attitude is not peculiar to Marxism, because it can be held by people of different philosophical orientations. Schaff therefore proposed a *differentia specifica*, a particular kind of social eudaemonism peculiar to Marxism which he called 'socialist humanism'.

> The follower of socialist humanism is convinced that happiness can only be achieved through social happiness. . . . [but] understands that the realization of this postulate requires a struggle, that the cause which he promotes is socially conditioned and requires a specific change of social relationships. . . . In the name of 'Love thy neighbour' he [the follower of socialist humanist] calls for a class struggle—although this appears to be a contradiction—calls for hatred towards all oppressors of man in the name of universal human love. . . . He is a dialectician and because of that, while calling for peace, he fights.[22]

This *differentia specifica* produces a distinct variant of social eudaemonism, but its distinctiveness is not its forte. The principle of hatred in the name of universal human love will be difficult to apply in concrete, everyday situations.

The work which more than any other establishes Schaff's membership in the positivist school of Marxism is his *Introduction to Semantics*,[23] the first book of its kind in Marxist literature, and one which ended the taboo surrounding semantics. In it the influence of the Polish analytical movement is striking and unconcealed. A clear statement is made that even a 'quotation maniac' can find no statements about semantics in Marx and Engels, simply because this discipline did not exist in their times. Because it is philosophically important, it should be developed, not criticized 'nihilistically'. Schaff observed that Marxism has produced many a critical publication on semantics; however he added: '. . . it can be definitely asserted that they were not creditable performances'.[24]

The *Introduction to Semantics* may appear to be too elementary,

---

[22] Op. cit., p. 93.
[23] A. Schaff, *Wstęp do semantyki* (Warsaw, 1960), English edition, *Introduction to Semantics* (Oxford, 1962).
[24] Op. cit. English edition, p. x.

rather like a textbook for undergraduates. It ought to be remembered that when a philosophical movement absorbs a new realm of problems, it must first fit them into an existing framework. The scope of the book is extensive; the author wished to examine semantics as (*a*) a branch of linguistics and (*b*) a branch of logic, and also to consider (*c*) semantic philosophy, and (*d*) 'general' semantics, as in Korzybski. However, the main purpose was to investigate those problems of semantics which are significant for Marxist philosophy.

Because semantics has nowadays become a complex and heterogeneous discipline, Schaff starts his investigation with a semantic analysis of the term 'semantics'. The first part of the book, entitled 'The Problem of Research in Semantics', is devoted to a review of general problems in contemporary semantics. In the second part, entitled 'Chosen Categories of Semantics', Schaff concentrates on several problems and attempts to give them a materialistic interpretation. For example, he discusses at considerable length Whorf's linguistic-relativity principle: No individual can objectively describe the world because he is conditioned to certain modes of interpretation, the result of having grown up in a given linguistic environment. Whorf observed an interdependence of environment and language, particularly with regard to languages remote from the Indo-European, such as Hopi Indian and Eskimo. The structure of the language of the Hopis reflects their environment, particularly the arduous agricultural conditions. Once the language was formed to describe the environment, it gradually began to form the *Weltanschauung* of the tribe. In Eskimo languages, to take another example, there is a multitude of different expressions referring to ice, whereas in the language of the Aztecs there is only one expression for both ice and cold. Schaff insists that Whorf has thus provided a materialistic interpretation of the specificity of non-Indo-European primitive languages. No such explicit interpretation can be found in Whorf's writings. However, the interpretation given by Schaff can be considered as a legitimate interpretation of Whorf's findings.

In the *Introduction to Semantics* Schaff is particularly absorbed by the problem of communication. In his view the unquestionable achievements of semantics cannot veil the fact that the social aspect of the problem has been neglected. The problem of communication, as rooted in the relationship environment-thought-language, cannot be solved without reference to the Marxist theory of 'basis and superstructure'. Thought and social institutions, i.e. 'superstructure', are shaped by environmental, material conditions, i.e. 'basis', and therefore 'superstructure' reflects 'basis'. This is succinctly summarized in Marxist terminology as 'being determines consciousness'. It is thus by examining the impact of environment on language and *vice versa* that Schaff was hoping to elucidate some entangled problems of human communication.

When compared with the high calibre work of Polish analytical philosophers, Schaff's *Introduction* is nothing special; it even leaves something to be desired in terms of exactitude. When compared with the semantic or rather 'anti-semantic' output of the other Marxists, Schaff's *Introduction* is something special. It may be reasonably hoped that this treatise will exert a significant influence on Marxist philosophy, lessening its dogmatism, and increasing philosophical penetration and sophistication.

If there was any shadow of doubt as to whether or not linguistic–analytic Marxism was a transient or evanescent phenomenon, Schaff's 1964 book, *Language and Cognition*,[25] dispels it. The title of the book is the same as that given to Ajdukiewicz's selected papers of 1961.[26] Its content is closer to semantic philosopy than Schaff's *Introduction to Semantics* of 1960.

In the introduction to the book he begins characteristically with a quotation from Marx. Important qualifications follow. Marx had formulated his opinions in times 'when philosophers were not restricted by, nor interested in, the rigours of strict thinking . . . Marx wrote in metaphors, using phrases and expressions most of which require elucidation and interpretation.'[27] The process of cognition and particularly the active rôle of language in this process were neglected or ignored by materialist philosophies before and after Marx; idealist philosophies, on the other hand, have contributed much to the understanding of this problem.[28] Schaff's intention is to fill this gap. His book is divided into three parts: (1) the history of the problem, (2) the empirical assumptions, and (3) the analysis of the problem.

The first part is subdivided into two sections. The first section

[25] Adam Schaff, *Język a poznanie* (*Language and Cognition*) (Warsaw, 1964). English translation is to appear in 1967 by McGraw Hill.
[26] K. Ajdukiewicz, *Język i poznanie—Wybór pism z lat 1920–1939* (*Language and Cognition—Selected Papers of the Years 1920–1939*) (Warsaw, 1960).
[27] Schaff, *Language and Cognition*, p. 5.
[28] Ibid., p. 6.

consists of a presentation and discussion of some most interesting theories of the philosophy of language from the eighteenth to the first decades of the twentieth century. It is a stimulating essay which, apart from one or two paragraphs, could have been written by a 'bourgeois' philosopher. It is worth consideration by anyone interested in the philosophy of language.

The second section of this first part is, however, not so illuminating. The analysis of Cassirer's 'symbolic forms' is oversimplified if not distorted. Also, the presentation of Ajdukiewicz's radical conventionalism, as an offshoot of neo-positivism, is mistaken. Under the label of neo-positivism many different things are discussed, but links which Schaff suggests as obvious seem to me rather dubious.

In the second part Schaff's indebtedness to Whorf is even more conspicuous than in the *Introduction*. The discussion is completed by Schaff's own admission that 'The linguistic system in which we think influences our comprehension of reality and consequently affects our behaviour (in the broad sense of the term "behaviour")'[29]. This standpoint is not quite reconcilable with the Sapir–Whorf hypothesis in its original wording, but it originated from it and was inspired by it; of this Schaff is quite aware. One can easily subscribe to Schaff's standpoint that 'whoever wishes to investigate in a scholarly and fair manner the problem of the active rôle of language in the process of cognition must relate his inquiries to this hypothesis (which does not of course mean a complete affirmation of the hypothesis in question').[30] This last point is addressed to 'strict' Marxist philosophers who wish to derive the solutions of all philosophical problems from the writings of Marx, Engels, and Lenin. To them is also directed a remark that it will not do to insinuate that the Whorfian hypothesis is a kind of idealism. 'The unquestionable problem which cannot be eliminated *a priori* by any materialist concerns the active rôle of language in the cognition and behaviour of people.'[31] The copy theory of truth as developed by Lenin, and incorporated in the Marxist theory of knowledge, admits a subjective element in the allegedly objective process of depicting reality. However, as Schaff rightly observes, it is one thing to declare that a subjective element is involved in our cognitive processes (due to our psychophysical constitution), but it is another to pinpoint this element in a concrete analysis of the process of cognition. Estimating the

[29] Op. cit., p. 124.   [30] Ibid., p. 125.   [31] Ibid., p. 34.

degree of the influence of our language on our comprehension of the world is a partial answer to this problem.

The third part of *Language and Cognition* is perhaps the most significant. The problem with which Schaff is basically pre-occupied is whether in the cognitive processes and in communication we should regard thinking and verbalizing of thoughts as two distinct and separate processes, or whether a sort of homogeneous linguistic-thinking process occurs. Schaff asserts that speech as it is conceived in civilized societies implies thinking, and therefore that speaking involves thinking is an analytic thesis. However, he goes further and claims that there are no thoughts without linguistic expression, and therefore thinking involves language. This, however, Schaff does not consider to be an analytic statement, but a synthetic one, and 'the central hypothesis of our consideration'.[32]

Schaff rightly observes that the empirical verification of his central hypothesis would be a tremendous undertaking involving the international cooperation of specialists over many years; it would require a sort of geophysical year in the humanities. In the meantime philosophy must bide its time; at present it may help to clear the ground by elucidating some basic categories involved.

The leap between *Introduction to Semantics* (1960) and *Language and Cognition* (1964) is quite significant; whereas the former was mainly expository in character and consisted basically of a presentation of problems, the latter has a more argumentative character and consists to a considerable degree of a discussion of problems.

In 1965 Schaff delivered yet another surprise; another imaginative reinterpretation of Marxist philosophy. The book of 1965, *Marxism and the Human Individual*,[33] is perhaps not as significant from the point of view of content as the previous two (of 1960 and 1964); however, it is the one for which Schaff was admonished and severely, if not vehemently criticized, by the leadership of the Polish Communist Party. Since the book is to appear soon in English translation, I shall offer only a few general comments.

In a nutshell, *Marxism and the Human Individual* is an attempt to rehabilitate the young Marx and to interpret the economic and

[32] Op. cit.. pp. 166, 133.
[33] Adam Schaff, *Marksizm a jednostka ludzka* (Marxism and the Human Individual), PWN (Warsaw, 1965); the English translation is to appear in 1967 by McGraw Hill.

other works of the mature Marx within the framework of the young Marx. It is a mistake, Schaff insists, to think that there were two Marxes. There was only one. The mature Marx executed and worked out in detail, perhaps in a slightly misleading idiom, the programme of the young Marx. Schaff writes: 'Economics for Marx, although he devoted his entire life to it, is not the end in itself. Marx was and remained the philosopher and sociologist for whom man is the central concern. This is the key to his studies in economics. . . . [Marx's] researches in economics are not the end in itself, . . . but only a means for achieving the main goal which is the *liberation of man*', (pp. 19, 21). This, according to Schaff, is the humanistic content underlying the whole teaching of Marx. It follows that in essence Marxism is a philosophy of Man. It also follows that one of the principal concerns of Marxist philosophy ought to be with the concrete human individual, with man in his individuality and *not* (as it has hitherto been the tradition in Marxist philosophy) with a 'statistical' man conceived as an abstract resultant of the interplay between economic and social forces.

It is not the philosophical reinterpretation of Marx that met with a storm from the party officials, but a practical application of the thesis that one of the main concerns of Marxist philosophy is with the concrete human individual, with the conditions of happiness of particular human beings. Being empirical enough on the one hand, and concerned with the human individual *in concreto* on the other, Schaff has found that many people in Poland lead miserable and frustrated lives, that, in other words, many people are alienated from society. This conclusion flagrantly violates one of the *a priori* dogmas of the communist ideology which states that there are no alienated people in a socialist society. Hence the friction between the leading exponent of Marxist philosophy and the ideological guardians of the sacred fire.

Schaff's evolution in thought, to sum up, has been extraordinary although not inexplicable. The germ of analysis which was once considered as malignant in Marxism now appears to be a source of growth. A respect for logic, the employment of modern semantics and research into the philosophy of language have led Schaff to a pioneering position in contemporary Marxism.

W. Krajewski is another Marxist of the new wave, one who shows a distinct analytical orientation. His essay, 'Schools and

Disputes Within Marxism', already mentioned, not only claimed recognition for the two major Marxist schools (scientists and humanists), but postulated a further division into sub-schools.

> If we recognize that philosophy should be developed creatively, and if developing it is not to be the privilege of a few established authorities, it is only natural that there must be controversies on particular problems, as well as divergences concerning the subject and structure of philosophy, its methods and ways of its advance. It would be odd if there were unanimity in these matters, and since there is not, who is to decide whose position is right?[34]

The aim of Krajewski's *Philosophical Essays* is to consider some problems of ontology, regardless of what the 'classics' said about them, since 'both in Engels and in Lenin we can find many inconsistencies'.[35] One of these inconsistencies, as Krajewski pointed out, lies in Engels' views on dialectics. In *Anti-Dühring* he stated that out of existing philosophy, the only independent discipline which is left is the science of *thinking*—formal logic and dialectical logic; in the same work and in others, Engels explicitly asserted that the laws of dialectics govern the sphere of thought as well as external reality. Another shortcoming, Krajewski continued, is Engels' assertion that 'the proofs of higher mathematics ... are, strictly speaking, from the point of view of elementary mathematics, erroneous'.[36]

In the essay, 'Sense Impressions and Reality',[37] after an exhaustive historical–analytical examination of the views on the relationship between sensory cognition and reality, Krajewski compiles a list of attitudes critical of the senses. (The examination and its results are very much in the style of Mme Kotarbińska in her works of the 1930s.)

1. The world exists objectively and our senses give us an accurate and complete picture. (A view held by naïve people unfamiliar with theoretical reflection.)

2. The world exists objectively and our senses give us an accurate picture of some of its features; this picture is, however, not

[34] W. Krajewski, 'Schools and Disputes Within Marxism', in *Szkice filozoficzne*, pp. 20, 21.

[35] W. Krajewski, 'O przedmiocie filozofii marksistowskiej' (On the Subject of Marxist Philosophy) in *Szkice filozoficzne*, p. 23.

[36] W. Krajewski, 'Dialektyka marksistowska a logika formalna' (Marxist Dialectics and Formal Logic), in *Szkice filozoficzne*, p. 144.

[37] In *Szkice filozoficzne*.

complete. There are some other features of the world inaccessible to sensory cognition. (Held by some ancient philosophers.)

3. The world exists objectively and our senses give us a truthful but approximate and incomplete picture of some of its features; the range of sensory perception is to a large degree subjectively conditioned. (Held by many Marxists.)

4. The world exists objectively and our senses give us a truthful (although approximate) picture of some of its features—so-called 'primary' ones. Other sensory impressions (secondary) are caused by certain features but do not resemble them. Besides these features of the world there are some others not accessible to sensory cognition. (Held by Lenin at times and by some Marxists.)

5. The world exists objectively but none of our sensory impressions (perhaps with the exception of impressions of time relations) resemble reality. They do symbolize certain features of the world and correspond to these features in a certain way. In particular the laws of impressions isomorphize the laws of the world, owing to which the world is cognizable. (Held by Helmholtz.)

6. The world exists objectively but none of our impressions resemble reality; laws in the world of impressions (the phenomenonological order) do not resemble the laws of reality (the ontological order); consequently the real world is uncognizable. (Held by Spencer.)

7. The world exists objectively but there is no order in it; the laws established by us are subjective, determined by the nature of our minds; therefore, the real world is completely uncognizable. (Held by Kant.)

8. The world does not exist objectively; our impressions are the only reality. (Held by Berkeley.)[38]

After this presentation, Krajewski remarks that it is not his aim to assert that only one of the positions mentioned is the Marxist one. 'I contend that the third position and . . . variants of the fourth are compatible with basic assumptions of dialectical materialism. But obviously only one of them can be true. The final solution will be provided by the further development of science.'[39]

In the essay, 'The Problem of the Truthfulness of Impressions and Concepts',[40] Krajewski attempted to analyse the causes of disagreement and confusion among Marxists concerning the concept of truth. At least two different concepts of truth are in current

[38] Op. cit., pp. 228, 229.   [39] Ibid., p. 231.   [40] In *Szkice filozoficzne.*

usage among Marxists—one 'narrower' or logical, another 'broader' or epistemological. In the conclusion, which is quite 'Ajdukiewiczian' in style, he wrote:

> Therefore the applicability of the term 'truthfulness' to impressions and concepts is finally a matter of convention—we must establish whether we shall use the term 'truthfulness' in the logical sense only or in the broader sense as well. The question is which of the decisions will be more practical.[41]

Krajewski has never been a 'revisionist', and has no intention of uprooting Marxism. His attitude is not that of a partisan nor of an eccentric, but rather it reflects certain tendencies which have been accumulating in Polish Marxism over a period of years.

To recapitulate: in Poland the tradition of analysis and the 'climate of logic' generated a new version of Marxism which is acquiring more and more distinct features. An analytic-linguistic tendency is not confined to the philosophers discussed above. It can be found in the works of younger Marxists, for example in Cackowski's *The Cognitive Content of Sensory Impressions*,[42] or in recent works of the leading Marxist aesthetician, S. Morawski.[43]

It is not possible at present to predict the future of this movement. At any rate, the basic principle of Marxist sociology, that environment influences thought, has been illustrated by the way in which a logical and analytical environment has distinctively affected dogmatic Marxist thought.

RÉSUMÉ

The collision between Marxism and analytical philosophy had two consequences. The first of these was that the Marxists' desire was fulfilled. Analytical philosophy is no longer a dominant trend in Poland; its strength has been diluted; its output drastically limited. This was mainly due to the remarkable help of circumstances rather than to the successful action of the Marxists. Secondly, however, the Marxists themselves were, in turn, infected by the germ of analysis; and with or perhaps without their consent, the analytical approach to philosophy and the ability to see a multitude of meanings (when the Marxist dogmatists would expect but one) have been thrust upon their minds. So analytical philosophy will be circulating in their veins even if the whole analytical movement is entirely extinguished.

[41] In *Szkice filozoficzne*, p. 239. [42] Z. Cackowski, *Treść poznawcza wrażeń zmysłowych* (The Cognitive Content of Sensory Impressions) (Warsaw, 1962). [43] See in particular 'Lenin as a Literary Theorist' in *Science and Society* (New York, XXIX, 1965).

IX

SOME COMPARISONS WITH BRITISH

ANALYTICAL PHILOSOPHY

Although the analytical movements in Britain and in Poland had much in common, only a limited number of *general* observations can be made. Most generalizations are bound to be true of only some philosophers, or true of most of them for some of the time. Each of the major philosophers in each country pursued problems in his own way. Therefore a comparison simply in terms of similarity of opinions would give an incomplete picture. The method of arriving at opinions, the structure of argument, the nature of the dilemma which motivated the philosopher, must also be considered. For the above reasons this chapter is divided into two sections. The first, more general in character, is concerned with two kinds of philosophers: those devoted to problems and those concerned with method. The second section, which is more detailed, contains a series of comparisons in which the British philosophers (Moore, Russell, Wittgenstein, and Ryle successively) are contrasted individually either with a corresponding Polish philosopher, or with the Polish analytical movement in general.

I PROBLEM—PHILOSOPHERS AND METHODOLOGISTS

Regarding their attitude towards traditional philosophy, analytical philosophers can be divided into two groups:

1. Those devoted to problems.
2. The methodologists.

236

The former do not usually condemn traditional philosophy; while criticizing it, they partially accept it and aim at its reconstruction rather than rejection. They wish to devise a better philosophy.

The methodologists denounce all traditional philosophy and claim to have found a method ideally suited for philosophical inquiry. They advocate a method which subsequently determines the scope and nature of philosophical pursuits.

In other words, problem-philosophers begin with problems and choose methods of inquiry appropriate to them, whereas methodologists start with a method and eliminate all problems but those which can be tackled by that method.

In Britain and in Poland analytical philosophy has included both kinds of philosophers. Problem-philosophers have been, in Britain, Moore, Russell, and Wittgenstein (with some qualifications), as well as Ayer, Kneale, Popper, and Ryle. In Poland they have been Twardowski, Kotarbiński, Ajdukiewicz, and Tatarkiewicz. The British methodologists were the radical Oxford linguistic philosophers, Austin in particular. They elevated the method of ordinary language analysis. The Polish methodologists were above all Łukasiewicz and Tarski; they elevated the method of logical analysis.

It is characteristic of many analytical philosophers that they have changed from a concentration on problems to concentration on method, and *vice versa*. Russell, in the years 1912–1915 when he professed scientific philosophy, understood as an inquiry into the logical form, was a methodologist. However, a passion for dealing with problems led him away from this obsession. In later years he did not trim philosophy to a shape suitable for his method, but on the contrary applied various methods in accordance with the variety of philosophical problems. Both Russell and Moore, although radical in their refutation of idealism, were not so radical in their rejection of all traditional philosophy. They were of course against 'bad', traditional metaphysics. However, they were not solely concerned with the novelty of their method. Their interest in certain philosophical problems persisted, and these problems could easily be classified as those of traditional philosophy.

Gilbert Ryle is considered by many to be a most prominent practitioner of the method of ordinary language analysis, particularly because of *The Concept of Mind*. However, I shall argue later on that he was more a problem-philosopher than a methodologist.

Although he described philosophical activity as drawing the map of usage, we can trace in his work a distinctive nominalistic current tending towards a radical elimination of all unnecessary entities. In other words, his work may be seen as in the main stream of traditional philosophy. Convergences between Kotarbiński and Ryle are more than apparent, as will be demonstrated in the last section of this chapter.

In Poland the most prominent problem-philosophers were Kotarbiński and Ajdukiewicz. Kotarbiński was primarily involved in the defence and justification of his materialist monism or semantic materialism. The neatness and precision in the formulation of his doctrine were due to a logical apparatus provided mainly by Leśniewski. The other two philosophical issues which absorbed him were his lay ethics and, of course, praxiology. When the wave of radicalism reached Poland, and mathematical logic was considered to be the backbone of future philosophy, he resisted it. Instead of a radical reform, he aimed at a partial one; instead of a new construction, he undertook a reconstruction of philosophy. Of course, he intended 'to cultivate small philosophy as a programme of intellectual reform'. The tenor of his undertaking was indeed methodological. None the less, after many years of removing philosophical rubble, he arrived at a philosophical system in the strict sense, monistic materialism. He arrived, that is, at an answer to a traditional philosophical problem.

Ajdukiewicz, a most painstaking analyst, made his name through incisive, highly technical analyses of separate philosophical issues. In his most original works the formulation of philosophical problems was related to his theory of meaning and expressed in terms of his semantics. The semantic apparatus was elaborate indeed. Quite a substantial part of all his inquiries was devoted to working out his own methods of tackling philosophical problems. Yet the techniques of mathematical logic which he applied, together with his own theory of meaning, were designed for a solution, or at least a formulation, of traditional problems. His radical conventionalism was undoubtedly a construction of a philosophical kind. He did not succeed in proving that all our knowledge is shaped decisively by the language we accept; and consequently that different pictures of reality are reflections of different conceptual apparatuses. In posing the problem and in reaching an extreme solution, Ajdukiewicz made us aware of the limits of the claim asserting that language has a decisive influence on our thought.

Semantic refutation of subjective idealism is another instance where Ajdukiewicz presents himself as a problem-philosopher. Here again the technical means involved were formidable. Starting with his theory of meaning Ajdukiewicz showed that the paradoxical thesis of subjective idealism can be held only if we are prepared to violate the rules governing the uses of language. Although Ajdukiewicz's investigations were always highly technical, and apparently included analyses for analysis' sake, his main purpose was to examine relationships between reality and its descriptions.

So much for problem philosophers.

Methodologists concentrated on those problems which fitted their methods. Possibly the most conspicuous among Polish methodologists was Tarski. He regarded himself as a philosopher so long as he could find philosophical problems which were capable of being framed within a highly specialized logical and mathematical apparatus—so long as procedures of mathematical logic could be superimposed on philosophical issues. After a success with the definition of the concept of truth in formalized languages, and partial success with some other semantic concepts, he withdrew from philosophy altogether. He did not cease to apply his method, but he applied it only in the realm most proper for it—mathematics.

Łukasiewicz was also a methodologist. In his paper, 'On Method in Philosophy', delivered in 1927, he proclaimed a programme of scientific philosophy and pointed out that its structure should coincide with the structure of systems of formal logic. However, he left the construction of this new scientific philosophy to future generations while he himself proceeded with ever more subtle and technical problems of formal logic. In 1946, when he still considered himself a philosopher, he claimed the object of philosophical inquiry to be a philosophical system, but said that he himself was unable to provide a system which would fulfil the criteria of scientific method. Like Tarski, he dropped philosophy altogether and remained faithful to his method. His philosophical career, from the paper 'The Analysis and Construction of the Concept of Cause' in 1907 to his investigation of modal logic in the 1950s, shows clearly his development away from philosophy.

In general, the prominent Polish methodologists gave themselves over to the method of mathematical logic and then found themselves doing mathematics; this was the result of their trust in method and their desire to be consistent. The more consistently they adhered to their method, the more consistently they ruled out problems of a philosophical nature.

The trust in method and the desire to limit the province of philosophy to the size embraceable by method is, incidentally, a version of the Cartesian quest for certainty. With analytical philosophers, it is method which gives the comfort of certainty.

It is evident that the British methodologists are to be found first of all among Oxford philosophers of ordinary language. Polish methodologists were mathematically minded; the British were 'classically' minded; it is therefore hardly surprising that their methods differed. The acceptance of the method of ordinary language analysis, together with the rejection of mathematical logical analysis, were both a reflection of the Oxford classicist tradition. No one carried these attitudes further and more consistently in philosophy than Austin. He conceived of the method of ordinary language analysis as the only method capable of bringing about progress in philosophy. Mathematical logic was discarded as distorting the real process of thought and as straining language. For the sake of certainty and homogeneity, philosophical inquiry was focused on certain areas of philosophy (philosophy of mind and some parts of moral philosophy). In addition, the nature of philosophical inquiry was so defined that the method of ordinary language analysis seemed perfectly appropriate. Only by these two operations, concentrating on selected problems, and redefining the nature of philosophical inquiry, could the method of ordinary language analysis be considered uniquely suitable for philosophy.

With the lapse of time, however, some adherents of the linguistic idiom felt a bit uncomfortable in such a restricted realm. So some philosophers moved to different fields (e.g., H. L. A. Hart to jurisprudence and Sir Isaiah Berlin to the history of thought); some others began to liberalize British philosophy from within (e.g. P. F. Strawson, *Individuals*, 1959, and Stuart Hampshire, *Thought and Action*, 1960). Austin himself remained faithful to his method, indifferent to other philosophies. In order to call his activities philosophical, however, he had to provide 'excuses', and these excuses were altogether not very convincing. The philosophical relevance of the new problems which Austin tackled may be disputed. Tracing a multitude of usages and recording nuances of meaning were considered by Austin to be the prerequisites for the solution of philosophical problems. It is now clear that his linguistic distinctions did not fulfil their promise.

Austin's unquestionable achievement is the discernment and analysis of 'performative utterances'. But it may be argued that this contribution in actual fact belongs to logic, or perhaps to grammar (as he sometimes suggested). He pointed out that language is systematically employed, not only for stating or describing, but for performing certain actions. Such utterances as 'I warn you to', or 'I promise you *x*' are performances rather than descriptions. In distinguishing this class of utterances, to be appraised not in terms of truth and falsity but in terms of 'felicitousness' and 'unfelicitousness', he in fact elaborated a logic of performance through linguistic acts. His theory was no doubt original, but not novel in the absolute sense. Other attempts have been made to elaborate the logic of interrogative as well as exclamatory statements. An awareness of the necessity to elaborate the logic of various types of utterances did not orginate with Austin.

Faithfulness to method might have led Austin to linguistics in the way that faithfulness on the part of Polish methodologists led them to mathematics. One of Austin's definitions of philosophy, as 'a true and comprehensive *science of language*', seems to indicate that had he lived longer he might have departed from philosophy and continued his practice, with illuminating results, within the boundaries of a new comprehensive science of linguistics.

2 PARTICULAR COMPARISONS

A. *Moore and Twardowski*

Moore and Twardowski are similar in the styles of their philosophizing and in the rôles they played in the respective analytical movements.

1. They both established realism as the basis on which analytical philosophy was to be developed. This realism seems to have come, directly or indirectly, from the same source, Brentano. At the time when Moore announced his refutation of idealism he was interested in Brentano and, it can be safely assumed, influenced by him.

2. Neither Moore nor Twardowski had much affection for mathematical logic. Moore was 'allergic' to it throughout his life,

although he appreciated its significance. He made the effort to acquire a basic knowledge of mathematical logic but, owing to his basically classical education, 'showed very little aptitude for it', as he himself admitted. Twardowski, although at one time favourably inclined towards mathematical logic, later turned away from it. In 1921 he wrote an article in which he claimed that it had been abused and also praised beyond its merit. Consequently, neither of the two participated in the development of analytical philosophy when it was dominated by mathematical logical analysis.

3. Another characteristic shared by Moore and Twardowski was philosophical scepticism. Neither openly professed any philosophical doctrine. Moore's restraint was a natural one. He mistrusted all doctrines all his life. Twardowski probably had a philosophy of his own, but did not advocate it for fear that he might not be able to justify it with the rigour and precision he thought necessary.

4. The significance of Moore and Twardowski lies not so much in *what* they said, but in *how* they said it. It was a cautious, meticulous, analytical approach that was of utmost importance in their philosophy. Moore's main concern was 'to get really clear as to what on earth a given philosopher *meant* by something which he said, and, secondly, the problem of discovering what really satisfactory reasons there are for supposing that what he meant was true, or, alternatively, was false'.[1] It was through minute and painstaking analyses that these questions were to be answered. In Moore's work a greater diversity of types of analysis can be found than in Twardowski's. The latter was in his element in the analysis of psychological propositions, a legacy of Brentano's school. As Moore did in England, so Twardowski in Poland initiated discussions about the 'meaning of analysis', 'the analysis of meaning', 'the meaning of meaning', and 'the analysis of analysis'—to use Broad's description.

There are, of course, a number of ways in which the two differed.

(1) Their rôles in the British and Polish analytical movements, respectively, were quite unlike, partly because of differences between British and Polish academic and intellectual traditions.

In Britain the phrase 'analytical philosophers' serves as a description for a great many individuals of diverse interests who

---

[1] Paul Schilpp (ed.), *The Philosophy of G. E. Moore*, The Library of Living Philosophers (New York, 1942), p. 14.

have shown some affinity in their ways of dealing with philosophical problems. It cannot be even said that they have shared the same method of inquiry; what was in common was an *attitude*. Therefore we can hardly apply the term 'school' to analytical philosophy in Britain. The term can be used only with regard to Oxford philosophy of ordinary language.

In Poland the school of analytical philosophy originated from Twardowski. Owing to the Continental methods of university teaching (under which a professor is responsible for each of his students up to the doctorate degree, and owing to the conformity of universities as to curriculum) the continuity of the analytical trend in Poland was smooth and undisturbed. This unity and, in a sense, uniformity of Polish analytical philosophy was also related to the political, social, and economic events which occurred in Poland after she regained her independence in 1918. There was very little by way of tradition to continue; but at the same time, there was little by way of tradition to inhibit new thought. The new philosophical movement was initiated by Twardowski in Lwów, but afterwards its centre moved to Warsaw. Lwów nevertheless remained a stronghold of analytical philosophy. Other universities, which were staffed by philosophers from Twardowski's school, were considered simply as branches of the same movement. Only the Jagiellonian University at Cracow, the oldest university in Poland and one of the oldest in Europe, kept rather apart. In short, the homogeneity of the development of analytical philosophy in Poland was one of its characteristic traits.

The British movement, on the other hand, included outstanding personalities of quite different concepts of philosophy. There was no similar continuity or heritage. During the first seven years at Cambridge, Moore lectured but little, and worked mainly on *Principia Ethica*. Next, he spent seven years in Edinburgh, lecturing only occasionally. Only after his return to Cambridge did he remain there for a considerable time. The story repeats itself with Russell and Wittgenstein. The development of British analytical philosophy is a development of similar tendencies rather than a development of a school.

(2) The influence of Moore on the history of twentieth-century philosophy was certainly greater than that of Twardowski. Though neither of the two was a prolific writer, a number of Moore's papers marked the beginning of new periods of discussion in Britain ('Refutation of Idealism', 'The Status of Sense

Data', 'A Defence of Common Sense'). Above all, Moore's *Principia Ethica*[2] opened a new and fruitful phase in English moral philosophy. Twardowski's main work, *Zur Lehre vom Inhalt und Gegenstand der Vorstellungen*, was not very influential. However, Twardowski exercised a significant influence in the theory of truth; his paper, 'On the So-Called Relative Truths', together with his teaching, marked the beginning of a period in which the theory of truth became one of the main concerns of Polish philosophers. After this, however, new ideas were introduced into Polish philosophy by his pupils rather than by Twardowski himself. Moore participated continuously in British analytical philosophy, writing papers until the 1950s. But his position is rather difficult to define precisely. On some occasions he made pronouncements which ordinary language philosophers assume to be anticipations and even the beginning of their movement.[3] On other occasions he made statements which can by no means be reconciled with the philosophy of ordinary language.[4] What is most important, however, is the fact that for five decades Moore made his presence felt in British philosophy in his specific, unmistakable way. Perhaps he should not be made a member of any group, but recognized as in a class by himself. Twardowski in the 1920s and 1930s produced nothing of real importance. He clearly began the analytical movement but when it reached its maturity, he stood apart.

3. It seems that for Moore, analysis of the meaning of philosophically important expressions was a source of knowledge. He said himself that, having discovered the meaning, he sought for satisfactory reasons to suppose that the statement was true or false. For Twardowski, analysis of the meaning of expressions was a means, a way to instil the technique of rigorous philosophical inquiry into the minds of his students.

To conclude, it may be suggested that both Moore and Twar-

---

[2] *Principia Ethica*, as a matter of fact, was translated for the first time into Polish in 1918, and undoubtedly exerted some influence.

[3] 'When we are engaged in the intricacies of philosophical discussion, . . . we are apt to forget what a vast number of arguments this interesting and important question must involve: we are apt to assume, that if one or two points be made on either side, the whole case is won.' (G. E. Moore, 'The Refutation of Idealism' *Philosophical Studies* (London, 1960), p. 2.)

[4] '. . . my business is not with . . . proper usage as established by custom.' '. . . verbal questions are properly left to the writers of dictionaries and other persons interested in literature; philosophy has no concern with them.' (G. E. Moore, *Principia Ethica* (London, 1960), pp. 2, 6.)

dowski exerted their greatest influence not through proclaiming revolutionary ideas, but through the sheer power of their personalities and through their insistence on simplicity, plainness, and the unparadoxical character of philosophical inquiry.

B. *Bertrand Russell and Polish analytical philosophy*

Among British philosophers, Bertrand Russell exercised the greatest influence upon the analytical movement in Poland. It was through Russell's *The Principles of Mathematics* (1903) that the first link was established between British and Polish analytical movements. When *Principia Mathematica* appeared it was much read, much admired, and much criticized in Poland for at least two decades; it became the 'bible' of the Polish logicians. *Principia* indirectly influenced the Polish analytical movement more than any other single work; from it Polish philosophers and logicians learned their mathematical logic. When they mastered the technique, it was in relation to and often against *Principia* that they developed their own ideas. Russell did not continue his investigation into the philosophy of mathematics after this work was completed in 1913. His 1919 *Introduction to Mathematical Philosophy* may be considered a summary of the *Principia* without the use of symbolic language. When Russell was finishing his work on the foundations of mathematics, the Poles began their logical researches. In 1910 Łukasiewicz discussed Russell's antinomy of classes in *On the Principle of Contradiction in Aristotle*. This antinomy and related ones captured the attention of many Polish philosophers and logicians, Leśniewski and Chwistek in particular. It may be said that the Poles took over the work on the foundations of mathematics and logic where Russell left off. The strictly formal approach in the philosophy of mathematics initiated by Frege, elaborated in detail and reinforced by Russell, was given a distinctive nominalistic interpretation by Polish logicians and was reintroduced to the Anglo-Saxon world via Tarski. There is little doubt that the work on the foundations of mathematics and logic conducted in recent years by Quine, Goodman, and other nominalistically minded philosophers shows traces of the influence of Leśniewski and Tarski both of whom owed much to Russell.[5]

[5] It is interesting to observe that Leśniewski in the last years of his life advocated a movement 'Back to Frege' as he (Leśniewski) was discouraged by Russell's 'oversimplifications and distortions' of Frege. In Leśniewski's view, Russell was too vigorous and too impatient in his expansions of Frege's ideas and made a number of blunders not to be found in Frege.

On the logical side, then, Russell's influence on Polish philosophy cannot be overrated. On the philosophical side the situation is less clear-cut. Russell's views were not influential. They did not even have much in common with those of Polish philosophers. It is true that his *attitude* towards philosophy coincided closely with the attitude of the majority of Polish analytical philosophers. The points in common were the following:

1. Analysis is the initial and indispensable part of philosophical inquiry. This for Russell was 'the strongest and most unshakable prejudice as regards the methods of philosophical investigation'. This was also the tacit assumption of almost all analytical philosophers in Poland.

2. Language is a medium which shapes ideas and as such should be an object of philosophical inquiry. It appears that the Poles followed up this insight more scrupulously than did Russell.

3. Language in philosophical investigation is none the less not to be considered as the sole object of philosophical inquiry, but is to be related to something which is non-linguistic. This point was given substance in the development of Polish semantics.

4. Everyday language is somewhat inadequate for conducting philosophical investigations with definiteness and precision. Therefore this language should be either 'improved' upon or replaced by artificial languages modelled on mathematical logic.

5. Important though common sense may be, philosophical inquiry can only be entrusted to it up to a certain point; logic and in particular mathematical logic also must take its place as a guardian of philosophical soundness.

6. The question '*How* do we know?' is only a part of the question '*What* do we know?'. Russell remarked once that he reversed the usual order of treatment common in philosophy since Kant, that of going from '*How* do we know?' to '*What* do we know?' In Polish philosophy the question '*How* do we know?' was not extensively discussed; it was taken for granted that 'we *can* know'. Efforts were almost entirely directed towards enlarging the scope of what we know.

In relation to Russell's philosophical opinions, hardly any Polish philosophers accepted his logical atomism or his theory of meaning, his 'neutral stuff' or his theory of perception, his resolution of the mind–matter problem or his theory of knowledge. It seems that the only two positions held in common were realism and the correspondence theory of truth. In Poland these views were acquired from Brentano via Twardowski; Russell, curiously enough, seems to have been similarly influenced. It is sufficient to read Russell's article, 'Meinong's Theory of Complexes and Assumptions', to realize the degree to which he was influenced by Meinong's realism, which derived from Brentano.

Russell's acceptance of a correspondence theory of truth came after he had espoused realism; and it was basically on the strength of his realism that he rejected monistic and pragmatistic theories of truth. In *Philosophical Essays* a clear stand was taken in favour of a correspondence theory of truth, which he defended later in a modified version in *An Inquiry into Meaning and Truth* (1940) and in *Human Knowledge* (1948). Although Russell accepted the correspondence theory explicitly and asserted that 'no other theory had any chance of being right', his formulation,[6] tied to his causal theory of meaning and reminiscent of his pictorial theory of truth (an offshoot of logical atomism), differs considerably from the correspondence theory in its classical or Aristotelian version as advocated in Poland: sentence s is true in language L if and only p. If $s =$ 'snow is white', then it is true if and only if snow is white (p).

There was no philosopher in Poland who could be compared with Russell in scope and accomplishment. Among Polish analytical philosophers, only Kotarbiński was of similar stature, but he lacked some of Russell's qualities. The two participated vigorously in public life and influenced general attitudes. They both advocated ethics free from religion. They both wrote on a wide range of subjects (Russell on happiness, education, marriage; Kotarbiński on lay ethics and praxiology). They were both secular to the core.

C. *Wittgenstein—a lack of impact on Polish analytical philosophy*

Wittgenstein, as compared with Russell, was at odds with Polish analytical philosophy. He had no influence, and received no recognition; his attitude to philosophy was alien to Polish philosophers and his results were considered dubious if not obscure.

[6] The following definition of truth is provided in *Human Knowledge*: 'Every belief which is not merely an impulse to action is in the nature of a picture, combined with a yes-feeling, or a no-feeling; in the case of a yes-feeling it is "true" if there is a fact having to the picture the kind of similarity that a prototype has to an image; in the case of no-feeling it is "true" if there is no such fact. A belief which is not true is called "false"' (p. 170).

The *Tractatus Logico-Philosophicus* seems to contain themes which were later developed in the Polish movement. However, the *Tractatus* had no influence, and was not studied seriously. It was considered to be an obscurely written 'dark' book, full of mysteries and riddles. The maxim expressed in the preface of the *Tractatus*: 'What can be said at all can be said clearly, and what we cannot talk about we must consign to silence' was not only known but also rather strictly observed in Poland, and because of this, the *Tractatus* gained no favour. In spite of some 'attractive' topics—the logical structure of propositions, the nature of logical inference—the overall unintelligibility of the work and its obvious metaphysics discouraged Polish philosophers completely.

Wittgenstein's *Philosophical Investigations* did not have much influence either. In this case, however, most of Wittgenstein's contentions were in contradiction to Polish positions.

1. Wittgenstein said that the things we are looking for 'already lie open to view', and have 'escaped remark only because they are always before our eyes'. In Poland it was contended that only through logical penetration can we arrive at significant philosophical results.

2. Wittgenstein said that 'we must do away with all *explanation*, and description alone must take its place'. In Poland it was believed that philosophy should attempt to explain as well as to describe.

3. Wittgenstein said that 'philosophy may in no way interfere with the actual use of language'. In Poland it was claimed that everyday language is inadequate for conducting philosophical inquiry and therefore should be improved upon or at least occasionally rectified.

4. Wittgenstein said that 'philosophy is a battle against the bewitchment of our intelligence by means of language'. In Poland it was held that philosophy is a work of reason, one aided by language.

5. Wittgenstein said that with philosophical problems 'definitions usually fail'. In Poland the problems investigated by analytical philosophers were meant to yield to definition and to unequivocal formulation.

This list could be prolonged. The differences seem to stem partly from different subject matters. Wittgenstein developed his discourse in reference to problems of the philosophy of mind. In Polish philosophy these problems were little discussed.

Yet there is something of importance shared by Wittgenstein

and the Polish movement. It characterizes twentieth-century analytical philosophers of various denominations: a pre-occupation with meaning and language. It is difficult to define Wittgenstein's philosophical position, but if we agree that what makes an analytical philosopher is first of all an attitude towards language, then Wittgenstein is an analytical philosopher.[7] This is his common ground with Polish analytical philosophy. In particular, the common assumption was that 'All philosophy is a critique of language'.

A more concrete common feature is this. Wittgenstein is considered to have initiated the so-called *de jure* theory of meaning, which determines meaning 'by looking into the workings of our language, and in such a way as to make us recognize those workings'. Ajdukiewicz proposed his theory of meaning in 1930 in much the same way, as we have seen in Chapter V. According to his view, to accept a language implies respecting the rules of its usage; if we do not respect usage (the workings of our language), we do not operate with the language in question. However, this recognition did not lead Ajdukiewicz to attach paramount significance to ordinary language. He contended that, within what is usually called ordinary language, several ordinary languages can be (and are) accommodated. Instead of compiling a catalogue of usages of one universal ordinary language, he concentrated on rules of sense which enable language to work as it actually does. With the help of rules of sense, he attempted to analyse ordinary as well as artificial languages, the languages of philosophy as well as those of science. The acceptance or promotion of the *de jure* theory of meaning does not necessarily lead to ordinary language philosophy.

In more recent times, Wittgenstein's *Investigations* have evoked some echoes in Poland, not so much among analytical philosophers as among linguistically minded Marxists. Adam Schaff discussed the *Investigations* in his *Introduction to Semantics*, and a doctoral thesis, devoted to the examination of the *Investigations*, was written by a follower of Marxist philosophy at the University of Toruń in 1961. Another doctoral thesis concerned with the philosophy of the later Wittgenstein was in hand at Warsaw University in the early 1960s.

[7] As a matter of fact, Wittgenstein's philosophizing fulfills the three further requirements (as stated in Chap. I) which are necessary to warrant giving him the name 'analytical philosopher'.

D. *Ryle and Kotarbiński*

The common core of Ryle's and Kotarbiński's philosophies is so substantial that it might be argued that Ryle's 'logical geography' was another name for Kotarbiński's 'concretistic reductivism', or that Kotarbiński's elimination of spurious categories was, in fact, an application of the idea of a 'category-mistake'.

Yet, in spite of almost the same methodological programme, and in spite of remarkably similar results (in Ryle opposition to the bifurcation of physical and mental worlds, in Kotarbiński the interpretation of all phenomena in terms of bodies), they differ on the cardinal issue of what their philosophy is about. Ryle firmly announced that 'ontologizing is out'. Kotarbiński never really abandoned the ontological consequences following from his concretistic semantics.

Because the philosophical assertions they held show an un-usual degree of likeness, the question arises whether Kotarbiński was too bold in drawing ontological conclusions, or whether Ryle was too reluctant to draw any ontological conclusions at all.

'To understand the work of an original philosopher,' Ryle wrote, 'it is necessary to see—and not merely to see but to feel—the logical *impasse* by which he was held.' The grasp of this 'logical impasse' necessitates an answer to the question: 'Just what was the conceptual fix that he was in? What dilemma was pinching him?'[8] By applying this maxim to the philosophy of Kant, Ryle was prompted to assert that the opinion is erroneous that Kant set himself the task of only analysing a number of concepts, such as *space, time, causation, duty, life*, and *purpose*. Ryle argued that 'First he did not set himself these tasks; they set themselves to him. Secondly, they did not attack him in a random sequence of local raids.'[9] In other words, it was a real dilemma that puzzled Kant, a logical *impasse* by which he was held up rather than a desire to elucidate concepts. I shall argue that Ryle also had his own logical *impasse* which has held him up, and that he was not only a linguistic philosopher concerned with a number of concepts, such as *seeing, picturing, fancying, imagining*, etc. *The Concept of Mind* is not

[8] G. Ryle, 'Formal and Informal Logic', *Dilemmas* (Cambridge, 1960), p. 125.
[9] Ibid., p. 126.

only the most extensive performance in Oxford ordinary language philosophy (distinctive for its 'orderliness, clarity and vivacity of style'[10]), but it is an expression of a dilemma that was pinching Ryle. What is perhaps the most striking similarity between Ryle and Kotarbiński arises from this fact.

Like Kotarbiński, Ryle started with a modest methodological programme aiming at the elimination of expressions in which, despite their grammatical correctness, the logical syntax is faulty. In 'Systematically Misleading Expressions' (1931) he argued that the grammatical subjects of statements, which purport to refer to something, do not always do so. Statements in which the grammatical subject-word or phrase (e.g. 'Reality', 'Being') *appears* to denote or refer to something, but where in fact there is no referent, Ryle called quasi-ontological. Such statements are at best systematically misleading, or at worst meaningless. If they are systematically misleading, the apparent subject-word 'is a concealed predicative expression, and what is really recorded in such statements can be re-stated in statements no part of which even appears to refer to any such subject.'[11] If they are meaningless, they must be rejected.

The convergence with Kotarbiński's position is quite clear. In both cases the intention was to unmask expressions which appear to be something different from what they actually are. For Kotarbiński the trouble-makers are apparent names or pseudo-names which, under the guise of grammatical noun-forms, confuse us. The statements which contain them are pseudo-existential statements; if they are taken literally, they are meaningless; if they are re-stated, they can become meaningful statements, but if and only if apparent names are replaced by other expressions. Ryle did not introduce any special phrase corresponding to Kotarbiński's 'apparent names' (onomatoids), but used a descriptive expression 'the grammatical subject or phrase which appears to denote or refer to something'.

A further striking similarity consists in the treatment of statements which are seemingly about universals. Ryle stated that by expressions such as 'unpunctuality is reprehensible', we do not

---

[10] 'These virtues,' G. J. Warnock continued, 'have been thought to be dispensable, or even undesirable, by some who share broadly the same philosophical aims.' (*English Philosophy since 1900* (London, 1959), p. 94.)

[11] G. Ryle, 'Systematically Misleading Expressions', *Logic and Language*, A. G. N. Flew (ed.) (Oxford, 1955), p. 18.

really suppose that unpunctuality ought to be ashamed of itself, but only that

> 'Whoever is unpunctual deserves that other people should reprove him for being unpunctual.' For it is unpunctual men and not unpunctuality who can and should be blamed, since they are, what it is not, moral agents.[12]

The style of this translation and its underlying motive could not be more Kotarbiński-like. Also, Ryle's general conclusion ('It is my own view that all statements which seem to be statements "about universals" are analysable in the same way, and consequently that general terms are never really the names of subjects of attributes'[13]) was precisely one of the theses of reism. However, Ryle was not quite so determined as Kotarbiński to find a definite resolution of these quasi-ontological statements. He only wished to show that in *some* cases statements whose grammar is correct must be restated in order to be logically correct. For example, when we say '"Honesty does so and so" . . . we are really saying in a formally improper way . . . "Whoever is honest, is so and so"'.[14] Kotarbiński, owing to his ontological commitment, was more determined and wished either to reject them as meaningless or to translate in such a way that apparent names were eliminated.

In the course of his essay, Ryle analysed phrases that appear to refer to such mental entities as feelings, ideas, and thoughts. The genuine logical subject of a statement, seemingly referring to a man's feelings, is the man himself.

> 'Jones hates the thought of going to hospital' only means what is meant by 'Jones feels distressed when he thinks of what he will undergo if he goes to hospital'.[15]

According to Ryle, other statements referring to alleged mental occurrences should be translated in the same sort of way. The class of misleading referential expressions that appear to refer to mental occurrences, only briefly discussed in the essay we are considering, was to become the main subject of Ryle's inquiry in *The Concept of Mind*, and was the subject-matter of his struggle with dualism.

[12] Op. cit., p. 20.   [13] Ibid., p. 21.
[14] Ibid., pp. 21, 22. In Kotarbiński's *Elements* very much the same examples are considered. 'Magnanimity is an attribute of noble people' Kotarbiński translates as 'Whoever is noble is magnanimous' (2nd edn., pp. 72, 73).
[15] Ibid., p. 29.

The essay is said to foreshadow Oxford ordinary language philosophy. This view seems to be much exaggerated. There are two main themes in Ryle's argument.

1. A concealed nominalistic one. Here, the object is a reduction of unnecessary semantic entities.

> Do not treat all expressions which are grammatically like proper names or referentially used 'the'—phrases, as if they were therefore proper names or referentially used 'the'—phrases.[16]

May we not ask at this point about the ontology underlying this recommendation? Why should we attempt to rule out these pseudo-names? Is this because they are vacuous?

2. There is also the obvious attempt at a systematic restatement of 'handy, idiomatic expressions' which are often misleading and need restating. 'Philosophy must then involve the exercise of systematic restatement.'[17] At no point did Ryle indicate that he accepted ordinary language as the basis for philosophical inquiry. On the contrary, because 'customary usage is perfectly tolerant of systematically misleading expressions',[18] he explicitly wished to restate them in a 'better form', which meant not 'more elegant or brief or familiar or more swiftly intelligible to the ordinary listener', but in a way which exhibits logical form. The analysis of logical form and 'the exercise of systematic restatement' were conceived by Ryle as one of the main aims of philosophy, and even 'the sole and whole function of philosophy'. So we may safely assert that Ryle was not a codifier of ordinary usage but a rectifier if not a reformist. There is no difference whatever between Ryle and Kotarbiński as to the need for restatements, 'controlled not by desire for elegance or stylistic correctness, but by desire to exhibit the forms of the facts into which philosophy is the inquiry'.[19]

As is evident in 'Systematically Misleading Expressions', Ryle is concerned basically and even solely with the systematic restatement of expressions which are logically faulty in spite of their grammatical and idiomatic correctness. This is the main though not the sole business of Kotarbiński's *Elements*.

In the paper 'Categories' (1937), Ryle continued the same line of inquiry. The idea of a category-mistake, which consists in the 'presentation of facts belonging to one category in the idioms

[16] Op. cit., p. 32. [17] Ibid., p. 36.
[18] Ibid., p. 34. [19] Ibid., p. 36.

appropriate to another', or in the allocation of 'concepts to logical types to which they do not belong', led Ryle to a sharp differentiation between logical and grammatical categories. A similar distinction is to be found in Kotarbiński's *Elements*. Under the name 'semantic categories', Kotarbiński and other Polish philosophers analysed and described the logical behaviour of expressions whose clear and unambiguous status from a grammatical point of view is confusing and misleading from a logical point of view. For Polish philosophers, 'mixing semantic categories' meant allocating concepts of logical types to categories where they do not belong. To do this is to commit, for Ryle, a category-mistake. In the *Elements* semantic categories are characterized in the following way:

> Phrase A and phrase B belong to the same semantic category if and only if a meaningful sentence remains so after A is replaced by B in this sentence. Contrariwise, phrase A and phrase B belong to different semantic categories if and only if a meaningful sentence ceases to be so after A is replaced by B in this sentence. For example, the words 'larger' and 'or' belong to different semantic categories because the meaningful sentence 'Paris is larger than Madrid' becomes meaningless when we insert 'or' in place of 'larger.' Then we have 'Paris is or than Madrid'.[20]

With Ryle the concept of category-mistake is explained by examples. If we consider an incomplete expression, a sentence-frame as '. . . is in bed', then it is clear that when we insert 'Jones' in the gap of the sentence-frame, we shall obtain a meaningful statement. If we insert 'Saturday' in the gap of the sentence-frame, we shall *not* obtain a meaningful statement. Therefore, 'Jones' and 'Saturday' belong to two different categories. However, the meaning of the term 'category' is left unspecified. It seems that a certain indefiniteness in Ryle's position resulted from his unwillingness to commit himself ontologically. With Kotarbiński the treatment of semantic categories and that of systematically misleading expressions is based on the principles of reistic semantics, which have a clearly ontological orientation.

The writings we have so far considered may be regarded as semantic overtures to Ryle's major undertaking, *The Concept of Mind*. In neither of the two essays did Ryle formulate ideas fundamental to the Oxford philosophy of ordinary language, as con-

[20] T. Kotarbiński, *Elements*, 2nd edn., p. 76.

ceived in the 1940s and 1950s. What is specific and novel in Ryle's early writings does resemble closely what was specific for Kotarbiński.

In *The Concept of Mind*, as I have suggested, Ryle attempts like Kant to escape from a dilemma. For Ryle it is the dilemma raised by Cartesian dualism, the bifurcation of mind and body. If a philosopher rejects dualism he may do it in various ways. He may assert the existence of 'neutral stuff' (Mach, Russell). He may simply assert that the problem in question is meaningless (Carnap). He may favour spiritualism (Berkeley) or materialism (Kotarbiński).

Ryle did not advocate spiritualism. On the contrary, he fought against it. He did not wish to blur the distinction between mind and body in favour of a neutral stuff. Nor did he consider the problem to be a meaningless one. He asserted that there is no intelligence but only intelligent people, no feelings but only people who feel, no mental processes but only experiencing people. This is the doctrine of a committed philosopher. The very idea of a category-mistake has sense in Ryle's discourse only when it has an ontological orientation. If there is no existential status attached to expressions about bodies, there is no category-mistake. If a category-mistake occurs, it is only because nonexistential expressions are mistaken for existential ones; expressions about alleged mental processes are mistaken for expressions about bodies. The names of alleged entities are rejected because they refer to nothing, whereas those of bodies and experiencing people are accepted because they refer to objects existing in the primary sense, i.e. in space and time. At the bottom of the idea of a category-mistake is an ontological commitment.

Whether Ryle wished to say this *expressis verbis* or not, the conclusions which follow from his arguments are that there *really exist* only physical objects, that there *really occur* only physical happenings (sometimes mistaken for so-called mental events and processes), and that *all* statements which refer to minds are *ipso facto* categorical statements about bodily behaviour or more often 'semi-hypothetical statements' about anticipated bodily behaviour. Everything about every individual can be expressed in body language.

Ryle's conceptual fix can be expressed in a methodological way. It then becomes a sort of radical nominalism. From the beginning the impetus towards an elimination of unnecessary entities has been apparent in Ryle's writings. Occam's razor is at work in almost all his essays. It was precisely this nominalistic drive that has given impetus to the whole of *The Concept of Mind*. This drive is the crux of all Ryle's semantic contributions—'Systematically Misleading Expressions', 'Categories', and 'The Theory of Meaning'—and gives continuity and cohesion to all Ryle's philosophy. The common thread is a desire to eliminate entities. Three main types of systematically misleading expressions, quasi-ontological and quasi-Platonic ones, and 'the'-phrases, were examined 'because all alike are misleading in a certain direction. They all suggest the existence of new sorts of objects. . .'[21] In the theory of meaning those theories were examined and rejected which postulate meanings as independent entities. The meaning of an expression is not, according to Ryle, an entity denoted by it. Consequently, 'it is not only repellent but positively misleading to speak as if there existed a Third Realm whose denizens are Meanings.[22]

There is conspicuously little ordinary language method in 'Systematically Misleading Expressions', as has been demonstrated, and there is conspicuously little employment of the method in 'The Theory of Meaning'. In the latter Ryle wrote:

> . . . From Transatlantic journals I gather that at this very moment British philosophy is dominated by some people called 'linguistic analysts'. . . . It falsely suggests, for one thing, that any sort of careful elucidation of any sort of complex or subtle ideas will be a piece of philosophizing. . . . But, even worse, it suggests that philosophical problems are like the chemist's or the detective's problems in this respect, namely that they can and should be tackled piecemeal. Finish problem A this morning, file the answer, and go on to problem B this afternoon. This suggestion does violence to the vital fact that philosophical problems inevitably interlock in all sorts of ways.[23]

That problems are important, and not method, Ryle argued further on:

> It would be patently absurd to tell someone to finish the problem of the nature of truth this morning, file the answer and go this

[21] G. Ryle, 'Systematically Misleading Expressions', *Logic and Language*, p. 32.
[22] G. Ryle, 'The Theory of Meaning', *British Philosophy in the Mid-Century* (London, 1957), pp. 262, 263.
[23] Ibid., pp. 263, 264.

afternoon to solve the problem of the relations between naming and saying, holding over until tomorrow problems about the concepts of existence and non-existence.[24]

It is thus clear that for both Ryle and Kotarbiński problems, not methods, were of the utmost importance, and that the major problem was to dispense with the existence of all entities but corporeal bodies.

Let us merely notice one final similarity. It has to do with the treatment given to such alleged mental entities as 'visual images', 'mental pictures', etc. Both Ryle and Kotarbiński emphasized that their doctrines should not be identified with primitive behaviourism, which denies the existence of mental life; but both insisted that the familiar truth that we are constantly seeing things in our minds' eye and hearing tunes in our heads is no proof that there exist things which we see and hear. Seeing things in our minds' eye does not involve either the existence of things seen or the occurrence of acts of seeing. For Kotarbiński alleged mental images are imitative descriptions of actual reactions.[25] The thesis of imitationism is that talk of mental images and other mental phenomena depends on concepts of a different sort. Ryle's account of these alleged mental entities is, as should be expected, not much different from Kotarbiński's. Characteristically, when making his point, Ryle does not give dry formulations, but rather vivid illustrations and convincing examples:

> . . . a person picturing his nursery is, in a certain way, like that person seeing his nursery, but the similarity does not consist in his really looking at a real likeness of his nursery, but in his really seeming to see his nursery itself, when he is not really seeing it. He is not being a spectator of a resemblance of his nursery, but he is resembling a spectator of his nursery.[26]

This is a beautiful illustration of the thesis of imitationism. And Ryle's other explanations of the so-called mental phenomena are quite Kotarbiński-like.

Perhaps the major difference between Ryle and Kotarbiński is in style of philosophical argument. What is striking in Kotarbiński is the conception of the concretistic picture of reality and his persistent and systematic refinement of this picture; his

[24] Op. cit., p. 264.
[25] See Chap. IV, section 3C—'Imitationism and extraspectionism'.
[26] Ryle, *The Concept of Mind*, p. 248.

arguments do not seem to bear the mark of unusual individuality. In Ryle, the most striking feature is the individuality and force of argument. Ryle's two basic techniques, *reductio ad absurdum* and *regressus ad infinitum*, have been commonly used in philosophy, but his application of these techniques was unmistakably individual. If Ryle is right that 'every rigorous philosophical argument is a discovery', then his discoveries are considerably more numerous than those of Kotarbiński.

It is rather paradoxical that Kotarbiński, despite his extraordinary precautions to avoid ambiguity and his tireless reformulation of statements, was perhaps less successful in stating convincingly and conclusively his position than was Ryle. One may conclude that metaphor sometimes serves clarity better than unembellished language, regarded by so many as the only possible vehicle for arriving at the definiteness and accuracy of thought.

FINAL REMARKS

It may be worth while adding some last general observations about the analytical movements in Britain and in Poland.

1. Britain, the cradle of analytical philosophy, has cultivated it longer, in more diversified forms, and with more illuminating results than any other country. The British analytical movement has inspired and influenced philosophers in all other countries.

Polish analytical philosophy has had little influence outside Poland; it was less diversified than the British, but more systematic in the examination of the problems it undertook.

2. British philosophy was a movement with many currents. In Polish philosophy, which was more homogeneous, a main theme was semantics. Semantics may be seen as having given rise to the formalistic endeavours of Polish logicians (e.g. Leśniewski), as well as having served as a foundation for the work of such philosophers as Kotarbiński and Ajdukiewicz.

3. In Britain all the four types of analytical philosophers (formists, reformists, rectifiers, and codifiers) were active. The formists, after Russell moved away from the philosophy of mathematics, were hardly represented. In Poland only the first three types could be found, the formists constituting an outstanding group and the reformists being philosophically most accomplished.

Let us combine two classifications, the first dividing analytical philosophers into formists, reformists, rectifiers, and codifiers and the second dividing them into methodologists and problem-philosophers. We can then see that the formists and the codifiers, the extremists of the first classification, are methodologists. The problem-philosophers, on the other hand, are either reformists or rectifiers.

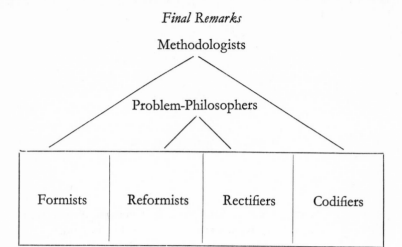

It is worth remarking that Polish methodologists are formists, and British methodologists are codifiers.

4. In Britain we may trace three main phases in the development of analytical philosophy. They are exemplified by Russell's Logical Atomism in the early 1920s, Ayer's *Language, Truth, and Logic* in the mid-1930s, and Austin's *Philosophical Papers* written in the 1950s. In Poland the continuous development of the analytical movement led to its finest results in the late 1920s and in the 1930s. The war shattered this continuity. After the war, analytical philosophy never regained its previous strength; the 1950s saw its definite decline.

5. Both in Britain and in Poland analytical philosophy appeared to many to be too dry and too 'unexciting'; it did not offer any solution to human problems or any consolation. On the other hand, it won a measure of respect not enjoyed by philosophies of the past.

6. The most significant influence of analytical philosophy in both countries seems to have been exerted through its method, through its critical and sober attitude. This influence still continues.

Analytical philosophy, of whatever denomination, suffers from being misrepresented as either a mere craft or as an unexciting account of dry and technical problems. However, by abandoning the dogmatic pretensions so characteristic of previous philosophies in favour of critical restraint, analytical philosophy does not cease to be philosophy or cease to perform its duty. On the contrary, in elevating the critical and rational faculties of man, it develops penetration and insight, and at the same time teaches responsibility, meaningfulness, and humility in the search for truth, understanding, and order. To serve mankind most fruitfully, analytical philosophy must free itself from one kind of dogmatism, namely the dogmatism of precision. It must follow the Aristotelian principle that we should not attempt to be more precise than the subject-matter requires; it must not insist that all problems should be treated with the highest rigour obtainable. Then it may construct philosophical edifices, not only meaningful and coherent, but also more embracing and more lasting.

SELECTED BIBLIOGRAPHIES

Since it is impossible to give the full bibliographies of all Polish analytical philosophers, only their major works are listed here. In most cases, full bibliographies are now available, and I have tried to indicate where they can be found. English, French, and German translations of some more important papers and books are also mentioned. It should be stressed that the bibliography given here is most rudimentary; a more comprehensive one can be found in Z. Jordan's *Philosophy and Ideology*, published in 1963. References to almost all of the works which served as sources for this book are to be found in the text.

AJDUKIEWICZ, Kazimierz. (A full bibliography of the works of Ajdukiewicz from 1913 to 1964 can be found in Volume II of *Język i poznanie*. Warszawa: PWN, 1965.)

Język i poznanie (*Language and Cognition*). Vol. I (Selected Papers of the Years 1920–1939), Warszawa: PWN, 1960; Vol. II (Selected Papers of the Years 1946–1964), Warszawa: PWN, 1965.

Z metodologii nauk dedukcyjnych (On the Methodology of the Deductive Sciences). Lwów: Polskie Tow. Filoz., 1921. English translation is to appear in 1968.

'O znaczeniu wyrażeń' (On the Meaning of Expressions), in *Księga Pamiątkowa Polskiego Tow. Filoz.*, Lwów, 1931.

'Sprache und Sinn', *Erkenntnis*, 4, 1934.

'Das Weltbild und die Begriffsapparatur', *Erkenntnis*, 4, 1934.

'Der logistische Antiirrationalismus in Polen', *Erkenntnis*, 5, 1935.

'Epistemology and Semiotic', *Proceedings of the Tenth International Congress of Philosophy*, Amsterdam, 11–18 August 1948.

'The Scientific World—Perspective', *Readings in Philosophical Analysis*, ed. by H. Feigl and W. Sellars, New York: Appleton-Century-Crofts, 1949.

'Logic and Experience', *Synthese*, 8, 1950 (6–7).

'Three Concepts of Definition', *Logique et Analyse*, 3/4, 1958.

'Le probleme du fondement des propositions analytiques', *Studia Logica*, 8, 1958.

Selected Bibliographies

'The Axiomatic Systems from the Methodological Point of View', *Studia Logica*, 9, 1960.

Logika pragmatyczna (Pragmatic Logic). Warszawa: PWN, 1965.

KOTARBIŃSKI, Tadeusz. (A full bibliography of the works of Kotarbiński from 1913 to 1965 can be found in *Fragmenty filozoficzne*, 3rd series. Warszawa: PWN, 1967.)

Wybór pism. Myśli o działaniu (Selected Papers. Thoughts about Acting). Vol. I. Warszawa: PWN, 1957.

Wybór pism. Myśli o myśleniu (Selected Papers. Thoughts about Thinking). Vol. II. Warszawa: PWN, 1958.

Elementy teorii poznania, logiki formalnej i metodologii nauk (The Elements of the Theory of Knowledge, Formal Logic and the Methodology of the Sciences). 1st edn., Lwów: Zakład Narodowy im. Ossolińskich, 1929; 2nd edn., Wrocław–Warszawa–Kraków: Ossolineum, 1961.

English translation of the second edition under the title *Gnosiology.* Oxford: Pergamon Press, 1966.

'The Development of the Main Problems in the Methodology of Francis Bacon', *Studia Philosophica*, 1, 1935.

'On Pansomatism', *Mind*, 64, 1955.

Traktat o dobrej robocie (A Treatise on Good Work). 1st edn., Łódź: Łódzkie Towarzystwo Naukowe, 1955; 2nd edn., Wrocław–Warszawa: Ossolineum, 1958; 3rd edn. 1965.

English translation under the title *Praxiology—an Introduction to the Science of Efficient Action.* Oxford: Pergamon Press, 1965.

Wykłady z dziejów logiki (Lectures in the History of Logic). Łódź: Łódzkie Towarzystwo Naukowe, 1957.

French translation under the title *Leçons sur l'histoire de la logique.* Paris: Presses Universitaires de France, 1964.

'The Concept of Action', *The Journal of Philosophy*, 57, March 1960.

ŁUKASIEWICZ, Jan. (A full bibliography of the works of Łukasiewicz from 1899 to 1954 can be found in *Z zagadnień logiki i filozofii.* Warszawa: PWN, 1961.)

Z zagadnień logiki i filozofii. Pisma Wybrane (On Problems of Logic and Philosophy. Selected Papers). Warszawa: PWN, 1961.

'Über den Satz von Widerspruch bei Aristoteles', *Bulletin International de Académie des Sciences de Cracovie, Classe de Philosophie*, 1910.

O zasadzie sprzeczności u Arystotelesa. Studium Krytyczne (On the Principle of Contradiction in Aristotle. A Critical Study). Kraków: Akademia Umiejętności, 1910.

Die logischen Grundlagen der Wahrscheinlichkeitsrechnung. Krakau: Akad-der Wissenschaften, 1913.

'Zur Geschichte der Aussagenlogik', *Erkenntnis*, 5, 1935–1936.

Selected Bibliographies

'Bedeutung der logischen Analyse für die Erkenntnis', *Actes du VIII Congrès International de Philosophie*, Prague, 1936.
'En défense de la logique. La pensée catholique et la logique moderne', Compte rendu de la session spéciale tenue le 26. IX. 1936 pendant le IIIe Congrès Polonais de Philosophie. Kraków: Wydawnictwa Wydziału Teologicznego UJ, 1937, Series 1, No. 2.
'The Shortest Axiom of the Implicational Calculus of Propositions', *Proceedings of the Royal Irish Academy*, 52 sect. A, 1948.
Aristotle's Syllogistic from the Standpoint of Modern Formal Logic. Oxford: Oxford University Press, 1951; 2nd enlarged edn., 1957.
'A System of Modal Logic', *The Journal of Computing Systems*, 1, No. 3, 1953.
'On a Controversial Problem of Aristotle's Modal Syllogistic', *Dominican Studies*, 7, 1954.

TARSKI, Alfred
Logic, Semantics, Metamathematics: Collected Papers. Oxford: Oxford University Press, 1956.
Pojęcie prawdy w językach nauk dedukcyjnych (The Concept of Truth in Formalized Languages). Warszawa: Towarzystwo Naukowe Warszawskie, 1933.
'The Semantic Concept of Truth', *Philosophy and Phenomenological Research*, 3, March 1944.

TATARKIEWICZ, Władysław. (A full bibliography of the works of Tatarkiewicz from 1910 to 1960 can be found in *Charisteria*, Warszawa: PWN, 1960.)
'Die Disposition der Aristotelischen Prinzipien', *Philosophische Arbeiten* IV, bd. 2, Giessen, 1910.
'On the Four Types of Ethical Judgements', *Proceedings of the Seventh International Congress of Philosophy*, Oxford, 1931.
'Les trois morales d'Aristote', *Séances et travaux de l'Académie des sciences morales et politiques*, Paris, 1931.
O szczęściu (On Happiness). 1st edn., Kraków: Wiedza-Zawód-Kultura, 1947; 2nd edn. Warszawa: PWN, 1949; 3rd edn., 1962.
Historia filozofii (A History of Philosophy). 1st edn., Vols. I and II, Lwów: Zakład Narodowy im. Ossolińskich, 1931; Vol. III, Warszawa: Czytelnik, 1950; latest edition of Vols. I, II, and III, Warszawa: PWN, 1958.
Skupienie i marzenie (Concentration and Contemplation). Kraków: Wydawnictwo M. Kot, 1951.
'The History of Philosophy and the Art of Writing It', *Diogenes*, Winter, 1957.
Historia estetyki (A History of Aesthetics). Vols. I and II, Wrocław–Kraków: Ossolineum, 1960.

Selected Bibliographies

'Abstract Art and Philosophy', *The British Journal of Aesthetics*, 2, 1962.

TWARDOWSKI, Kazimierz. (A full bibliography of the works of and on Twardowski up to 1938, compiled by D. Gromska, was published in *Ruch Filozoficzny*, XIV, 1938, pp. 14–39.)

Wybrane pisma filozoficzne (selected Philosophical Papers). Warszawa: PWN, 1965.

Rozprawy (*Essays*). Lwów: Polskie Towarzystwo Filozoficzne im K. Twardowskiego, 1938.

Rozprawy i artykuły filozoficzne (*Philosophical Papers*). Lwów: Drukarnia 'Prasa', 1927.

Idee und Perzeption, Wien, 1892.

Zur Lehre vom Inhalt und Gegenstand der Vorstellungen, Wien, 1894.

Wyobrażenia i pojęcia (*Images and Concepts*), Lwów, 1898.

'O tzw. prawdach względnych' (On the So-Called Relative Truths), *Księga pamiątkowa Uniwersytetu Lwowskiego*, Lwów: Senat Akad. Uniw. Lwowskiego, 1900.

German translation in *Archiv für systematische Philosophie*, 1902.

2nd Polish edn., *Polskie Towarzystwo Filozoficzne*, Lwów, 1934.

'Über begriffliche Vorstellungen', *Beilage zum XVI Jahresbericht der philosophischen Gesellschaft an der Universität zu Wien*, Leipzig, 1903.

INDEX OF SUBJECTS

INDEX OF NAMES

Index of Names

International Library of Philosophy & Scientific Method

Editor: Ted Honderich
Advisory Editor: Bernard Williams

List of titles, page three

International Library of Psychology Philosophy & Scientific Method

Editor: C K Ogden

List of titles, page six

ROUTLEDGE AND KEGAN PAUL LTD
68 Carter Lane London EC4

International Library of Philosophy and Scientific Method
(Demy 8vo)

Allen, R. E. (Ed.)
Studies in Plato's Metaphysics
Contributors: J. L. Ackrill, R. E. Allen, R. S. Bluck, H. F. Cherniss, F. M.
Cornford, R. C. Cross, P. T. Geach, R. Hackforth, W. F. Hicken, A. C. Lloyd,
G. R. Morrow, G. E. L. Owen, G. Ryle, W. G. Runciman, G. Vlastos
464 pp. 1965. 70s.

Armstrong, D. M.
Perception and the Physical World
208 pp. 1961. (2nd Impression 1963.) 25s.

Bambrough, Renford (Ed.)
New Essays on Plato and Aristotle
Contributors: J. L. Ackrill, G. E. M. Anscombe, Renford Bambrough,
R. M. Hare, D. M. MacKinnon, G. E. L. Owen, G. Ryle, G. Vlastos
184 pp. 1965. 28s.

Barry, Brian
Political Argument
382 pp. 1965, 50s.

Bird, Graham
Kant's Theory of Knowledge:
An Outline of One Central Argument in the *Critique of Pure Reason*
220 pp. 1962. (2nd Impression 1965.) 28s.

Brentano, Franz
The True and the Evident
Edited and narrated by Professor R. Chisholm
218 pp. 1965, 40s.

Broad, C. D.
Lectures on Psychical Research
Incorporating the Perrott Lectures given in Cambridge University in 1959
and 1960
461 pp. 1962. 56s.

Crombie, I. M.
An Examination of Plato's Doctrine
I. Plato on Man and Society
408 pp. 1962. 42s.
II. Plato on Knowledge and Reality
583 pp. 1963. 63s.

Day, John Patrick
Inductive Probability
352 pp. 1961. 40s.

International Library of Philosophy and Scientific Method
(Demy 8vo)

Edel, Abraham
Method in Ethical Theory
379 pp. 1963. 32s.

Flew, Anthony
Hume's Philosophy of Belief
A Study of his First "Inquiry"
296 pp. 1961. 30s.

Goldman, Lucien
The Hidden God
A Study of Tragic Vision in the *Pensées* of Pascal and the Tragedies of
Racine. Translated from the French by Philip Thody
424 pp. 1964. 70s.

Hamlyn, D. W.
Sensation and Perception
A History of the Philosophy of Perception
222 pp. 1961. (2nd Impression 1963.) 25s.

Kemp, J.
Reason, Action and Morality
216 pp. 1964. 30s.

Körner, Stephan
Experience and Theory
An Essay in the Philosophy of Science
272 pp. 1966. 45s.

Lazerowitz, Morris
Studies in Metaphilosophy
276 pp. 1964. 35s.

Merleau-Ponty, M.
Phenomenology of Perception
Translated from the French by Colin Smith
487 pp. 1962. (2nd Impression 1965.) 56s.

Montefiore, Alan, and Williams, Bernard
British Analytical Philosophy
352 pp. 1965. 45s.

Perelman, Chaim
The Idea of Justice and the Problem of Argument
Introduction by H. L. A. Hart. Translated from the French by John Petrie
224 pp. 1963. 28s.

Schlesinger, G.
Method in the Physical Sciences
148 pp. 1963. 21s.

4

International Library of Philosophy and Scientific Method

(Demy 8vo)

Sellars, W. F.
Science, Perception and Reality
374 pp. 1963. 50s.

Shwayder, D. S.
The Stratification of Behaviour
A System of Definitions Propounded and Defended
428 pp. 1965. 56s.

Smart, J. J. C.
Philosophy and Scientific Realism
168 pp. 1963. (2nd Impression 1965.) 25s.

Smythies, J. R. (Ed.)
Brain and Mind
Contributors: Lord Brain, John Beloff, C. J. Ducasse, Antony Flew,
Hartwig Kuhlenbeck, D. M. MacKay, H. H. Price, Anthony Quinton and
J. R. Smythies
288 pp. 1965. 40s.

Taylor, Charles
The Explanation of Behaviour
288 pp. 1964. (2nd Impression 1965.) 40s.

Wittgenstein, Ludwig
Tractatus Logico-Philosophicus
The German text of the *Logisch-Philosophische Abhandlung* with a new
translation by D. F. Pears and B. F. McGuinness. Introduction by Bertrand
Russell
188 pp. 1961. (2nd Impression 1963.) 21s.

Wright, Georg Henrik Von
Norm and Action
A Logical Enquiry. The Gifford Lectures
232 pp. 1963. (2nd Impression 1964.) 32s.

The Varieties of Goodness
The Gifford Lectures
236 pp. 1963. (2nd Impression 1965.) 28s.

Zinkernagel, Peter
Conditions for Description
Translated from the Danish by Olaf Lindum
272 pp. 1962. 37s. 6d.

International Library of Psychology, Philosophy, and Scientific Method
(Demy 8vo)

PHILOSOPHY

Anton, John Peter
Aristotle's Theory of Contrariety
276 pp. 1957. 25s.

Bentham, J.
The Theory of Fictions
Introduction by C. K. Ogden
214 pp. 1932. 30s.

Black, Max
The Nature of Mathematics
A Critical Survey
242 pp. 1933. (5th Impression 1965.) 28s.

Bluck, R. S.
Plato's Phaedo
A Translation with Introduction, Notes and Appendices
226 pp. 1955. 21s.

Broad, C. D.
Ethics and the History of Philosophy
Selected Essays
296 pp. 1952. 25s.

Scientific Thought
556 pp. 1923. (4th Impression 1952.) 40s.

Five Types of Ethical Theory
322 pp. 1930. (8th Impression 1962.) 30s.

The Mind and Its Place in Nature
694 pp. 1925. (7th Impression 1962.) 55s. See also Lean, Martin.

Buchler, Justus (Ed.)
The Philosophy of Peirce
Selected Writings
412 pp. 1940. (3rd Impression 1956.) 35s.

Burtt, E. A.
The Metaphysical Foundations of Modern Physical Science
A Historical and Critical Essay
364 pp. 2nd (revised) edition 1932. (5th Impression 1964.) 35s.

International Library of Psychology, Philosophy, and Scientific Method

(Demy 8vo)

Carnap, Rudolf
The Logical Syntax of Language
Translated from the German by Amethe Smeaton
376 pp. 1937. (6th Impression 1964.) 40s.

Chwistek, Leon
The Limits of Science
Outline of Logic and of the Methodology of the Exact Sciences
With Introduction and Appendix by Helen Charlotte Brodie
414 pp. 2nd edition 1949. 32s.

Cornford, F. M.
Plato's Theory of Knowledge
The Theaetetus and Sophist of Plato
Translated with a running commentary
358 pp. 1935. (6th Impression 1964.) 28s.

Plato's Cosmology
The Timaeus of Plato
Translated with a running commentary
402 pp. Frontispiece. 1937. (4th Impression 1956.) 35s.

Plato and Parmenides
Parmenides' *Way of Truth* and Plato's *Parmenides*
Translated with a running commentary
280 pp. 1939 (5th Impression 1964.) 32s.

Crawshay-Williams, Rupert
Methods and Criteria of Reasoning
An Inquiry into the Structure of Controversy
312 pp. 1957. 32s.

Fritz, Charles A.
Bertrand Russell's Construction of the External World
252 pp. 1952. 30s.

Hulme, T. E.
Speculations
Essays on Humanism and the Philosophy of Art
Edited by Herbert Read. Foreword and Frontispiece by Jacob Epstein
296 pp. 2nd edition 1936. (6th Impression 1965.) 32s.

Lange, Frederick Albert
The History of Materialism
And Criticism of its Present Importance
With an Introduction by Bertrand Russell, F.R.S. Translated from the German by Ernest Chester Thomas
1,146 pp. 1925. (3rd Impression 1957.) 70s.

International Library of Psychology, Philosophy, and Scientific Method
(Demy 8vo)

Lazerowitz, Morris
The Structure of Metaphysics
With a Foreword by John Wisdom
262 pp. 1955. (2nd Impression 1963.) 30s.

Lean, Martin
Sense-Perception and Matter
A Critical Analysis of C. D. Broad's Theory of Perception
234 pp. 1953. 25s.

Lodge, Rupert C.
Plato's Theory of Art
332 pp. 1953. 25s.

The Philosophy of Plato
366 pp. 1956. 32s.

Mannheim, Karl
Ideology and Utopia
An Introduction to the Sociology of Knowledge
With a Preface by Louis Wirth. Translated from the German by Louis Wirth
and Edward Shils
360 pp. 1954. 28s.

Moore, G. E.
Philosophical Studies
360 pp. 1922. (6th Impression 1965.) 35s. See also Ramsey, F. P.

Ogden, C. K., and Richards, I. A.
The Meaning of Meaning
A Study of the Influence of Language upon Thought and of the
Science of Symbolism
With supplementary essays by B. Malinowski and F. G. Crookshank.
394 pp. 10th Edition 1949. (4th Impression 1956) 32s.
See also Bentham, J.

Peirce, Charles, *see* Buchler, J.

Ramsey, Frank Plumpton
**The Foundations of Mathematics and other Logical
Essays**
Edited by R. B. Braithwaite. Preface by G. E. Moore
318 pp. 1931. (4th Impression 1965.) 35s.

Richards, I. A.
Principles of Literary Criticism
312 pp. 2nd edition. 1926. (16th Impression 1963.) 25s.

Mencius on the Mind. Experiments in Multiple Definition
190 pp. 1932. (2nd Impression 1964.) 28s.

Russell, Bertrand, *see* Fritz, C. A.; Lange, F. A.; Wittgenstein, L.
8

International Library of Psychology, Philosophy, and Scientific Method
(Demy 8vo)

Smart, Ninian
Reasons and Faiths
An Investigation of Religious Discourse, Christian and Non-Christian
230 pp. 1958. (2nd Impression 1965.) 28s.

Vaihinger, H.
The Philosophy of As If
A System of the Theoretical, Practical and Religious Fictions of Mankind
Translated by C. K. Ogden
428 pp. 2nd edition 1935. (4th Impression 1965.) 45s.

von Wright, Georg Henrik
Logical Studies
214 pp. 1957. 28s.

Wittgenstein, Ludwig
Tractatus Logico-Philosophicus
With an Introduction by Bertrand Russell, F.R.S., German text with an
English translation en regard
216 pp. 1922. (9th Impression 1962.) 21s.
For the Pears-McGuinness translation—*see page 5*

Zeller, Eduard
Outlines of the History of Greek Philosophy
Revised by Dr. Wilhelm Nestle. Translated from the German by L. R. Palmer
248 pp. 13th (revised) edition 1931. (5th Impression 1963.) 28s.

PSYCHOLOGY

Adler, Alfred
The Practice and Theory of Individual Psychology
Translated by P. Radin
368 pp. 2nd (revised) edition 1929. (8th Impression 1964.) 30s.

Bühler, Charlotte
The Mental Development of the Child
Translated from the German by Oscar Oeser
180 pp. 3 plates, 19 figures. 1930 (3rd Impression 1949.) 12s. 6d.

Eng, Helga
The Psychology of Children's Drawings
From the First Stroke to the Coloured Drawing
240 pp. 8 colour plates. 139 figures. 2nd edition 1954. (2nd Impression 1959.) 25s.

Jung, C. G.
Psychological Types
or The Psychology of Individuation
Translated from the German and with a Preface by H. Godwin Baynes
696 pp. 1923. (12th Impression 1964.) 45s.

International Library of Psychology, Philosophy, and Scientific Method
(Demy 8vo)

Koffka, Kurt
The Growth of the Mind
An Introduction to Child-Psychology
Translated from the German by Robert Morris Ogden
456 pp. 16 figures. 2nd edition (revised) 1928. (6th Impression 1952.) 45s.
Principles of Gestalt Psychology
740 pp. 112 figures. 39 tables. 1935. (5th Impression 1962.) 60s.

Köhler, W.
The Mentality of Apes
With an Appendix on the Psychology of Chimpanzees
Translated from the German by Ella Winter
352 pp. 9 plates. 19 figures. 2nd edition (revised) 1927. (4th Impression 1956.) 25s.

Malinowski, Bronislaw
Crime and Custom in Savage Society
152 pp. 6 plates. 1926. (7th Impression 1961.) 18s.
Sex and Repression in Savage Society
290 pp. 1927. (4th Impression 1953.) 21s.
See also Ogden, C. K.

Markey, John F.
The Symbolic Process and Its Integration in Children
A Study in Social Psychology
212 pp. 1928. 14s.

Murphy, Gardner
An Historical Introduction to Modern Psychology
488 pp. 5th edition (revised) 1949. (5th Impression 1964.) 40s.

Paget, R.
Human Speech
Some Observations, Experiments, and Conclusions as to the Nature, Origin, Purpose and Possible Improvement of Human Speech
374 pp. 5 plates. 1930. (2nd Impression 1963.) 42s.

Petermann, Bruno
The Gestalt Theory and the Problem of Configuration
Translated from the German by Meyer Fortes
364 pp. 20 figures. 1932. (2nd Impression 1950.) 25s.

Piaget, Jean
The Language and Thought of the Child
Preface by E. Claparède. Translated from the French by Marjorie Gabain
220 pp. 3rd edition (revised and enlarged) 1959. (2nd Impression 1962.) 30s.

10

International Library of Psychology, Philosophy, and Scientific Method *(Demy 8vo)*

Piaget, Jean *(continued)*
Judgment and Reasoning in the Child
Translated from the French by Marjorie Warden
276 pp. 1928 (3rd Impression 1962.) 25s.

The Child's Conception of the World
Translated from the French by Joan and Andrew Tomlinson
408 pp. 1929. (4th Impression 1964.) 40s.

The Child's Conception of Physical Causality
Translated from the French by Marjorie Gabain
(3rd Impression 1965.) 30s.

The Moral Judgment of the Child
Translated from the French by Marjorie Gabain
438 pp. 1932. (4th Impression 1965.) 35s.

The Psychology of Intelligence
Translated from the French by Malcolm Piercy and D. E. Berlyne
198 pp. 1950. (4th Impression 1964.) 18s.

The Child's Conception of Number
Translated from the French by C. Gattegno and F. M. Hodgson
266 pp. 1952. (3rd Impression 1964.) 25s.

The Origin of Intelligence in the Child
Translated from the French by Margaret Cook
448 pp. 1953. 35s.

The Child's Conception of Geometry
In collaboration with Bärbel Inhelder and Alina Szeminska. Translated from the French by E. A. Lunzer
428 pp. 1960. 45s.

Piaget, Jean and Inhelder, Bärbel
The Child's Conception of Space
Translated from the French by F. J. Langdon and J. L. Lunzer
512 pp. 29 figures. 1956 (2nd Impression 1963.) 42s.

Roback, A. A.
The Psychology of Character
With a Survey of Personality in General
786 pp. 3rd edition (revised and enlarged 1952.) 50s.

Smythies, J. R.
Analysis of Perception
With a Preface by Sir Russell Brain, Bt.
162 pp. 1956. 21s.

van der Hoop, J. H.
Character and the Unconscious
A Critical Exposition of the Psychology of Freud and Jung
Translated from the German by Elizabeth Trevelyan
240 pp. 1923. (2nd Impression 1950.) 20s.

PRINTED BY HEADLEY BROTHERS LTD 109 KINGSWAY LONDON WC2 AND ASHFORD KENT